Prairie Grass Roots

The Henry A. Wallace Series on Agricultural History and Rural Studies

Richard S. Kirkendall, SERIES EDITOR

The American Farmer and the New Deal, *by Theodore Saloutos*

Roswell Garst: A Biography, *by Harold Lee*

Railroad Development Programs in the Twentieth Century, *by Roy V. Scott*

Agricultural Science and the Quest for Legitimacy:
Farmers, Agricultural Colleges, and Experiment Stations, 1870–1890,
by Alan I Marcus

To Their Own Soil: Agriculture in the Antebellum North,
by Jeremy Atack and Fred Bateman

Corn and Its Early Fathers, *by Henry A. Wallace and William L. Brown*

Toward a Well-Fed World, *by Don Paarlberg*

Prairie Grass Roots: An Iowa Small Town in the Early Twentieth Century,
by Thomas J. Morain

Prairie
Grass Roots

An Iowa Small Town
in the Early Twentieth Century

THOMAS J. MORAIN

THE HENRY A. WALLACE SERIES
ON AGRICULTURAL HISTORY AND RURAL STUDIES

IOWA STATE UNIVERSITY PRESS ● Ames

THOMAS J. MORAIN was born and raised in Jefferson, Iowa, where his father and brother have edited the local newspaper for over fifty years. He earned his doctorate in American Civilization at the University of Iowa in 1974 and taught Iowa history and the history of women at Iowa State University for five years before accepting his current position as director of research and interpretation at Living History Farms in Des Moines in 1981.

© 1988 Iowa State University Press, Ames, Iowa 50010

Photo credits: Greene County Historical Society

Iowa State Historical Department

Composed by Iowa State University Press from author-provided disks
Printed in the United States of America

First edition, 1988

Library of Congress Cataloging-in-Publication Data
Morain, Thomas J., 1947–
    Prairie grass roots: an Iowa small town in the early twentieth century/Thomas J. Morain.–1st ed.
    p. cm.–(The Henry A. Wallace series on agricultural history and rural studies)
    Includes index.
    ISBN 0–8138–0068–4
    1. Jefferson (Iowa)–Social conditions. 2. Jefferson (Iowa)–Rural conditions. I. Title. II. Series.
HN80.J44M67 1988
306'.09777'466–dc19   88-652
                                                                                      CIP

To the three generations of Jefferson Morains
who were and are an important part of my life,

Perce and Myrtle

Fred and Lois

Rick, Bill, Steve, and Debbie

GREENE COUNTY, 1875. From earliest days, railroa
played a vital factor in the development of the county. With
a decade after this 1875 map appeared, a third rail line, t
Chicago, Milwaukee, and St. Paul connecting Des Moine
with the Okoboji–Spirit Lake region, ran north and sou
through Jefferson. The towns of Churdan, Farlin, and Coop
appeared along it in the early 1880s. *Courtesy of Gree*
County Historical Society

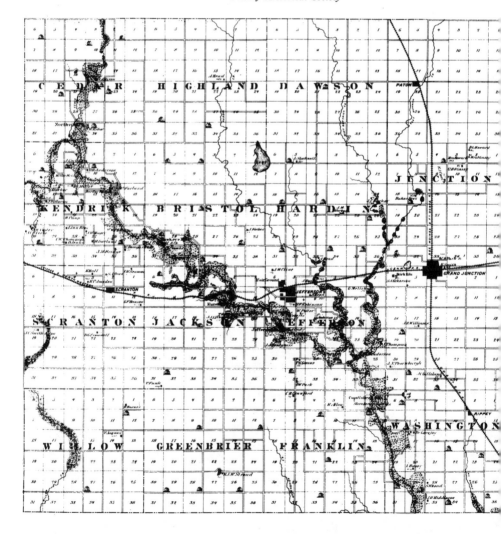

CONTENTS

Editor's Introduction, ix
Preface, xiii

1   INTRODUCTION: *A Land of Milk and Honey*, 3

2   SOCIAL IDENTITY: *To Whom Much Is Given*, 33

3   GENDER: *Created He Them*, 72

4   TECHNOLOGY: *Rise Up as Eagles*, 109

5   MORALITY: *Thine Infinite Iniquities*, 147

6   WORLD WAR I: *The Noise of War*, 177

7   BOOM AND BUST: *The Water of Gall*, 212

8   CONCLUSION: *Days Should Speak*, 247

Notes, 263
Index, 281

EDITOR'S INTRODUCTION

THE HENRY A. WALLACE SERIES on Agricultural History and Rural Studies is designed to enlarge publishing opportunities in agricultural history and thereby to expand public understanding of the development of agriculture and rural society. The Series will be composed of volumes that explore the many aspects of agriculture and rural life within historical perspectives. It will evolve as the field evolves. The press and the editor will solicit and welcome the submission of manuscripts that illustrate, in good and fresh ways, that evolution. Our interests are broad. They do not stop with Iowa and U.S. agriculture but extend to all other parts of the world. They encompass the social, intellectual, scientific, and technological aspects of the subject as well as the economic and political. The emphasis of the Series is on the scholarly monograph, but historically significant memoirs of people involved in and with agriculture and rural life and major sources for research in the field will also be included.

Most appropriately, this Iowa-based Series is dedicated to a highly significant agriculturist who began in Iowa, developed a large, well-informed interest in its rural life, and expanded the scope of his interests beyond the state to the nation and the world. An Iowa native and son of an agricultural scientist, journalist, and secretary of agriculture, Henry A. Wallace was a 1910 graduate of Iowa State College, a frequent participant in its scientific activities, editor of *Wallaces' Farmer* from 1921 to 1933, founder in 1926 of the Hi-Bred Corn Company (now Pioneer Hi-Bred International, Inc.), secretary of agriculture from 1933 to 1940, and vice-president of the United States from 1941 to 1945. In the agricultural phases of his wide-ranging career, he was both a person of large importance in the development of America's agriculture and the leading policymaker during the most creative period in the history of American farm policy.

As founder of what became Pioneer, Wallace hoped to increase farm productivity; as secretary of agriculture, he emphasized the restoration of profit to the farm business; but as a farm leader, he was interested in more than the economics of agriculture. His thinking had been influenced in large ways by his grandfather, the first Henry Wallace, who had been a leader of the Country Life Movement early in the twentieth century and a member of President Theodore Roosevelt's Country Life Commission. That commission had advocated the development of a "distinctively rural civilization" that would be much more than merely a producer of food and fiber. Henry A. picked up that concept and became a champion of such a civilization during his years as editor of *Wallaces' Farmer.* The concept encompassed all aspects of rural life, including the social as well as the economic. Henry's goal, as Joel Kunze has demonstrated, was the formation of a "distinctive and satisfying rural civilization."

In this latest addition to the Wallace Series, Thomas J. Morain deals with rural life during the years in which the Wallaces and their farm paper were a force in Iowa. Morain focuses on one part of the state, the town of Jefferson, the place in which he was born and raised and his family ran the newspaper. His book fulfills a promise of the Series, expressed at the beginning and repeated since, to be concerned with rural as well as agricultural history. *Prairie Grass Roots* represents the "new rural history," which Robert P. Swierenga has defined as "the systematic study of human behavior over time in rural environments." That history is part of a "new social history" that has emerged among professional historians over the past three decades, shifted attention away from elites, focused on broad social groups, and expressed a determination to achieve, as Peter N. Stearns has written, "historical perspective on the everyday activities of ordinary people." Morain employs a method of the new social historians—community studies—and deals with themes that interest such historians, including class, race, gender, and modernization.

Morain's book is an unusual work of its kind. The author has a very close and positive relationship with the community he has studied. It is his community; he did not come to it as an outsider. Yet he did return to it armed with the questions being asked of communities by modern historians.

The author seeks to show what life was like in an Iowa small town in the first third of this century. He assumes that small-town life was very important at the time. He shows that it was changing in major ways, in large part because of the impact of technological developments such as automobiles and telephones. The chief virtue of the book is its illustration of the changes in rural life during the period.

The volume suggests that the Wallace vision of a distinct rural civilization was going down to defeat by the forces of modernization.

Rural life was being incorporated into another civilization dominated by the city. ". . . rural and small town residents continued their chronic concern with the growing influence of the city," Morain reports near the end of his book. "In more and more ways it was obvious that the urban centers, not the farm and small town, were coming to dominate American life. . . . In the decade following World War I, . . . the cities . . . took the offensive. Urban culture invaded the farms and small towns as technology brought city and country into daily contact."

RICHARD S. KIRKENDALL

Henry A. Wallace Professor of Agricultural History and Rural Studies
Iowa State University

PREFACE

In at least two ways, this is an amazing book. I am amazed that I began it, and my wife is amazed that I completed it.

While I never planned to concentrate on local history, I never seemed to get too far from it. I grew up with a century of Jefferson, Iowa, history in the basement where my father, who edited the local newspaper, stored the volumes of back issues in tall cases. The *Jefferson Bee* began publication in 1866, and the bound set is nearly complete. It was fun to pull down a volume, spread it out on the Ping-Pong table, and laugh at the fashions, the patent medicine ads, and the prices. In 1966 the *Bee* celebrated its centennial and published a special edition. My summer job was to produce enough historical features to fill six eight-page sections. For three months I returned to those old volumes and copied out articles that helped to tell the story of the community. Flowery obituaries, draft calls, automobile records, famous visitors—day after day, I transcribed items from those fading sheets.

However, I never used any of the material in my own undergraduate or graduate history courses. It simply never occurred to me that what happened in Jefferson was "real" history. It was fun and kind of "cute," but it was not what anyone outside of Jefferson would have found relevant to the great issues of the day, and in my college years, "relevance" was everything.

My first academic encounter with Iowa history came nearly a decade later. In the summer of 1975, Dr. Louis Geiger, chairman of the Iowa State University history department, asked if I would teach an Iowa history course. Student demand had been so heavy in preregistration that the department needed to add several sections. Though I wanted the job, I blurted out that I had never taken a course in Iowa history and was not sure I knew enough about it to teach it. He brushed aside my confession of ignorance and assured me, "If you've lived here all your life, you must know something about it." Oh great, I thought, I can be red hot from 1947 on. I survived the first year, thankful that malpractice suits against teachers are rarely successful, and continued at Iowa State for four more years.

In the summer of 1978 I stumbled into my first local history project since the newspaper centennial. I was hired by the Iowa Department of Transportation to study how the coming of automobiles affected life in Iowa small towns. For six weeks I was again back in Jefferson, this time with a tape recorder interviewing longtime residents about their experiences with early cars. At the end of the study I wrote up a report but knew I had barely scratched the surface. The automobile ushered in a revolution in daily routines of both farm and town. I was also aware that my home town was a gold mine of information about this subject and many others.

I wanted to continue and expand the study. Early in 1979 I explained my interest to Karen Rush at the Home State Bank. Would the bank help to underwrite a study of Jefferson history? They would, and with evidence of local support, the Iowa Humanities Board provided additional funding to support a six-month project. It was not strictly a research grant. The project placed a historian in Jefferson to assist community residents in a study of their past. A historical series appeared in the newspaper, and we conducted and transcribed a series of oral history interviews with longtime residents. At the conclusion of the project in October, there was a three-night chautauqua that combined historical entertainments with lectures on the community's past.

The project was designed to involve community residents as partners in the research and interpretation of data. It combined a historian and a community in a joint endeavor. The project was entitled "The Autobiography of Jefferson, 1900–1930," a deliberate emphasis to involve those who had lived through the era in the process of interpreting it as history. Data generated by the project became the nucleus of this book.

I have found the project rewarding for several reasons. First, the small town has been a neglected area among professional historians. Since the sixties, the new growth in the field of history has been away from the traditional mainstream. It has been the politically active groups that have attracted historians. Black history, women's history, and ethnic and urban history have come to the front in the wake of their respective social and political movements. Main Street was much too mainstream to interest historians looking for evidences of American diversity and previously neglected perspectives. The small town was too quiet to attract much attention. Nevertheless, the small town has been tremendously important in American history, most definitely so in Iowa. In his history of Iowa written for the bicentennial, Joseph

Wall reminds us that "almost from the beginning, the townspeople have exerted an influence far beyond that which their numbers would suggest . . . (I)t has been the influential people in Iowa's small towns who have molded the state in their own image" (p. 150). Prior to the rise of the urban metropolis in the twentieth century, America was in a very real sense a nation of small towns, and American institutions, even in the cities, were dominated by small town standards.

The time period covered by the study was chosen partly because of its dynamic characteristics. The real transition from the Victorian to the modern era occurred in the early years of the twentieth century. The perspective of those who came of age before World War I is often significantly different from those who grew up after. The postwar decade has been dubbed the "Roaring Twenties," but underneath some noisy, short-lived fads, some fundamental transformations of daily life were occurring. Population shifts, technological innovations, and revolutions in transportation and communications were opening new opportunities and forcing some painful reevaluations. Another reason for choosing this time period was that the resources for community involvement were abundant. Though most of the residents I interviewed insisted that they knew nothing of any historical value, I knew better. Those born before World War I had a marvelous perspective on the transition from the days of buggy travel and denominational rivalries to automobiles, radio, and the "new morality."

The familiarity of the terrain of this project carried advantages and disadvantages. The groundwork was easy because it was my hometown, and I knew who and where my resources were. On the other hand, this affects the final product. Those who were giving me information had already "placed" me in the community picture and sometimes shaped their responses accordingly. This does not mean that the data I collected was better or worse than an "outsider" might have gathered, but it was different. Some told me things that they would never have revealed to a stranger, and I have tried to respect those confidences. Therefore, there are times when I revert to journalistic credentials and do not footnote my sources of information, and I do so with no apologies. I have invited several local residents to read the work before publication to tell me if specific examples I used seemed typical of the common experience. In the long run, knowing that a perspective was widely shared is more significant than knowing which individual mentioned it.

In addition to the way the project was structured, two other factors shaped the work. The first is that while Jefferson is my subject, I have been more interested in what might be typical of the midwestern small town than in ways Jefferson was unique. Many local histories are written for a local readership only. They are filled with dates of "firsts" and lists of names that interest only those who feel a personal connection with the subject. While this book is a study of Jefferson, the topics with which it deals were critical for residents of small towns throughout the region. What was occurring in Jefferson was also happening in Atlantic, Grundy Center, and Chariton and in similar towns in Illinois, Minnesota, and Nebraska. What this work attempts is to describe how broad social changes that happened everywhere in general happened somewhere in particular.

For that reason, however, Jefferson readers may be in for a slight letdown. They may be expecting more of the anecdotal. Yes, I have included how Mike Brunner was perhaps the only Catholic to march in a Ku Klux Klan parade and how Model-T drivers had to back up Danger Hill to keep from running out of gas. But there are some stories every red-blooded Jefferson High graduate knows that did not make it into print. There is only passing reference to Louie's Candy Kitchen, and not one word about Mrs. Herman or Miss Mabel. There is certainly more Jefferson history than what is included in the following pages. With a focus on Jefferson the typical rather than Jefferson the unique, however, some good stuff had to go.

The second factor is that I have tried to describe the era from the perspective of those who lived it. I tried to let the data suggest what were the important issues and what were not. There is sometimes a temptation to assume that national events are most important and that a local history should record how local residents responded to important (i.e., national) events. However, events that affect all of us may not be the ones that affect any of us most personally. Most of us "live" at the local level most of the time. A flu epidemic that knocks out a babysitter for three days makes more of an impression on our lives than a shift in the administration's Central American policy, and we remember it longer. Likewise, prosperity or depression means more to most of us as it is expressed in the monthly family budget than in terms of the Gross National Product. Jefferson residents did not recall the twenties primarily as the time of Calvin Coolidge, the Scopes trial, and the Teapot Dome scandal. More often in the transcripts were the memories of the double date to the Cooper High School class play or swimming in Spring Lake, and it is from these recollections that the local historian must construct the larger patterns of social change.

Taking the local perspective, however, does not mean that the historian simply reconstructs how local residents remember the issues. The historian has the advantage of perspective and the responsibility to use it. The farm kids dreading their first day in town schools may not have analyzed why they felt so defensive. The women who organized the Friday Club in 1888 did not see themselves as the vanguard of a movement to enlarge women's horizons. Nor did the merchants who bought the first automobiles see in their purchase the introduction of future competition from big city shopping centers. Whether they understood them or not, however, these were significant issues. Such incidents rarely made headlines, but cumulatively they fashioned new patterns of activity that led to new ways of looking at the world.

One dimension of the title, *Prairie Grass Roots,* reflects this concern for the local perspective on issues. The book is an attempt to reconstruct the "grass roots" view of life of those who occupied the midwestern prairies. A second interpretation also reflects a local perspective, but a personal rather than a collective one. One of the most satisfying aspects of the work throughout the project has been the deeper insight I have gained into my own past and perspectives, my "roots," for I am keenly aware that I am a product of the "prairie grass" community I describe. I no longer live in Jefferson, and the world has changed a great deal even since my high school graduation in 1965. Nevertheless, we measure change against certain standards. For me, this study has been the opportunity to explore the origins of beliefs I once accepted as givens and against which, even now, I usually must justify deviations. It has been a very rewarding venture.

ACKNOWLEDGMENTS

I owe a debt to the many people who assisted in the preparation of this work. Financial support was provided by the Iowa Department of Transportation, the Iowa Humanities Board, the Home State Bank of Jefferson, the American Association for State and Local History, and the National Endowment for the Humanities. Bessie McClelland, curator of the Greene County Historical Society Museum and a treasure of information on details of local history, provided numerous photographs from the museum collection. Mary Bennett of the Iowa State Historical Department assisted in the location of photos from the Iowa City collection. Office and research space was donated by the *Jefferson Bee* and *Herald,* the Ames law firm of Curtis, Finn, and Pattinson, and Living History Farms of Des Moines. During the project, while I commuted daily from Ames to Jefferson, my grandmother Myrtle served me six months of lunches and made sure I cleaned up my plate.

I owe a special thanks to several historians for their constructive comments on selected chapters. They include Dorothy Schwieder, Richard Kirkendall, William Murray, Kenneth Pins, and Joseph Wall.

My parents and several other family members read drafts of each chapter and improved the work with their corrections and suggestions for further research. Ron Troyer and Jeff Marck of Drake University provided valuable statistical data on Greene County from a computer file compiled from Iowa census records.

Without the help of two typists, the project would never have seen the light of day. Deb McGinn transcribed the oral histories from the Jefferson project. Blanche Breen, a volunteer at Living History Farms who had lived through many of the events I was describing, not only typed several drafts of each chapter but provided a running and spirited commentary on where I had and where I had not got the story right. Suzanne Lowitt and Carol Kromminga of Iowa State University Press edited the work with careful attention.

Of course, the real credit for the work goes to the community of Jefferson. Over forty-five local residents supplied information through oral history interviews, and many more contacted me with an anecdote or fact they thought might be useful. To all those who were willing to share their experiences and insights, I am very grateful.

Prairie Grass Roots

CHAPTER 1

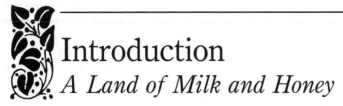

Introduction
A Land of Milk and Honey

> The Lord sware unto their fathers that He would give us a
> land that floweth with milk and honey.
>
> — JOSHUA 5:6

JAMES DAVIS WAS TWO YEARS OLD in 1849 when his parents, Truman and May Davis, left their farm in northeast Missouri and took the family to its new home in central Iowa. The Davises were the first white settlers in Greene County. James and a new civilization grew up together on the Iowa prairies. He was six when the county was incorporated. He was fourteen when the Civil War broke out. The first railroad chugged through the county when he was nineteen. When he was thirty-five, men at the saw mill on the Raccoon River talked on a telephone to an office a mile and a half away. He was forty-seven when electric lights in Jefferson were first switched on. The land into which the Davis family moved in 1849 was unoccupied. In 1900 there were 17,820 residents of Greene County.

In 1904 a crowd of thirty-five hundred local residents gathered in Jefferson for a meeting of the Old Settlers' Association. James Davis's older brother, Charles, was a charter member when the group organized in 1889. Not all the celebrants personally qualified as old settlers as well as Charles Davis, of course, but that was no problem. They were there to demonstrate their pride in their local citizenship, which they did quite succinctly in the following resolution: "*Resolved,* That the good Lord possibly might have made a better county than Greene, but He probably never did."[1]

How everything had changed, "from the log house period to the day of the well-appointed modern residence with the comforts and conveniences the early settlers never dreamed possible" was the big topic of the day.[2] How those changes came about was not significantly different in Greene County than elsewhere in Iowa. Just as a biography of Charles or James Davis would read like that of any of a thousand other early Iowa settlers, the history of Jefferson is typical of most Iowa local histories. For those who think of history in terms of wars, famous people, and important events, Jefferson has few claims to historical distinction. (Some might disagree, of course, for it was in Jefferson that Harold Stassen formally kicked off his 1948 presidential campaign.) For those who can think of history in the larger terms of changing patterns, however, the annals of the community offer a rich and fascinating historical resource.

This is an exploration of how a typical Iowa community experienced the first third of the twentieth century, the three decades following that Old Settlers' gathering. "Typical" is a slippery term, but those who know the town seem to have no problem with that description. In one sense, Jefferson is typical by default in that it lacks the unique. It has no foreign ethnic flavor and no unusual industries. Its streets lie in that rigid grid pattern common across the Midwest. It is a county seat town, the business district circling a courthouse square. Sixty miles northwest of Des Moines, it is far enough from a larger city to maintain a life of its own but not so distant as to be completely immune from urban influence. It was predominantly Protestant in the early twentieth century but had a visible Catholic element. Its merchants and professionals provided the same basic services to the surrounding rural population that one found in most small towns. In short, a salesman to Jefferson who happened to step off the train at the North Western depot when the Old Settlers' reunion was in progress would have discovered little in the town that he had not encountered in the dozens of similar communities through which he had already passed.

To understand the world of those local residents who gathered that afternoon in 1904, one must examine how they viewed the changes that dominated their discussions. Three developments during the latter half of the nineteenth century had significantly molded the nature of the community. The first was the triumph of the "Yankee" wing of evangelical Protestantism in impressing its own particular character upon community opinions, norms, and institutions. The second was the establishment of Jefferson as a retail trade and service center for the surrounding agricultural community. The third was the transformation, in only fifty years, of open prairies into a highly productive and prosperous farming region. These developments created the lenses through which residents viewed the dawn of the twentieth century and the background against which they would measure future change.

The opening lines of the creation myth are the same for all Iowa communities. In 1803 the United States gained possession of the region as part of the Louisiana Purchase. For $15 million, about $.02 an acre, France sold its claim to the vast expanse between the Mississippi River and the Rocky Mountains. American settlement in Iowa began after an 1833 treaty with the Sauk and Mesquakie tribes. It was not until 1842, however, that a treaty extinguished Indian title to central Iowa, and the western half of that tract was not opened to American settlers until 1845. Even then, there was no rush of pioneers into the upper Raccoon River valley. When the Truman Davis family arrived in 1849, they found the land empty. The Indians who had once occupied it had left, except for an occasional hunting party. Five years later there were only 150 people in the whole county.

In most cases the early white settlers in Greene County were small farmers from the Ohio River valley and the states of the Upper South. The Davis family was typical. Heading north from Missouri in 1849, they stopped at Fort Des Moines for a few days to replenish their supplies and then made their way about twenty miles along the Raccoon River to Adel, "a town of about 20 inhabitants, including dogs," one of the Davis children recalled.[3] Mrs. Davis and the younger children stayed with an Adel family while Truman and the two older sons headed up the Raccoon in search of a cabin site. Moving north about forty miles along the east side of the river, they found a spot with a flowing stream in a beautiful grove of oak and maple trees.

There they drove stakes into the ground to locate a homestead and at once began cutting logs for a cabin. The walls were covered with oak clapboards. The windows had shutters but no glass. The floor was puncheon, split logs laid with their flat side up and the holes between the logs filled with clay. Davis and his sons constructed the hearth and firewall of flat rocks, and the chimney was fashioned from sticks plastered heavily with blue clay to keep them from catching fire.

When the cabin was finished, the three returned to the family in Adel and reloaded the wagon. Truman and May Davis arrived at their new cabin with "one yoke of oxen, one cow, one horse, twelve chickens, eight sheep, two pigs, one dog, a few necessary housekeeping utensils, and six children."[4] And in their new home, a one-room cabin seven feet high, sixteen feet long, and twelve feet wide, they spent the winter—with six children.

Second to arrive was the Enos Buttrick family, neighbors of the Davises from Sullivan County, Missouri. They too made their way to Fort Des Moines and Adel where they inquired about the location of their friends. They learned that the Davis cabin was "some forty miles to the northwest" and, with that scanty information, took off to find it.

Enos Buttrick was born in Vermont in 1812 while his father was a soldier in the United States Army, but when Enos was three, the family moved to Sullivan County where the boy grew up. He married

Catherine Dillevon, and by the time they decided to move to Iowa with the Davises, the couple had seven children. Enos was thirty-six. Thus, between the Davis and Buttrick families, there were thirteen children. It was not only the Iowa topsoil that was fertile.

In 1852 Enos Buttrick accepted an invitation to accompany an Indian hunting party heading up the Raccoon valley. He liked the land he saw. Truman Davis had made his last move, and today a plaque on a large rock near the site of his cabin marks his grave. Buttrick, however, decided to pull up stakes again, "even over the protests of his wife Katie who was content in her new found home" near her friends. In the spring of 1854 the Buttricks moved to a new claim about twenty miles west and became the first white settlers of Carroll County.[5]

Davis and Buttrick were typical of the small farmers from the Upper South and the Ohio valley who settled along the banks of the Raccoon and the Des Moines rivers in the 1840s and 1850s. As discomfiting as the news might be to their descendants, most of the founding fathers of Greene County were Democrats. (So were founding mothers, but they could not vote.) They heartily approved of American expansion and the elimination of any barriers (human or otherwise) to the opening of new land for settlement. The Mexican War had been a popular cause, and they were pleased with the Oregon Treaty in 1846, which ended the dispute with Great Britain in the Pacific Northwest. They were suspicious of financial institutions. Too many of them had lost money in bank panics or shady dealings. The Iowa Constitution adopted in 1846 reflected their suspicions and specifically prohibited banks from operating within the state. Farming, not manipulating other people's money, was the most noble occupation, and it did not require a lot of book learning.[6]

These first Greene County settlers brought with them their religious beliefs as well as their political loyalties. While many came to Iowa with no membership in any denomination, the region proved to be a fertile mission field for Methodist, Baptist, Christian, and other evangelical preachers who could paint vivid pictures of Judgment Day and lay out the steps to salvation in simple terms. Early settlers were suspicious of ministers who read sermons on the finer points of theology. They were also cool to smug reformers so certain of their own righteousness that they assumed they should set the standards for everyone else. Among those settlers who first settled along the Raccoon, religion was an individual thing, a matter between each person and God. They did not like government regulation in morals any more than in economics.

By the terms of the Missouri Compromise of 1820, the land north of Missouri was closed to the slave system, and Davis and Buttrick clearly understood that they were moving into free territory. The small southern farmers who moved into the Iowa river valleys were not advocates of slavery, but neither were they clamoring for an immediate end to it. Most of them were willing to allow slavery to continue where it existed. By no means were they advocates of racial equality. The 1846 Iowa Constitution put limits on black citizenship in Iowa to discourage black migration.[7]

Moving away from a slave state did not exempt them from the slave controversy, however. Early in 1854, in an attempt to open the Great Plains for settlement, Sen. Stephen A. Douglas of Illinois drafted a bill for the incorporation of the Kansas and Nebraska territories introducing the doctrine of popular sovereignty. Let the settlers of each new territory decide for themselves whether to allow slavery, the bill argued. Organizing those two areas as separate territories, the Kansas-Nebraska Act introduced the possibility that westward migration from Iowa might be into slave country. Nevertheless, Iowa's two senators, both Democrats, supported the bill.

The act aroused immediate and intense hostility in areas of Iowa and many other northern states. Angry groups felt betrayed over the repeal of the Missouri Compromise and began forming political coalitions to run candidates against officials who supported the measure. In Iowa the anti-Nebraska faction nominated James Grimes for governor to run against the Democrats' Curtis Bates. Grimes was known for his outspoken hostility to slavery, and while he did not yet advocate its outright abolition, he bluntly opposed its extension into any new territory.

Greene County voters knew where Grimes stood, but they did not agree with him. In 1854 the population was composed almost entirely of southern farm transplants. In a nearly unanimous verdict the county supported the Democrats' Bates over Grimes, 102–2. Grimes won in statewide returns by a slim majority, however, and those of similar persuasion captured a majority of seats in the state House of Representatives.[8]

Local developments were of more concern to the settlers than national politics, however. From 1854 to 1856 Iowa experienced a flood of settlers pouring onto the newly opened prairies. Rail lines reached the Mississippi in 1854 and came as far west as Iowa City by 1856. Highways through Illinois and Indiana were crowded with wagons of settlers heading for Iowa. In 1850 the population of the state was 192,214. By 1856 the figure stood at 517,875, with the heaviest growth coming after 1854.

Greene County was also welcoming new arrivals. From 1854 to 1856 the population swelled from 150 to 1,089. The panic of 1857 slowed migration, but by 1860 there were 1,374 people living on land that ten years earlier had been occupied by only a few scattered families.[9]

In the fall of 1854 county judge William Phillips appointed a three-member commission to select a location for the county seat. The men staked out a plot of upland prairie, two-and-a-half miles square, in the very center of the county. Since the Greene County treasury had no money, Phillips arranged for a two hundred dollar loan from Des Moines financier Hoyt Sherman to buy the land at the federal government land office. The commissioners named the new community for Thomas Jefferson, the patron saint of both American rural life and the Democratic party. However, since a town in Dubuque County had already registered that name for itself, the Post Office Department refused the second petition. Consequently, the name was amended to "New Jefferson," a move that satisfied postal authorities. Gradually, however, as the Dubuque community disappeared from maps and memory, so did the prefix, and the county seat of Greene County came to be known simply as Jefferson. [10]

The new town grew steadily. B. F. Robinson opened a dry goods store in 1854. George Walton also offered merchandise for sale and brought his wife and children to Jefferson in the summer of 1855. For a few months the Waltons were the only family in town. In the fall of 1855 Judge Robert Rippey built the first frame house and established his office there. A physician arrived but died a few months later. In the spring of 1856 some fifteen families arrived, and several set up craft shops. Much to the satisfaction of local residents, a weekly mail route from Adel was established.[11]

Regardless of what the county history books would lead the reader to believe, relations among early residents were not always harmonious. Indeed, the frontier attracted people of widely diverse values and goals, and in a context of minimal social or legal restraint, some conflict was inevitable.[12]

Included among the new arrivals to Jefferson was a species of settler strikingly different in outlook from small southern farmers like Davis or Buttrick. The latter wanted most of all to be left alone, an aspiration undoubtedly strengthened by their contact with the new arrivals. From the southerners' perspective, these newcomers not only displayed a disgusting predilection for self-improvement schemes but were also fond of pointing out their virtues to those who took life at a less feverish pace. In short, the Yankees were coming.

Azor R. Mills was the first schoolteacher in Jefferson. He arrived in 1855 at the age of twenty-eight. Mills's ancestors eight generations back had landed in New England in 1628, and Azor was a son of whom a Puritan ancestor could be proud. Born in 1827 in Wadsworth, Ohio, Mills received an excellent formal education, unlike Davis and Buttrick. The son of an army officer, he attended boys' academies in Ohio and enrolled in the first class of the University of Wisconsin. He taught school for a few years and then decided to move west. He bought several tracts of unimproved Iowa land, and with his background in mathematics, did much of his own surveying work on them. One deed was for a half section lying directly north of Jefferson, which, at the time of his purchase in 1855, boasted only the residence of George Walton. It was on his Jefferson tract that Mills made his new home.[13]

In Mills, one sees many traits that characterized Yankee settlers. It was the Yankees who were described as "yearning to constitute a social and cultural elite that would sponsor and support higher education, literary societies, and lecture courses, and follow their inclination to regulate the morals of the whole society." Historian Richard Power discussed the "cultural imperialism" of the Yankees, their zeal to impress the character of New England upon the growing population of western states. Painfully aware that democracy is a numbers game, New England Yankees knew that political power was shifting to the West. They were dismayed at the prospect, as one contemporary put it, of being subject to "people strong in their impulses, conscious of their rapidly growing strength . . . ambitious of using it . . . but comparatively undirected and unrestrained by the influence of institutions of religion and education."[14]

Knowing that they could not stop the westward migration, New Englanders set out to convert the West to Yankee standards. The American Home Missionary Society supported hundreds of Congregational and Presbyterian missionaries to the western states where they worked to establish local congregations. Catherine Beecher, daughter and sister of famous New England preachers and herself a well-known educator and author, sounded the call for young Christian women to enlist as teachers to combat the fearful scourge of ignorance among children growing up on the western frontier. Yankee loyalists were instrumental in the creation of scores of colleges in the Old Northwest and the upper Mississippi valley.

Cultural uplift Yankee style also meant attacking sin and sloth. The initial settlement of Iowa coincided with three very active decades for American reform movements. Health fads, prison reform, women's rights, crusades for new standards of dress – the northern states teemed with advocates of one cause or another. Most important among the reform movements of the day were the issues of abolition and temperance, both with roots deep in New England. Imbued with the notion that theirs was a superior vision, Yankees dutifully accepted their responsibility for the moral and intellectual life of the nation and set about to do what needed to be done, with or without an invitation from the uneducated, the undisciplined, the disinterested, or the unmotivated.

Azor Mills worked as a carpenter in his first year in Jefferson and taught school in the winter of 1856 in the newly constructed courthouse. He continued teaching until the Civil War broke out. Elected to the state legislature after the war, he supported a measure providing funds for new buildings at the state agriculture college in Ames. Six of his daughters graduated from Iowa State over the next several decades.[15] In 1872 he was elected county superintendent of schools. For more than two decades Mills was a central figure in the educational life of Greene County.

Mills was also a pivotal figure in the early religious life of the community. He was a charter member of the Jefferson Methodist Church. The congregation was under the direction of Rev. Joseph Cadwallader with whom Mills organized an interdenominational Sunday school. It existed from 1857 to 1867 when individual congregations took on their own Christian education programs.

During Mills's first winter teaching school, his friend, Ambrose Holland, organized a New England–style singing school to help pass away the long evenings. It is unlikely that the students learned any drinking songs that session as Mills and Holland were both ardent prohibitionists. When it was discovered that one Washington Allen was selling whiskey illegally, it was Mills who visited Allen to inform him of the violation and "to suggest that he had better keep a whiskey saloon out of it." The next day, George Walton, who had become sheriff, and a party of men approached the Allen home with a search warrant, but Allen loaded up his barrels on a sled and headed out of town. In 1857, the same year that he helped to organize the Sunday school, Mills was instrumental in the formation of the Greene County Temperance Society and served as its first secretary. A few years later, he became the first chairman of the county board of supervisors, which had replaced the county judge as chief county authority, and insured that that body would be hostile to liquor interests.[16]

The early success of "drys" like Mills had a lasting impact on the community. It set the tone of the community, attracting those who found it agreeable and encouraging those of a different perspective to choose a more congenial habitat. In a referendum on statewide prohibition in 1882, Greene County voted dry by a two-to-one margin, 1,572–773.[17]

Naturally, Mills was also active in local politics. Governor James Grimes helped to forge antislavery factions into the new Republican party, to which Mills was a devoted partisan. The Republicans championed the two important causes of the day: the antislavery and anti-liquor movements. The Iowa legislature under Republican control passed a stringent prohibition law in 1855, while New England and Quaker strongholds in Iowa became stations for the underground railroad, which transported runaway slaves to freedom. Mills was, in short, a typical Yankee. With his education and zeal, he worked hard to impress his own standards on the young town.

Men of Mills's persuasion, however, were not a majority before the Civil War. Democratic farmers along the Raccoon River still continued to control the county. In the 1856 presidential contest the Democrats ran James Buchanan against the Republicans' John C. Fremont. Greene County maintained its Democratic tradition, giving Buchanan a decisive 177–74 margin. Elsewhere around the state, however, Republicans prevailed and Iowa's electoral votes went to Fremont. Four years later, on the eve of the Civil War, the county was still loyal to the Democrats. In 1860 voters supported Sen. Stephen Douglas, author of the Kansas-Nebraska Act, over that other candidate from Illinois, Abraham Lincoln. The tally was 146–121.[18]

When the Civil War began in the spring of 1861, Republican elements responded enthusiastically to Lincoln's appeal for troops. Jefferson men organized military units and drilled daily. At Fourth of July celebrations, Mills, who was teaching a school in Washington Township, brought to Jefferson a company of his students whom he had organized as an army unit. From a population of 1,374 in 1860, Greene County supplied 150 soldiers for the Union army, which one source estimated to be about one-half of all able-bodied adult males.[19] Per capita, Iowa furnished more soldiers to the Union army than any other state.

Support for the northern cause was not universal, however, particularly among farmers along the Raccoon River. When Congress passed a law permitting states to draft men into service, local tensions mounted. The "neutrals," as those opposed to the war were called, met in Jefferson to discuss their situation. A fracas almost erupted over reciprocal insults between them and U ion loyalists. Though there is no record of local violence, there is evidence that the county contained a substantial element that had little zest for a war against the South.[20]

Not until 1864, after four years of civil war, did Lincoln and the Republicans carry Greene County. Even then, Lincoln's margin was only fifty votes, and local Republican candidates ran better than the president did. Sixty years later the county placed a statue of the Great

Emancipator on the courthouse lawn and enthusiastically supported naming a transcontinental highway after him, but during his lifetime the small farmers along the Raccoon consistently voted for whoever ran against him.[21] Significantly, Republican elements were far stronger in Jefferson, the center of county communications and organization. Rural Democratic elements found it far more difficult to organize and to keep in contact with each other.

More than any other single factor, the Civil War shaped the political life of the community over the next sixty years. For many who supported the Union cause, the war became a religious crusade as well as a military campaign. According to an account by his daughter, it was Mills's opinion that the war "welded the greatest fraternity that ever existed – the Grand Army of the Republic – now the Grand Army of the Redeemed."

Mills was wounded in Georgia in the battle of Altoona Pass, and he lost the use of his left arm. For the rest of his life it would be a constant reminder of the struggle. In the years after Appomattox, soldiers from more than sixty GAR regiments migrated to Greene County, and the number of Union veterans rose to over 250. They organized a GAR post in 1880 and continued to meet as often as twice a month for several decades to keep alive the memory of their participation in the grand cause.[22]

As late as the first world war, George Gallup's grandfather was still regaling his family gathered around the supper table with accounts of Civil War battles and the glory of the Union cause. Gallup, a Jefferson native who later founded the prestigious Gallup Poll, recalled that, for some reason no one knew, his grandfather's orientation never took with the next generation. George's father maintained an independent political status while his uncle Josephus was a frequent candidate for local office as a Democrat.[23]

The Gallups were the exception in this respect, however. Most local residents swallowed Republican principles right along with their green beans and tomatoes. The war brought victory for the Republicans and dishonor for the Democrats. The Democrats were tarred as the party of secession and rebellion, a charge that Republican candidates kept alive at every election. When Lincoln was assassinated, he became a martyr. Union soldiers, their families, and sympathizers saw the hand of Providence in the defeat of the South, a confirmation of the righteousness of their cause.

The political developments surrounding the war put men like Mills into power in small towns all across the state and in the state legislature and governor's office. Though they had opposition at the local level, Republicans clearly held the upper hand and used that influence to mold the infant state into a creature after their likeness. As individuals, Davis, Buttrick, and Mills were not towering figures in early Jefferson history, but in them one sees two powerful forces in conflict on the Iowa frontier: a fierce individualism and a moralism that thrived on community and regulation. While advocates of both values were present in the town's early history, it was the Yankee moralists who would impress their vision most forcefully on the community's character.

In 1909 retired Jefferson editor E. B. Stillman (himself as much a representative of the Yankee tradition in his generation as Mills was a generation before) wrote a history of Greene County in which he boasted that "three great agencies connected with everyday life of the American people are working together for the social, educational, and moral improvement of the homes of this favored land."[24] That trio consisted of the school, the pulpit, and the press. In Jefferson all three were definitely in the Yankee mold, much to Stillman's satisfaction.

Education was a combination of public and private effort. In 1871 Jefferson "seceded" from the surrounding township school district to organize an independent district. Jefferson voters promptly approved a levy for the construction of a six-room brick building on a full city block three blocks north of the square. The district maintained a graded common school, which taught the equivalent of the first eight grades of the modern system. In 1875 the Presbyterian minister, J. S. Dunning, opened a private academy offering classes beyond what the public schools provided. The academy continued for ten years until 1885 when Dunning left to take a position as financial agent at a new college in Fort Dodge. In that year the Jefferson school system established a public high school, insuring local students a continuing educational opportunity.

In 1889 the schoolhouse burned, and an even larger structure was constructed in its place. With insurance money from the old building and a new bond issue, Jefferson built a three-story school house complete with lofty bell tower. This housed the entire system, elementary through high school, until 1905 when a separate high school building was constructed.[25]

Jefferson churches also flourished. From the beginning, Protestants dominated the religious landscape. Four major evangelical denominations—Methodist, Baptist, Christian, and Presbyterian—organized strong congregations in those early days. "The Four" were a powerful force in the community.

Churches filled an important social function for they brought people together on a regular basis. Members of a particular congregation met together as often as three or four times a week, and church meetings were by far the largest regular assemblies in community life. Especially for women, the church and its auxiliary associations were likely to be the only organizations to which they belonged outside the home, and close friends were often drawn from sister members.

In a community that had few means of enforcing limits on the behavior of residents, the early churches played a strong role in fostering order. The intense rivalries among Protestant denominations of the early nineteenth century had subsided by the time of the Civil War. Although Protestant denominations justified their separate existences by differences in theological emphases and church organization, they shared a common evangelical perspective on most moral issues. Eager for new members, the congregations welcomed newcomers to the community into their fellowship. They stressed personal behavior over strict denominational doctrine and were less interested in their new members' views on the abstract questions of doctrine than their standards of conduct. Some, like the Baptists, held regular inquiries into members' behavior. While they divided the town into separate and competing congregations, the churches united the community on a deeper level by promoting a common code of conduct based on personal restraint.

The churches also instilled convictions of individual responsibility for the welfare of others.[26] Some Protestant denominations, viewing the world as hopelessly corrupt, spent little effort on social reform but urged members to seek their personal salvation through faith and piety. Another wing of Protestantism, reflecting the Yankee influence and including the major Jefferson denominations, felt a moral obligation to promote righteousness throughout society wherever possible. Although Jefferson Protestants advocated the formal separation of church and state, by no means did they intend to ignore the conduct of their neighbors. Religious freedom did not absolve the state from its responsibility for the behavior of its citizens. It meant primarily that the government was forbidden from taking a position on distinctives which separated denominations from each other. What they all shared in common, what they regarded as the fundamentals of Christianity and the foundations of morality, they regarded as essential for an orderly society. According to historian William G. McLoughlin, "few nineteenth-century evangelicals saw any inconsistency in supporting laws to enforce prohibition, laws against blasphemy and profanity, laws against lotteries, gambling, theater-going (and) dancing."[27] As the strongest institutions in the community, the Four were a considerable

TRUMAN AND MAY DAVIS. Typical of the small farmers from the Upper South who poured into Iowa in the 1830s and 1840s, Truman and May Davis, the first white settlers in Greene County, built a cabin along the Raccoon River. *Courtesy of Greene County Historical Society*

AZOR MILLS. The first schoolteacher in Greene County, Azor Mills represented the early wave of Yankee elements in the county. He helped found the first Sunday school and worked hard for temperance, abolition, the Union cause, and the Republican Party. *Courtesy of Greene County Historical Society*

· M A P ·
· SHOWING · ROUTE · OF ·
· TRANSCONTINENTAL · TELEGRAPH · LINE ·
· ACROSS · STATES · OF ·
· MISSOURI · AND · IOWA ·
· 1861 · 1862 ·

EARLY TELEGRAPH LINES. From its infancy, Jefferson has been located on major communication and transportation lines. A telegraph wire followed on the Chicago and North Western railroad route and linked Jefferson into a national communication network. *Courtesy of Iowa State Historical Society*

Christmas Ball.

—AT THE—

REVERE HOUSE,

Jefferson, - - Iowa.

The company of Yourself and Lady is respectfully solicited to attend a Christmas Ball,

Friday Evening, December 25th, 1868.

COMMITTEE OF INVITATION:

D. J. Sheldon, Carroll.
Wm. Merriam, Grant City.
Thos. Stiles, } Jefferson.
Geo. Lawrence, }
A. L. Thompson, } Boonsboro.
Sam. Johnson, }

G. Y. Cook, Glidden.
John Allen, Rippey.
H. Hamilton, } Montana.
E. E. Webb, }
Lem. Coldren, Dunlap.
Dr. Elwood, Carrollton.

COMMITTEE OF ARRANGEMENTS:

D. Northway,   John Skirving,   C. F. Lanham.

FLOOR MANAGERS:

J. Legore,   Capt. Yerger.   M. B. McDuffie.

Music--Hubble Bro's. Quadrille Band.

Tickets, Including Supper, $2.50.

CHRISTMAS BALL. *Courtesy of Iowa State Historical Society*

THE DUNNING ACADEMY. The Dunning Academy typified the Yankee emphasis on religion and education. The Presbyterian minister, J. S. Dunning, organized the Dunning Academy to provide higher learning beyond the curriculum of the common school and ran it until the community built a high school. *Courtesy of Greene County Historical Society*

THE JEFFERSON SCHOOL. The ornate spire pointing upward symbolized the aspirations of a people committed to a partnership between education and religion. This building, constructed in 1888, housed the entire system, elementary through high school, and was still in use as a grade school a century later. *Courtesy of Iowa State Historical Society*

PAUL STILLMAN AND VICTOR LOVEJOY. Paul Stillman (left, ca. 1896) and Vic Lovejoy (ca. 1930) loyally promoted the community through the weekly columns and editorials of the *Jefferson Bee*. Stillman served as Speaker of the Iowa House from 1911 to 1913. Both men, devout Presbyterians, were active in local Republican politics. *Courtesy of* Iowa Illustrated *and Greene County Historical Society, respectively*

The CULTURE CLUB Cook Book!

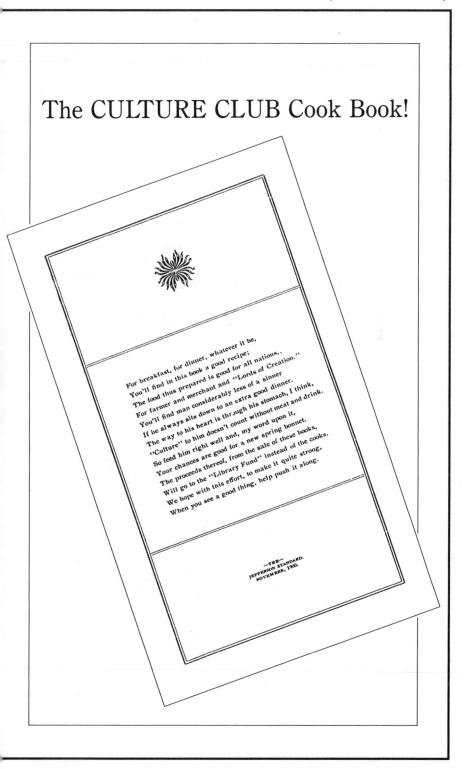

For breakfast, for dinner, whatever it be,
You'll find in this book a good recipe;
The food thus prepared is good for all nations,
For farmer and merchant and "Lords of Creation."
You'll find man considerably less of a sinner.
If he always sits down to an extra good dinner.
The way to his heart is through his stomach, I think,
"Culture" to him doesn't count without meat and drink,
So feed him right well and, my word upon it,
Your chances are good for a new spring bonnet.
The proceeds thereof, from the sale of these books,
Will go to the "Library Fund" instead of the cooks.
We hope with this effort, to make it quite strong,
When you see a good thing, help push it along.

—THE—
JEFFERSON STANDARD.
NOVEMBER, 1900.

ADVERTISEMENTS often offer an excellent window onto the community scene. About a decade after their founding in 1891, the Jefferson Culture Club produced a cookbook financed in part by ads from local stores. The ads reveal much about the business outlook of local merchants. Competing with the mail-order catalogue, they boasted of low prices. Fearing traveling salesmen, they reminded buyers of their relilability. Sensitive to the larger inventories of big city stores, they claimed that their fashions were as current as any. And always aware of local rivals, they supported club projects to win favor with local patrons. A few attempted a humorous approach, but most stressed business integrity and quality products.

Angel Cake.

Whites of eleven large, fresh eggs, or twelve small ones, one and one-fourth cups granulated sugar, sifted several times, one-half teaspoon cream of tartar, one cup flour, sifted several times, pinch of salt added to eggs before beating, beat whites of eggs about half, add cream of tartar and beat until very, very stiff, stir in sugar, then flour very lightly. Flavor with vanilla. Put in angel cake pan with slides, bake very slowly at first, then with an increasing heat till done, from forty to fifty minutes. After taking from oven turn upside down on slides, cover with a cloth and let stand in pans until cold, frost with boiled icing.—MRS. G. B. McCULLY.

Black Chocolate Cake.

Boil until it thickens, one-half cake Baker's chocolate and yolk of one egg, also one-half cup sweet milk. (Let the above cool.) One cup of butter, two cups of sugar, yolks of two eggs, three-fourths cup sweet milk, three cups flour, one teaspoon of soda, flavor with vanilla, then add the whites of two eggs beaten separately. One cup sugar, five tablespoons of water, boil until it drops from spoon, then put this into the beaten white of one egg, and ice when cool.—MRS. GEO. W. SMITH.

Chocolate Loaf Cake.

Dissolve two ounces of chocolate in five tablespoonfuls of boiling water, beat half a cupful of butter to a cream, add gradually a cupful and a half of sugar, beating all the while, add the yolks of four eggs, beat again, then add half a cupful of milk, then the melted chocolate and a cupful and three quarters of flour, beat the whites of the eggs to a stiff froth and stir them carefully into the mixture, add a teaspoonful of vanilla and a heaping teaspoonful of baking powder. Mix quickly and lightly, turn into a greased cake pan and bake forty-five minutes in a moderate oven.—MRS. HOTT.

Devil's Cake.

Custard part: One cupful of grated chocolate, one cupful of brown sugar, one-half cupful of sweet milk, yolk of one egg, stir together and cook slowly, set away to cool. Cake part: One cup brown sugar, one-half cup butter, two cups flour, one-half cup sweet milk, two eggs, mix cake and custard together, adding the last thing a teaspoonful of soda, dissolved in a little warm water. Filling: One cup brown sugar, one cup water, one cup white sugar, one tablespoonful vinegar, boil until thick like candy and stir in the beaten whites of two eggs and one-fourth pound of marshmallow, beat up and place on cake.—MRS. D. MILLIGAN.

For Good Goods at a Right Price, SEE FLESHER,

4   CULTURE CLUB COOK BOOK.

MRS. D. W. OLIVER. While women's ready-to-wear clothing grew in popularity and gradually reduced the demand for the local dressmaker, women's hats remained a local product. Mrs. D. W. Oliver ran a successful millinery in Jefferson in 1900.   GAMBLE'S CLOTHING STORE. Even before automobiles, local merchants feared the lure of the big-city store and tried to retain the loyalty of local shoppers with promises of quality and service.

force in defining local standards of conduct on a statutory as well as a personal basis.

The story of the Roman Catholic church in Jefferson, as in Iowa as a whole, is closely tied to European immigration. It was the Irish who accounted for most of the early Catholic population in Greene County. For the most part they lived either on small farms or worked for the railroad. Until well into the twentieth century there were only a few Catholic families in Jefferson, and the local Catholic congregation was much smaller than the major Protestant denominations. A roundhouse in Grand Junction attracted a sizable Irish component of rail workers to that community. At one time Greene County, the western half of Boone County, and a small strip of Calhoun County were all one Catholic parish. In 1873 a resident priest was appointed for the Jefferson congregation, but later he moved to Grand Junction to be nearer the larger Catholic population there. In the latter community, the church established a parochial school but never did so in Jefferson.[28]

A system of lodges and fraternal orders, quasi-religious in nature, complemented the churches. As in many midwestern small towns, the Masons and International Order of Odd Fellows were the largest and best organized. An 1887 county history notes that the Odd Fellows had one hundred members while the Masons had ninety-six. The latter included most of the Protestant clergy among its membership.

In addition, the history mentions chapters of the Knights Templar, the Knights of Pythias, and the Royal Arch Masons. The Young Men's Christian Association held debates, readings, declamations, music, and other elevating entertainments every other Friday night. For Protestant women, the Eastern Star chapter organized in 1891 as an auxiliary to the Masons and around the turn of the century had ninety members.[29]

Like churches, the lodges emphasized religion and morality. Free from traditional denominational lines, however, they attracted members from different churches, although Protestants and Catholics had their own orders. According to Lewis Atherton's study of small town life, "lodges were popular in part because they emphasized mutual help and accepted respectable men regardless of wealth or prominence. The religious and moralistic nature of their rituals appealed to churchmen, and even to many who believed in God and morality without being affiliated with churches."[30]

Unlike the churches, however, most lodges and fraternal orders maintained a system of highly stratified ranks and offices. Local men who dealt with each other as fellow businessmen, customers, or just friends through the day addressed each other during lodge meeting as "worshipful master," "chancellor commander," or "generalissimo."[31]

Meetings were conducted in elaborate and formal ritual. However loudly members may have sung the praises of democracy over aristocracy and the common man over the titled nobility, they were attracted by the exaggerated ritual and patterns of deference. For one glorious evening a month, they escaped the bland landscape of democracy, equality, the common man, and classless society into a prefabricated world of myth, ritual, exalted rulers, fancy costumes, and noble causes.

In addition to the schools and the religious organizations, the third source of support for the Yankee tradition in Jefferson was the local press. The role of newspapers is of special importance in a study of local history because early issues are such a ready source of information. While Jefferson editors have had their individual perspectives, they have also been, to a remarkable degree, representative spokesmen for the community.

This is especially true through the first third of the twentieth century in the case of the *Jefferson Bee.* The forerunner of the *Bee* was the *Jefferson Star,* a publication of questionable journalistic merit and integrity. V. B. Crooks brought the first printing press to town in 1860 to satisfy a state law requiring the publication of annual tax lists in three consecutive issues of "a newspaper." Crooks published the lists every year in three issues of the *Star,* submitted a bill for the service, and then ceased publication until the lists were ready the following year. The *Star* carried tax lists for not only Greene but also for Carroll, Calhoun, Sac, and other counties, making it a profitable undertaking. Stillman, with his background as a newspaper editor, expressed this opinion in his 1909 history: "The modern term 'graft' was not found in the vocabulary of the early period, but the fact remains that the methods of a lot of newspaper men in printing newspapers just three weeks during the year, would come powerful near fitting squarely to the term used above."[32] Crooks died shortly after beginning the *Star.* In 1863 the enterprise was taken over by new owners who changed the name to the *Jefferson Record.*[33]

In 1866, the venture achieved stability when a husband and wife team, M. H. and M. L. Money, became its editors. M. L. Money, the wife, received Stillman's vote as "the better newspaper man of the two." In its first edition, the new *Jefferson Era* pledged "great care will be employed in the selection of miscellaneous reading matter, pertaining to Morals, Education, Domestic Economy, Wit, Humor &c, &c; in a word, we shall endeavor to present something, in each issue, that will be interesting and useful to all."[34] In 1872 they changed the name to the *Jefferson Bee,* under which title it has been published ever since. The offspring of Crooks and Money, the newspaper maintained a congenial alliance with the Republican party, a loyalty unbroken to the present. The *Bee* is the oldest continuous business firm in Greene County.[35]

The Moneys sold the newspaper in 1872, and after a series of publishers, the *Bee* in 1884 came under stable ownership. E. B. Stillman moved to Jefferson from Chicago and operated the business by himself until 1891 when his son Paul graduated from the University of Michigan and purchased a half-interest. Paul's older brother Frank purchased his father's remaining interest in 1895 and shared editorial responsibilities for eight years. Frank departed to take a federal job in Washington, D. C., leaving Paul as sole editor.

Competing newspapers came and went during the latter decades of the century, but none seriously threatened the *Bee* as the leading journal in the county. When the Greenback party was formed from the agricultural discontent in the 1870s, party followers promoted the *Greene County Gazette,* but that lasted only a few years. The *Jefferson Citizen,* the *Jefferson Democrat,* the *Iowa Advocate,* and the *Iowa Argus* all tried the field from 1870 to 1885, but none had much success. In 1885, the *Souvenir* issued its first edition as a "society paper," with the financial backing of the powerful Head family, and continued publication until 1903 when it merged with the *Bee.*

Victor Lovejoy, brother-in-law of the *Souvenir*'s publisher, got his first taste of small-town journalism on that paper around 1895 and joined the *Bee* staff when the two papers merged. In 1908 he left the *Bee* and started the Jefferson *Standard* (later the *Free Lance*), returning to his desk at the *Bee* in 1912 where he remained for over thirty years until his retirement.

The *Jefferson Herald* began publication in 1917. To save production costs, the *Bee* and *Herald* merged their production plants in 1931, but even though both were printed in the same shop, they retained separate editors. The *Bee* was printed on Tuesday and the *Herald* on Thursday. A. J. Kirkpatrick took the *Herald* editorship in 1926 and continued until 1937 when he sold out to Victor Nesheim and Fred Morain. Nesheim ran the shop while Morain took over *Herald* editorial duties. In 1946 both papers came under common editorship when Lovejoy sold his interest in the *Bee* to Morain and Nesheim.[36]

What makes the *Jefferson Bee* an exceptionally good source of information for a study of the first third of the twentieth century are the personalities of editors Paul Stillman and Vic Lovejoy. In many ways, they were a great deal alike. Both were active in the Republican party. Stillman was elected to the Iowa House of Representatives for three terms and served as speaker of the house in 1911. Lovejoy continued full-time with the newspaper but held the post of Republican county chairman for several years. Both were devout Presbyterians and consistently used the newspaper to promote projects or positions they considered to be consistent with evangelical Protestant standards. Lovejoy wrote a popular weekly column entitled "Seasonable Sermons" from which quotes appeared in other newspapers around the state. The columns were, in fact, secular sermons, often quoting Scripture and calling for public action on what Lovejoy considered to be moral issues. Like Azor Mills a half century earlier, Stillman and Lovejoy combined their religion and politics to champion the morality they espoused and practiced. Their views were not shared by everyone, but they were clearly representative of the dominant religious, political, and economic perspectives of the community. Yankee roots grew deep in prairie soil.

At the end of the Civil War Greene County resumed its rapid growth. In 1865 the census placed the population at 2,036. During the next two decades the tempo of settlement increased. These were the years when acres of upland prairie sod were turned for the first time, farmhouses and barns were built, roads were laid out, and townships organized. Towns around the county were incorporated: Jefferson in 1872, Grand Junction in 1873, Scranton in 1880, Paton in 1883, and Churdan in 1884. Rippey, Dana, Cooper, and Farlin were platted, but only the former two would incorporate as distinct political entities. By 1890 the townships, communities, and school districts were in place and functioning. According to state census studies, the Iowa rural population peaked in 1880. In western Iowa, however, the crest came later. The population of Greene County reached its highest mark in 1900 at 17,820 before it began the long and gradual decline through the twentieth century.[37]

It was the railroad that brought the new waves of settlers to the county after the Civil War. A route through Greene County, connecting with Marshalltown, Cedar Rapids, and Clinton to the east and Carroll, Denison, and Council Bluffs to the west, had been surveyed in 1856, and Jefferson residents built with the promise of future rail service. The company that eventually became the Chicago and North Western began its arduous westward construction. By the Civil War it had reached Cedar Rapids. By 1865 it was as far as Boone, only thirty miles to the east of Jefferson. In the summer of 1866 the waiting finally ended. On 30 July the railroad to Jefferson became a reality. The *Jefferson Era* could hardly find words to express its joy. "The locomotive has finally overcome all obstacles and made its advent in Jeff. We are no longer in a wilderness of prairie, but on the great thoroughfare leading from the Atlantic to the Pacific coast – one of the most desirable roads on the continent. Why should we not rejoice over this good freak of fickle fortune?"[38]

The directors of the rail company arrived the next day to inspect the work. Cherry Street (later changed to Wilson Avenue) connected the C and NW depot with the courthouse and became the principal north-south avenue.

There was little delay in establishing regular rail service. By 20 August two trains ran each way on a daily basis. The line reached Denison in 1866 and Council Bluffs in 1867, becoming the first railroad in Iowa to connect the Missouri and Mississippi rivers. As a county seat town guaranteed of courthouse business and with a railroad to supply merchants and to carry livestock and grain to eastern markets, the future of Jefferson looked bright.

Rail service to Jefferson increased. In 1880, the Wabash, St. Louis Pacific Railroad Company established a rail line northwest from Des Moines. Twenty-seven miles of the north-south track ran through Greene County, with stations at Cooper, Jefferson, and Churdan. Several townships through which it passed voted a tax upon themselves to support the construction in order to lure a favorable route location. With these two lines through Jefferson and a third route, the Des Moines and Fort Dodge, which cut across the eastern part of the county, Greene County residents were well supplied with rail service. A 1905 daily timetable for Jefferson depots listed five westbound and six eastbound trains on one line and four northbound and four southbound trains on the other.[39]

Spurred by the new railroad connections, Jefferson grew rapidly. In 1865 the population was only about 200, but by 1870, with four years of rail service and a postwar economic boom, it had grown to 779. During the war, the courthouse and a shoe shop had been the only buildings on the square, but by 1870 many more establishments were either operating or negotiating with builders. In 1875 the population stood at 895. During the next ten years, the community experienced even faster growth. In 1880 there were 1,444 residents, and by 1885 the number had grown to 1,730, almost double the number of ten years earlier (Table 1.1).[40]

TABLE 1.1. Population of Greene County towns, 1880–1950

	1880	1890	1900	1910	1920	1930	1940	1950
Jefferson	1,444	1,875	2,601	2,477	3,416	3,431	4,088	4,326
Churdan	...	377	626	667	763	616	677	593
Grand Junction	752	932	1,113	1,012	1,010	1,025	1,125	1,036
Paton	84	245	328	358	414	388	394	404
Rippey	...	...	395	407	409	357	421	354
Scranton	...	715	963	845	843	1,058	1,014	891

In the 1850s, before the arrival of a railroad line, Judge Rippey and two associates, anticipating future building needs of the young town, financed the construction of a sawmill. To obtain the steam engine, saw blades, and other equipment for the mill they hired drivers and twenty yoke of oxen to make the forty-two day round-trip to Burlington, which is located two hundred miles to the southeast on the Mississippi River. That six-week trip represents a fact of frontier life that was both bane and blessing. Freight transportation before railroads was both slow and expensive, but those with capital to set up a frontier operation, like Rippey and his associates, were assured of a local market once the mill was in operation.[41]

The railroads changed the economic equation by sharply lowering the cost of freight transportation. Goods produced cheaply in eastern factories could undersell local manufacturers, spelling the doom of many local craftsmen and industries. Jefferson business directories detail the transformation. Small industries were a more important factor in the economy in 1856 than they were in the 1880s. Before the arrival of the railroad, Jefferson boasted a carriage maker, two sawyers, a tinner, a tailor, a milliner, a shoemaker, a barrel maker, a basket maker, and a tanner. After two decades of rail service, the 1886 business directory listed as local industries only two milliners, a tailor, a shoemaker, a harness shop, a wagon shop, and rolling mills. Since hats, shoes, and clothing were still being made to personal specifications, these artisans remained in business. The harness shop was involved in both retail and repair work as well as harness manufacture. While the rolling mills were still producing flour in 1886, their future was limited. Greene County farmers were putting more and more acres to corn, leaving the wheat market to the farmers on the cheaper lands of the Great Plains. Minneapolis became the great milling center of the Midwest, and Greene County housewives were soon baking their bread with flour made from Dakota or Nebraska wheat.[42]

The Iowa small town increasingly became a retail and service center for the surrounding farm community. As early as 1856 a local business directory had listed five carpenters, three merchants, two lawyers, one blacksmith, one physician, one teacher, one artist, and one surveyor.[43] The 1886 directory detailed a greatly expanded retail and service network. That 1886 listing included two banks, two newspapers, eight lawyers, five physicians, and two dentists. The school principal supervised eight teachers. There were five restaurants, two meat markets, and seven groceries, four of which also sold dry goods. There were three hardware stores, three general stores, two feed stores, two clothing stores, and one establishment that sold clothes, boots, and shoes. Two more specialized in boots and shoes only. There were two blacksmiths, three drugstores, two furniture stores, two jewelers, and two barbers. There were two hotels and two opera houses. The directory listed a creamery, a saloon, a post office, a bookstore, secondhand store, a billiard parlor, an abstracts and loan office, a photographer, several painters, and a sewing machine and organ shop. For a town of 1,750 people, the list reveals a diversity of retail and service establishments.[44]

What that 1886 directory did not include, however, was a unique new business that had begun operation in town. This one was practically invisible. Sears, Roebuck, and Company began in that year to compete for a share of the rural market through its mail-order operations. Montgomery Ward and Company had pioneered the concept a decade earlier with catalog sales at discount to members of farm organizations, specifically to the Grangers. It was now the turn of the local retailers to feel the outside pressure that had already undercut the local craftspeople.

Small town merchants fought back by opposing rural mail service. Lewis Atherton's account states: "(Local merchants) were convinced that if mail-order houses continued to prosper, every country town would be reduced to a post office, blacksmith shop, doctor's office and a grain elevator. Land values would decline and monopoly would rule the land. Only the railway depot would grow in size under the new regime."[45]

The battle created hard feelings and distrust between merchants and farmers. Rural residents felt that the merchants were trying to prevent them from taking advantage of the lower prices of the mail-order houses (which was a pretty good assessment of the situation). The merchants argued that the farmers had a civic responsibility to shop at stores that paid local taxes, supported community projects, and allowed customers to buy on credit. Though parcel post was eventually enacted, Jefferson merchants survived. In spite of outside pressures, the small town continued to be the retail and service center for the surrounding rural population.

The Yankee influence and retail trade were two important factors in the young community. A third major development of the latter nineteenth century was the agricultural transformation of the upper Mississippi valley. Millions of acres of fertile prairies put to crops and pasture became one of the most productive agricultural regions in the world. The most rapid expansion of farming operations in Greene County occurred between 1875 and 1895, with heaviest growth occurring in the first decade. When postwar deflation and the panic of the early 1870s ended, money became available once again to finance farming ventures. The number of improved acres shot up as farms were established on the fertile prairies. It was the rapid growth of farms that accounted for the population increase of the final quarter of the century. (See Table 1.2.)

TABLE 1.2. Greene County farm acreage, population, and density, 1856–1895

	Improved acres	Unimproved acres	Total acres	Population	Persons per square mile
1856	3,104	34,942	38,046	1,089	1.19
1860	7,227	20,860	28,087	1,421	2.41
1870	33,759	10,708	44,467	4,627	8.13
1875	59,940	49,838	109,778	7,037	12.37
1880	161,114	50,981	212,095	12,727	22.37
1885	189,214	109,757	298,971	15,923	27.98
1890	267,485	59,334	326,819	15,797	27.76
1895	275,439	58,374	333,813	16,299	28.64
1900	329,617	36,508	366,125	17,820	31.32

Source: U.S. and Iowa Census. Thanks to Ron Troyer and Jeff Marck of Drake University Department of Sociology for supplying a compilation of Greene County census data.

Not all the new farm families owned the land they worked. As the open prairies disappeared, the value of the land rose. The cheap lands were farther from the railroads, more difficult to farm, or both. Some families were willing to rent improved lands rather than to undertake the arduous task of developing their own. The cost of machinery, buildings, and drainage, in addition to the price of the land itself, also discouraged many new farmers from striking out on their own. Furthermore, as the first generation of farmers retired, they often rented their farms to children who did not yet have the resources to buy the land outright. As a result of all of these factors, the numbers of farm tenants rose (Table 1.3).[46]

The farm operation itself underwent substantial modification also. The cash crop of many early settlers was wheat, supporting several flour mills along the Raccoon River as late as the mid-1880s. By the 1870s, however, corn began to replace wheat as the basic crop. In 1874 Greene County farmers planted 22,313 acres in corn. In 1884 they put

TABLE 1.3. Number and percentage of farms operated by owners, managers, and tenants, Greene County, 1885–1905

	1885		1895		1905	
	Number	%	Number	%	Number	%
Owners	1,456	74	1,450	69	830	51
Managers	25	1	48	2	35	2
Tenants	478	24	617	29	748	46
Total	1,959		2,115		1,613	

Source: U.S. and Iowa Census.

in 88,945 acres, and by 1894 the census reported 117,338 corn acres. The production of oats, a natural rotation with corn and a feed for the growing number of work horses, grew simultaneously. The corn was fed to hogs for which there was a strong market in eastern cities. By the turn of the century Iowa led the nation in both corn and hogs. The Corn Belt had become a reality.

Most farmers diversified their operations. By 1900 Iowa had surpassed New York as the leading butter producer. Farm women churned and traded their butter to local merchants. Creameries gathered cream on milk runs through the countryside and produced large quantities of butter for eastern shipment. Iowa farms also developed an excellent stock of horses. By the 1890s Iowa ranked second only to Texas in the number of horses, but in the value of horses the Hawkeye State led the nation.[47]

None of those facts was the most exciting part of the story to the ones who lived on the farms, however. The real news was the new machinery, the incredible revolution in farm technology, which they could see, hear, smell, and touch. It was a revolution in power, and power is always exciting. The Davis family had arrived in Greene County with a yoke of oxen and a horse to pull their wagons and plows. They hoed their fields by hand. By 1900 Greene County farmers possessed an incredible array of implements driven by steam engines or pulled by horses. It was a time of "sit down" farming, as farmers rode sulky plows, check-row planters, and cultivators pulled across the fields by handsome teams of Belgians, Percherons, or Clydesdales. According to census figures, the value of implements and machinery on Greene County farms rose from $230,623 in 1880, to $385,160 in 1890, and to $584,070 in 1900.

Nowhere was the transformation more dramatic than in the small grain harvest. Before the Civil War, harvest was entirely by hand in a process that had not changed substantially since Old Testament times. The stalks were cut by hand, tied into small bundles, and shocked in the fields to dry. The shocks were later hauled to the barn where a few bundles at a time were spread out on a large canvas. Flails pounded the head of the grain from the stalks. The grain and chaff were gathered into winnowing trays and tossed into the wind, which blew away the lighter chaff until only the ripe grain was left. The grain was then poured into sacks to be ground into flour.

By 1900 the flail and winnowing pan were ancient relics. A mechanical binder pulled by three or four horses moved through the field cutting and binding the oat stalks in one operation. The bundles were still shocked by hand. They dried in the sun, awaiting the arrival of that new symbol of farm industrialization, the threshing machine. Several families in a neighborhood often purchased a threshing machine and a steam engine jointly and formed a threshing circle. Each year the men joined together for two to three weeks to harvest the oats on each farm. They loaded the shocks onto wagons and pulled them up next to a mechanical monster with a voracious appetite that looked something like a cross between a rhinoceros and a giraffe. Bundles were pitched head first onto a conveyor belt and fed through a knife to cut the twine and separate the stalks. The oats were then literally pounded and shaken from the stalks. Chaff flew out one end, and the clean oats emptied from a half-bushel measure that kept track of the day's production.

Providing power for the operation was a shiny black steam engine pouring out black smoke from its chimney and occasionally sounding off with a shrill whistle. The pioneer farmer with his flail and winnowing pan could thresh eight bushels if he worked hard for a long day. A threshing machine could dump out eight hundred bushels a day.

The revolution in agricultural technology of the latter nineteenth century foreshadowed two crucial developments in the first half of the twentieth. The first was a decline in the rural population as machine power replaced human labor on the farm. The population of the county peaked in 1900 at 17,820 persons but then began a steady decline. The second was an increase in productivity, not only in Greene County, but throughout the nation's heartland. Rapidly growing eastern cities had provided immediate markets for the increasing production, and improved transportation had opened world markets to midwestern farmers. There would come a time in the not-too-distant future, however, when the farms would produce more than the cities could consume. Then, farmers would discover that their threshing machines and corn planters were like the Trojan horse: what first appeared to be a gift from the gods carried destruction in its belly. Overproduction and ruinous prices were in the future, and how to control the farm surplus produced by an ever-declining rural population would be the rural dilemma of the coming century.

However, farmers thought the future looked good as the century ended. With the capital to take advantage of the new inventions and a better financial picture than that of the newer farmers of the western plains, Greene County farmers were not drawn into the agricultural protest movements of the latter nineteenth century. In 1876 the Greenback party wanted the government to issue cheap money to help relieve farm debt, but Greene County gave Greenback candidate Peter Cooper only 9 percent of its vote. Republican candidate Rutherford B. Hayes received a solid 66 percent majority.[48] In 1896 in the heat of the "free silver" debate, the county continued its Republican tradition with a 2,607–1,628 tally, a 61 percent margin for Republican William McKinley and "sound money" over William Jennings Bryan. Greene

County farmers were not without their discontents, but they did not view their situation as so desperate as to warrant an alliance with "radical schemers."[49] Not yet.

The final decade of the nineteenth century witnessed a new optimism around the state. The Spanish American War was a popular cause that launched the United States as a rising world power. The century ended with a second defeat for Bryan and western radicalism, which confirmed for Greene County that the country was in the safe hands of men with common sense (i.e., Republicans). In 1900 incoming governor Leslie Shaw addressed the state legislature in buoyant terms. "(It is) a matter worthy of note that our industrial and financial skies are brightening. After the experience of unrest, distrust, doubt, fear, disaster, and much of ruin through which we have passed, no thoughtful mind questions the truth of the proposition that we are entering upon a period of improved conditions."[50]

Other symbols of that faith in the future included the several crop "palaces" around the state. The Corn Palace in Sioux City was the most famous. It hosted exhibits from as far away as Louisiana and boasted of the productivity of Iowa farms. The Blue Grass Palace in Creston celebrated the hay fields and pastures of south central Iowa, while the Coal Palace in Ottumwa reminded the world that Iowa had profitable industries other than farming. According to Iowa State historian Earl Ross, the palace fad was more than local boosterism. "The serious side of these splurges . . . was in demonstrating something of the productive possibilities of the state. Together, the 'palace' exhibits were indicative of the extent and variety of diversification that the Corn Belt economy made possible and they were thus more significant for future possibilities than for present achievements."[51]

By most accounts the situation at the turn of the century looked promising. Greene County residents who attended that 1904 Old Settlers gathering were aware of their pioneer heritage. They were proud of what they had accomplished in only fifty years. It seemed to be the general consensus at the meeting that in Greene County the Good Lord had himself a choice piece of real estate upon which the tenants were making some valuable improvements. They could talk about the "good old days" freely because the issues that had divided county pioneers were, on the threshold of the twentieth century, far less sensitive. The old agenda was buried under the technological and political developments of the past four decades. From prairie grass origins fifty years earlier, Jefferson had grown into a prosperous retail center with established churches, schools, and civic organizations in the heart of a thriving agriculture setting.

CHAPTER 2

Social Identity
To Whom Much Is Given

For unto whomsoever much is given, of him shall be much required.

—LUKE 12:48

HISTORIAN JOSEPH WALL WRITES that "there is a smugness of attitude within the small town that is a constant source of exasperation to the farmer and of bemused wonder to the city dweller."[1] Jefferson residents at the turn of the century would have been startled to hear themselves called smug, or self-satisfied to an unwarranted degree. Of course, if pressed, they would have admitted that it was true that in literate, white, Anglo-Saxon, evangelical Protestants converged the highest evolutionary forms thus far produced by the most progressive political, economic, and intellectual impulses of western civilization. In that they understandably took a certain degree of satisfaction, and they expected even better things in the future. Rev. Josiah Strong, a spokesman for evangelical Protestantism, wrote confidently in 1893: "We have seen that the world is evidently about to enter on a new era, that in this new era mankind is to come more and more under Anglo-Saxon influence, and that Anglo-Saxon civilization is more favorable than any other to the spread of those principles whose universal triumph is necessary to that perfection of the race to which it is destined; the entire realization of which will be the kingdom of heaven fully come on earth."[2]

Yet theirs was not a self-confidence that expressed itself in a complacent acceptance of the status quo. Those at the top of the evolutionary ladder had a duty toward those on the lower rungs. They felt called to be instruments to lift the ignorant and less fortunate, a task that tempered their appreciation of their most favored status. It was no coincidence that they sang of themselves as "Christian soldiers, marching as to war." They were never allowed to forget that they had battles to fight. The price of progress was eternal vigilance against foes both

33

without and within. The cause would succeed, but no individual was immune from falling away or immune to temptations. There were anxieties behind the self-confident facade.

To understand how Jefferson residents experienced the remarkable changes of the early twentieth century, it is necessary to recreate their vision of the world and how it operated, the setting into which these changes were introduced. Two important concepts helped to explain how things worked and to confirm their conviction that they were in the front rank of the march of progress.

The first was a theory of how the human personality is formed that granted far more influence to genetic inheritance than does modern psychology. Intelligence, industriousness, and sometimes even a disposition to morality were thought to be carried to some extent in the same genetic combinations that influence skin color and height.

Nor was this folk wisdom only. Leading scientists and social theorists of the day gave the theory support. For example, Henry A. Wallace, editor of the influential *Wallaces' Farmer* in the early 1920s and an early advocate of hybrid corn, freely adapted genetic theories to explain human differences. He once said "the farmer who is experienced in the breeding of grains and live-stock has come to have a more genuine appreciation of hereditary characteristics than any other class of our nation. Even tho they lose money by it, farmers can see the peril of allowing admission of large numbers of people of low grade intelligence from southern and eastern Europe."[3] Southern and eastern Europeans were of low-grade intelligence in comparison, of course, to the high-grade intelligence of the people of northern Europe, which included most Greene County residents.

Closely related was the theory of progress through social evolution. Those races with the best characteristics from both heredity and environment advanced faster. It was "survival of the fittest" on a group level. Vic Lovejoy, editor of the *Jefferson Bee,* expressed his own understanding of evolution in a 1925 column. "That there is 'evolution' in the world no sane person will deny," he wrote. "Man himself 'evoluted' from a primitive state, a period when he was half wild and barbarous, and had little or no education. This can be proved by history of the peoples of northern Europe, from whom most Americans descended . . . (T)he change of man to his present state of intelligence and civilization was 'evolution.' The Negro and the Indian have 'evoluted' from savagery to a civilized state."[4]

Because evolution proceeds through time, history becomes the test of superiority. Since England, France, Germany, and the United

States were world leaders of the day, history thus certified the superiority of the Anglo-Saxon peoples. Protestantism had grown out of
Catholicism and, at least in the Midwest, was on the rise. Capitalism
and industrialization had replaced feudalism. All were signs of progressive evolution.

Reconstructing how local residents applied these concepts in daily
living is difficult, but one woman who was interviewed tossed out a
useful starting point during a discussion of high school social life in the
1920s. She joked that her mother would let her date anyone she
wanted, as long as he was not black, a Catholic, or a farm kid. She
chuckled as she said it. Nevertheless, in one breath she identified three
(and with a little stretch, four) of the fundamental factors by which
Greene County residents understood who they were: race, religion,
occupation, and gender. The four strongly influenced what people did
through the day, where they did it, who their friends were, where they
lived, and even to which political party they belonged. Change any one
of them, and you altered that person's community identity. Understand
them, and you comprehend a great deal about how that mechanic,
editor, teacher, housewife, lawyer, or clerk perceived the world and his
or her own position in it.

The issue of race was a significant factor in the social order of
1900. This was not because there was a large nonwhite population in
Greene County. In fact there was almost none. Of 17,820 residents
reported in the 1900 census only eleven were black. Five of these lived
in Jefferson. The 1910 census listed only one mulatto, a person of
mixed black and white parentage, as the entire nonwhite population
for the county. The number increased slightly by the 1920s but remained exceedingly small (Table 2.1).

TABLE 2.1.   Population of Greene County by race, 1870–1925

	White	Nonwhite
1870	4,624	3
1875	7,036	1
1880	12,711	16
1885	15,923	0
1890	15,786	11
1895	16,294	5
1900	17,809	11
1905	16,086	3
1910	16,022	1
1915	16,337	2
1920	16,451	16
1925	16,076	18

Source: 1925 Census of Iowa.

Ideas about race are informative, nevertheless. They reflect local residents' view of themselves and their place in the natural order of things. Certain notions about blacks necessarily implied notions about whites. Blacks had remained in a primitive state except when they had come under the influence of whites. Therefore, blacks must be inferior. Conversely, whites must be superior.

The conviction that racial differences beyond skin color were inherent created some uneasiness in a community whose formal ideology emphasized that "all men are created equal." As long as the discussion remained at the ideological level, it was easy to condemn the southern white for institutionalized discrimination and frequent brutalities toward southern blacks. Outspoken southern Negrophobes made it easy to sympathize with the blacks' situation. South Carolina's senator "Pitchfork Ben" Tillman spoke at a Jefferson chautauqua in 1907 and drew a spirited denunciation in the local press for his extreme hostility to racial integration.[5]

Indeed, there was evidence of occasional local integration. A 1904 write-up of a football game between Jefferson and Redfield mentions that a black man named Cottam was playing right guard for Jefferson. Integration in athletics was an issue around the state at the time, and high school or town teams in some communities refused to play opponents who suited up blacks. The article, however, noted that Cottam had been "the victim of both verbal and physical abuse on the part of some of the Redfield players."[6] The color line had not disappeared.

Most Jefferson residents were not completely comfortable with the idea of racial equality or full integration in either ideology or practice. In 1902 it was with obvious satisfaction that the *Bee*'s Frank Stillman, writing from the nation's capital, reported that Booker T. Washington's Tuskegee Institute was studiously avoiding the issue of social equality.

The two questions of politics and social equality are entirely cut out of the curriculum of the institute. Politics is never mentioned and the students have no thought of social equality and are not working to that end. On the contrary, they are sensible young people, who have become thoroughly imbued with the spirit of the institution as directed and inspired by Mr. Washington to wit; That the thing for the colored man to do is to work out his own destiny, make the most of himself and pass up the question of society, social equality and politics. Mr. Washington has impressed his students with the fact that the first thing the negro must do is to prove that he has the stuff to take care of himself and be a man among men; a mechanic, a farmer, a lawyer, a doctor or merchant. When he has worked out that problem, it will be time for him to give attention to politics and social questions.[7]

The report claimed that Washington "has unquestionably solved the negro problem so far as the negro is personally concerned" if blacks would follow his lead. Postpone the decision about the problem of social equality until the Negro has "worked out" the problem of education. In other words, postpone racial equality.

Until that time came, blacks were both Negroes and "niggers." The term "nigger" found its way into the language in a variety of expressions, none of them complimentary to the black. Rough granite boulders in the fields were "nigger heads," and Brazil nuts were "nigger toes." When the city code banned slingshots, it termed them "nigger shooters." A swindler was a "nigger in the woodpile," and children chose up teams by chanting, "Eeny, meeny, miny, moe; catch a nigger by the toe." "Uncle Tom's Cabin" played at the Jefferson Opera House in 1917, accompanied by a jazz band of "seven, singing, dancing pickaninnies."[8]

In 1916 D. W. Griffith's film classic "Birth of a Nation" played in Jefferson and prompted discussion of racial issues. An epic depiction of American history, its most controversial interpretations were the Reconstruction years following the Civil War. In a favorable review of the film, the *Bee* asserted that criticism expressed by national black leaders about the way blacks were depicted was "not well founded." "True," the writer agreed, "the negro is not shown up in a favorable light in most of the pictures, and yet one cannot help applauding the kindly acts and protection afforded by the old family servants who are depicted as remaining so faithful and true to their former owners." Furthermore, the review went so far as to *forgive* blacks for the trouble they created. After all, it said, they were not responsible for their own acts since whites were to blame for "every crime committed by the negro race, either then or since." The Negro should therefore forget the past.

The negro, after years of slavery and horrible persecution, could not have been expected to be much else than brutal, when power was placed in his hands. He thought only of his own deep wrongs and some way of being revenged. The negro of today should fully appreciate this, and not look upon the pictures as something portraying the character of the present day black man. That period has passed and gone, and with it the misguided and mistaken "carpetbaggers," most of the racial wrongs of the colored people, and no excuse exists for any revival thereof by reason of moving pictures based upon happenings in the reconstruction period.[9]

The concept of race extended beyond differences based on skin color. Sometimes nationality or ethnic groups were considered to be races, such as the "Nordic" or "Slavic" races, though both were white skinned. This dimension expanded the racial issue into questions of foreign policy and domestic issues by creating a hierarchy among nations that was also assumed to be a part of the natural order. Advanced races had a moral obligation to assist primitive ones, whether or not the latter requested it. This was international relations Yankee style.

For example, when the United States in 1916 was faced with an unstable Mexican government on its southern border and Mexican bandits were harassing American citizens, the argument for U.S. intervention was made not only on the basis of American self-interest but on its potential benefit to the Mexican people themselves. The *Jefferson Bee* voiced this sentiment in a 1916 editorial.

The *Bee* is of the opinion that this country owes the same duty to Mexico from the standpoint of humanity that it has already performed for Cuba, and Haiti, and Nicaragua, and Panama and the Philippines. It is a moral duty. The Mexican nation has destroyed itself. Nobody but the United States can resuscitate it and put it upon its feet. . . . We have done a hundred times as much for each of them as they can ever do for us. We have done it because we are big, and strong, and able; while they are weak and irresolute and unguided. Can anyone doubt that the people of Cuba and the Philippines and Haiti are happier, and more comfortable and more secure than they were before we intervened to help them? No more can we doubt that the imposition of American will upon the affairs of Mexico gives to these wretched people the only possible chance to ultimately redeem and re-establish themselves.[10]

Similarly, the basis for U.S. intervention in the Philippines was not self-interest but something like a parental responsibility toward a childlike race. "The Filipinos are about as capable of self-government as a herd of tomcats and the worst crime this country could commit against them would be to put them on their own resources," one Iowa editor commented.[11]

Neither the "Negro problem" at home nor American intervention abroad upset Jefferson residents unduly. In each case the problem posed no immediate threat to their sense of the proper order of things or to their own sense of security. There was, however, a dimension to the race question that did generate some uneasiness. It began to undermine their confidence that the "best people" were firmly in control at the national level. Beginning in the 1880s, the number of immigrants to the United States from southern and eastern Europe increased dramatically, a shift from earlier immigration sources from northern and western Europe. In the 1870s immigrants from western Europe totaled 2,000,000 and from eastern Europe, 181,000. Between 1901 and 1910 western European immigration remained at 2,000,000 while eastern

European figures jumped to 6,100,000. At the turn of the century Italy, Russia, and Austria-Hungary alone were supplying three out of every four immigrants.[12]

The "new immigrants" increasingly concentrated in ethnic pockets in eastern cities. Historian Charles Beard notes that the rise of these "foreign cities" within American urban centers was an extraordinary characteristic of the period. In 1900 about 14 percent of the total American population was foreign-born, but the immigrant population was increasingly concentrating in the cities. In urban centers of more than twenty-five thousand inhabitants, the foreign-born accounted for 25 percent of the total. Above one hundred thousand the proportion was 35 percent, and in the largest cities of the nation, immigrants actually constituted a majority.[13] Neither blacks at home nor Filipinos were challenging white, Anglo-Saxon, Protestant control of school boards, city halls, and state legislatures, but Jefferson residents were less sanguine about the immigrant blocs of the cities. It was not a local presence of immigrants that was the source of the unrest. Greene County had never had a large immigrant population. Rather, it was the image of the foreign-born crowding into eastern cities that disturbed the rural and small town residents.

Historian Don Kirschner's excellent study of midwestern rural attitudes toward the city explains that urban immigrant blocs posed a threat to the dominance of "American" (white, rural, Protestant) values in three ways.[14] This was especially true in the 1920s when postwar political upheavals rocked eastern Europe, and alarmed Americans were willing to believe that the disruptions were the results of radical scheming.

First, there was an economic challenge represented most clearly by the labor union. In the months immediately following the armistice, the nation underwent a series of labor strikes, some of which directly affected rural Iowa. In the fall of 1919, for example, as Jefferson was heading into a cold winter, a nationwide coal strike so cut production that the town drew up emergency plans for coal distribution. An emergency coal committee set up a rationing plan to spread existing supplies as efficiently as possible. The electric plant reduced its hours of production. Several railroads reduced the number of trains. The strike ended before residents faced real hardship, but the town was made keenly aware of its vulnerability to disputes between far-off unions and their employers.[15]

To the small town the labor union often appeared as the spokesman for the immigrant. It was easy to link the immigrant to the radical demands of some unions at a time when eastern and southern Europe struggled with socialist and communist uprisings. The *Bee* reprinted a

Chicago Tribune editorial relating immigrants to labor unrest. "It is small wonder that radicalism takes such ready root among non-American speaking residents when we reflect that speech is coined thought. Our newcomers, many of them, have come out of countries that boil with social tumult. They have been born in the midst of revolutionary agitation, nourished upon hatred of autocratic institutions, and into their consciousness have been seared the experiences of unjust domination."[16]

On the same editorial page, a reprint from *New York World* denied that labor radicalism "was the work of ignorant foreigners." It was a struggle between radical and conservative labor in the United States, the author claimed, but this strenuous effort to deny its foreign origin implied a substantial public belief to the contrary.[17]

There was a second challenge. In their swelling numbers and urban concentration, the new immigrants also posed a political threat to the countryside. Democracy is a numbers game, and that fact, once a source of comfort to rural residents who made up the majority, was beginning to take on an ominous ring. Their position of power was being challenged. This prompted a *Bee* editorial in 1919 defending the status quo and opposing foreign interlopers.

This country is a democracy, and a democracy is ruled by majorities. . . . Those who find intolerable our laws, as provided by the majorities, will have to seek other countries where the laws are to their liking. We are beginning to believe, in view of events now transpiring, that we shall be forced into a position where we must declare that America is for Americans, and for those others who are absolutely loyal to American law and American institutions, and for nobody else. We can adjust ourselves to labor conditions in which every foreign malcontent is eliminated and sent back to the place from whence he came, and we are not sure but that we should be infinitely better off if that very thing were done.[18]

But the immigrants did not go home, nor did they meekly assent to rural domination. In 1928 they captured the nomination of the Democratic party for one of their own, Gov. Al Smith of New York, a Catholic son of an immigrant "wet." Through the first third of the twentieth century, the political clout of the city became an unsettling reality to small town residents.

The third challenge, so closely interwoven with the economic and political, was the cultural. Rural Americans saw the immigrant as a real threat to traditional American values. The genetic arguments applied not only to the Negro but to the southern and eastern European as well. The Nordic was superior in intelligence, and it was Nordic (i.e., Anglo-Saxon) civilization that had developed Christianity and democracy more fully than any other people. A 1919 "Seasonable Sermon" in the *Bee* saw the Prohibition issue as a symbol of American superiority.

We saw an item in the daily papers the other day that thirty foreigners had applied for passports to Europe, giving as their reason, "no work, no booze." Thank God for small favors. The faster prohibition causes the shipping home of citizens of the syphilitic countries of Europe, the better it suits us. They can't be deported any too fast. . . . The scum of Europe is not going to flow to this country as it has in the past, for the boozer of the old world would much rather put up with the disagreeables of his own syphilitic land, than come here where the flowing cup is barred and stopped. So let the good work go on.[19]

The economic, political, and cultural images of the new immigrants combined to make them appear as a threat to the rural community. By the 1920s local residents had begun to fear that the national achievements of which they were most proud were endangered by immigrants crowding into the cities who did not appreciate American institutions. Whether the cause was genetic or cultural, the rise of the new immigrants in the cities threatened the proper order of things in two ways. There was the long-standing rural suspicion that city life was corrupting and less wholesome than life in small towns and the farm. Added to this now was the fact that the new urban ethnics had no background in, nor even respect for, traditional American values. In earlier times, rural-urban antagonisms were a family feud, differences between farmers and their city "cousins." The rapid growth of the urban immigrant populations changed that, and the cities began to take on an alien image.

Kirschner reconstructs the vicious circle into which cities like Chicago and New York had fallen, according to the rural Midwest. He calls it a "shorthand of interrelated symbols . . . the mention of any . . . of which was likely to evoke hostile feelings toward the others." As he phrased it, "immigrants were dirty and radical and vice-prone opponents of the American way whose drinking supported the criminal and murderous bootleggers who corrupted city officials who fawned before laborers and sold their souls for the votes of dirty and radical and vice-prone immigrants."[20]

Through the small towns and farms ran the unshaken conviction that their kind of people with their kind of values had made America great. The future of American progress and preeminence in world affairs depended on keeping the nation under the control of the right kind of people. The rise of other ethnic groups never suggested to midwestern Anglo-Saxons that their assumptions about themselves were wrong or needed to be revised in light of new evidence. While there was no immediate danger at the local or state level, there were distressing signs that they were losing control of the cities and that the cities were rapidly growing more powerful at the expense of rural areas. Not only did this new pluralism threaten them personally, but it spelled doom for the march of progress in which, until then, Anglo-Saxon America had been so nobly engaged.

A century earlier, New Englanders had viewed the rise of the West as a threat to not only their own preeminence but also to the survival of American institutions. Their fears motivated a massive campaign to convert western settlers to New England standards. In the early twentieth century, midwestern small town residents perceived a similar threat, this time, from the rising tide of immigrants in the city. Genetics, however, was the wild card in the new situation. Could the peoples of southern and eastern Europe ever become 100 percent Americans like Anglo-Saxons? The future of the republic hinged on the answer.

Race, as the issue was understood in the early twentieth century, was important in the way Jefferson residents understood who they were. To be a white Anglo-Saxon meant that one was among the most highly advanced people in human history and could share the honors for the highest level of civilization yet achieved. That was no small distinction. It was a heritage worth defending.

Religion was another factor by which Jefferson residents organized the world around them. While the population of Greene County was racially homogenous, it divided into numerous Christian denominations whose members took their church affiliations seriously.

The 1905 Iowa census reports a total church membership in Greene County of 5,569, or 35 percent of the total population.[21] These statistics need to be taken cautiously since they do not distinguish formal membership from denominational preference, nor do they adjust for differences among denominations in what constitutes membership. Nevertheless, the data provide a rough measure of the relative strength of the denominations.

In 1905 Catholics were the most numerous single denomination in the county with 1,680 members, located for the most part in Grand Junction and on farms across the northern tier of townships. Infant baptism helped to swell the Catholic membership rolls relative to those of some evangelical Protestant churches in which young children were not counted as members until baptism. The Catholic population in Greene County was primarily Irish, and outside of Grand Junction, Catholics were mostly farmers. Ten years later, a census reported that

Catholic membership had fallen off about 20 percent to 1,330.

Methodists were second in 1905 with 1,421 members but first in 1915 with 1,758. They had more congregations than any other denomination, often supporting several rural churches with the same pastor. Presbyterians were third, followed closely by Baptists and Christians (Disciples). There were around 125 German Lutherans in a small congregation southwest of Cooper, and two small rural congregations of Friends, one near Paton and another north of Scranton. Total church membership declined slightly in the ten years following 1905, from 5,569 to 5,260, consistent with a small population decline of that period.

The strength of Protestant denominations relative to each other was not as significant as their united size relative to Catholics. The religious cleavage in Jefferson, as elsewhere in Iowa and the Midwest, was between evangelical Protestantism and Catholicism. Historian Richard Jensen has convincingly argued that the major social and political division in the Midwest through the early twentieth century was a reflection of the Protestant-Catholic schism.[22] Differences among the Protestant churches were minor when compared with the long-standing hostility that separated Protestants and Catholics on such matters as repentance, salvation, and the role of the church and clergy. The former placed strong emphasis on the responsibility of the individual not only for his or her own salvation but for the moral environment of the community. The Catholic faith placed the church as a necessary mediator between God and the individual.

In Greene County the four major evangelical Protestant groups — the Methodists, Presbyterians, Christians (Disciples), and Baptists — had a total membership of 3,319 in 1905, almost twice the Catholic population. In Jefferson itself the margin was far greater. A church membership survey in 1904 reported that of 1,998 residents in town, only 129 were Catholics. Jefferson Protestants outnumbered Catholics nine to one.[23]

To understand the denominational environment of the community, however, one must keep in mind that church affiliation was only one dimension of community life. Members of different faiths also related to each other as neighbors, business associates, friends, classmates, and teammates, all of which cut their own lines through the community. Denominations were important, but no church was large enough to insulate its faithful from contacts with members of other denominations. In particular, the small size of the Catholic population in Jefferson prevented it from establishing a parochial school. Grand Junction, a town not half the size of Jefferson, supported both a public and a parochial high school. In 1915 a bishop speaking at Catholic confirmation ceremonies urged the Jefferson parish to build a parochial school as soon as possible, "a necessary auxiliary to the church if they had a regard for the spiritual and moral interests of their children."[24] It never materialized. For better or worse, Protestants and Catholics mixed in public schools and worked out their accommodations.

In part because parochial institutions failed to appear, the distinctions between Protestants and Catholics were expressed more clearly in ideological or symbolic terms than in everyday relations between the two groups. That is, Protestants tended to denounce Catholicism more than they did Catholics. On their part, Catholics distrusted Protestantism but generally lived in harmony with their Protestant neighbors. This is not to say that there were no antagonisms; there were. But the record also shows that while there were definite social distinctions between the two groups, individual relations generally proceeded amiably.

For example, the McCormicks and the Brunners were both Catholic members of the country club, which met twice a month for supper and recreation and included prominent Jefferson families. Friday night potlucks raised the issue of Catholics not eating meat on that day, but the necessary accommodations were made. Margaret McCormick Baker played violin in the Methodist orchestra. A. J. Finn, a Catholic, had a photography business and was well respected. The Kendalls and their six children lived across the street from the Rev. A. E. Slothower family in the Methodist parsonage. When Mrs. Kendall died, the Slothower family often helped care for the children, and the Methodist minister and his wife frequently were the ones who saw to it that the Kendall children got to catechism on time with their lessons learned.[25]

It was the impression of Roy Mosteller, raised as a Baptist on a farm northwest of Jefferson, that Protestants "had nothing against average Catholics, but they were afraid of the Pope and the higher ups."[26] The more abstract symbols of Catholicism, "the Pope and the higher ups," seemed more threatening than the actual Catholics they knew, "the average Catholics."

Evangelical Protestantism placed much less emphasis on the role of the sacraments than did the liturgical denominations, like the Lutherans and the Catholics, and the authority of the evangelical denominations to refuse the rites to members was correspondingly less critical. For the Catholic the sacraments of baptism, confession, communion, and last rites were critical steps in salvation. The church played a mediating role between the individual and God. Catholic "superstitions" about the sacraments gave the hierarchy an unwarranted hold on the lay member, according to Protestants. In the Protestant view the Catholic lay member was perceived as something of a victim;

it was the priest and the higher ups who used their members' credulity to maintain and strengthen the church. Nevertheless, could anyone be a 100 percent loyal American, Protestants asked, who owed spiritual allegiance to a foreign power, the Pope in Rome? There were even rumors that Catholics were storing guns in the basement of the rural St. Patrick's church west of Churdan, "waiting for the order from the Pope to take over the government."[27]

Catholics on their part had their own reasons for distrusting Protestants. A Yankee legacy was the impulse among evangelicals to feel a responsibility for the morality of the entire community, and it was, of course, a Yankee moral standard that served as the measure of righteousness. Whatever their differences on matters of theology or church government, most Jefferson Protestants subscribed to what might be called the Yankee Confession, an unwritten credo in four parts.

Article One maintained that life is a struggle, a test of will. Article Two declared that the individual, not the government or any other social unit, is responsible for his or her own well-being. Democracy and capitalism were the highest political and economic systems yet devised because they gave the fullest exercise of expression to individual decisions.

Article Three said that in most cases, success is a measure of character. Those with the will and the character to succeed will rise in a free-enterprise system. A 1924 editorial in the *Jefferson Herald* intoned the familiar rhetoric: "There is no such thing as failure to the man who refuses to see failure. There is no such thing as quitting to the man who believes a quitter is a failure, and the man who keeps his head up and eyes open can always make the hill in a manner better than the man who is nearly always looking for some reason to quit. There's a good living for anyone who honestly and truly wants to make it, and there's failure for those who are ready to quit fighting."[28]

It was Article Four that gave the creed its reform momentum. The righteous are responsible for the welfare of the community. St. Luke states: "For unto whomsoever much is given, of him shall much be required." While conversion of the sinner to the higher path was the preferable means of reform, it was sometimes necessary to use the legal authority of the state by making immoral activities illegal. Protestants dominated legislatures, city councils, and school boards, and it was a Protestant moral code that was written into the statute books.

While Protestants extolled the virtues of the separation of church and state, theirs was a Protestant interpretation of what that separation meant. Normally, it meant that no single denomination could use public institutions like the school or government offices to promote itself. It did not mean a ban on all religious teaching.

For example, an evangelist who was holding an evening revival series in the Methodist Church for a week in December in 1915 was also allowed to speak each afternoon at the high school on the general topic of Christianity.[29] Since he did not promote distinctly Methodist doctrines, only the great "truths" of the Christian religion, he was not violating the rule demanding the separation of church and state. However, no Catholic priest was ever accorded such an opportunity since the Catholic church was a single denomination. Protestant ministers could thus use the schools while Catholic spokesmen could not.

Yet for the most part, local Catholics made the necessary accommodations and learned to get along with a minimum of friction. For both groups the more distant or ideological the religious issue was made to appear, the greater the antagonism, but on most matters— with a few significant exceptions—daily relations between Catholics and Protestants were friendly.

Furthermore, the Protestant community was by no means monolithic in its attitude toward either Catholicism or Catholics. Protestant expressions of hostility frequently generated angry reactions among other Protestants in defense of Catholic friends. Unlike the race issue in which there was almost no sympathy for integration, there were both Catholics and Protestants who strongly objected to efforts to exacerbate religious antagonisms.

For example, several Jefferson Protestants recalled a vicious anti-Catholic newspaper entitled the *Menace*. Judging from the number who remembered it, one must conclude that the newspaper circulated freely. Its themes were predictable: the immorality of the priesthood, the Catholic plan to undermine American democracy by an armed revolution and to replace it with a Catholic theocracy subservient to Rome, and the nearly absolute power of the church over its superstitious members.

Yet by no means did all Protestants approve of such a publication. Jefferson resident Kellogg Thomas recalls that his father certainly did not.

I'll never forget the time to this day when I picked up a copy of the *Menace*. Well, it was probably the most scurrilous religious propaganda that anybody ever put out and it was a magazine that was widely circulated. . . . And I read it with avid interest because it had things like how the priests were storing Springfield rifles in the basement of the church, having affairs with the nuns. It was vicious. So I took it home to show my father, and I said, "Gosh, these guys are sure carrying on, aren't they?" And he read it, and I remember he tore it into four or five pieces, and he said, "Do you think Mr. Coyne would do that?" Old Michael Coyne was beyond question of a doubt my father's closest friend. . . . And I said, "Well, no not him." . . . "Well, they have certain things they have to do. For instance . . . they don't eat meat on Friday; they eat fish." (I remember this as if it were yesterday.) "When we had your birthday party last week and (Andrew) was over, the reason we had salmon sandwiches was that (he) was not supposed to eat meat on Fridays. That's one of the things his church believes." And then he said, "Don't ever you repeat anything to anybody or bring anything like that home again." And it was on the pain of getting paddled, and it made a vast impression on me.[30]

If Thomas's illustration is representative, the sensationalism of the publication was part of its appeal. While one cannot ignore its popularity, it is also true that it sometimes provoked angry reactions among Protestants in defense of Catholic friends.[31]

One could draw similar conclusions about Jefferson's experience with the Ku Klux Klan in the 1920s, the most glaring example of anti-Catholic sensationalism. After the Civil War the Klan formed in the South as a vigilante group to intimidate former slaves. After World War I, labor unrest, political radicalism, and the rising tide of immigration from Catholic countries in southern and eastern Europe convinced some that there was an international conspiracy directed against the United States. The Klan expanded its hate list to include Catholics, Jews, immigrants, and any other "un-American" group (i.e., anyone but white Protestants) and recruited a substantial following throughout the Midwest. In Des Moines, where the Klan had its greatest strength in the state, three KKK-sponsored candidates won election to the school board in 1925, but soon after, the power of the Klan faded rapidly.[32]

Greene County had its own Klan chapters. Details are scarce since the group took precautions to protect the identity of its members and to shield its internal organization from public scrutiny. Even its members were not sure who else belonged since they wore sheets and hoods during their gatherings. Sometimes rumors identified certain individuals as Klan leaders. Two pastors of Protestant churches in small towns around the county were reputed to be important Klan figures.[33]

Around 1924 and 1925 the Klan strength was at its peak. There were several meetings around the county, including a march around the courthouse square and several rallies west of Jefferson. Pauline McCormick Russell vividly remembered a near encounter with the Klan when she was a Catholic girl of seven or eight. It frightened her. "We'd taken a Sunday ride . . . out on old Highway 30 up there at Danger Hill and there were three men dressed in white and they had torches . . . they were having a meeting some place down there in the timber. My dad always protected us, so we got by there in a hurry. . . . And so that's all I can remember. And it was kind of in the fall of the year. I know the car was open and the men were standing out there with their white outfits on, and I can see them yet. Their outfits didn't go clear to the ground, you know. The only one we'd ever seen (in outfits like that) was my dad's sister (who) was a nun, and so, gosh, we just hadn't ever seen anybody in anything like this."[34] (It would be poetic justice if those three Klansmen could somehow be informed that they were remembered for a half century because they looked so much like nuns.)

Another account described a Klan rally west of town on the hill where the hospital now stands. Around a fiery cross, Klansmen in white robes listened to speakers denounce all un-American groups while a few hooded guards stopped cars along the highway and questioned the drivers. A funeral at the Methodist Church in Cooper was taken over by Klansmen who sat in their robes and hoods during the services and then provided an escort for the casket as it left the church on the way to the cemetery.[35] Nevertheless, despite its sensationalist rhetoric, trappings, and secret oaths, the Klan apparently left no record of any actual violence against any individuals in the local area.

Moreover, while the Klan's hostility was no laughing matter, memories of it did contain some humorous anecdotes. Several residents claim that Mike Brunner, the operator of the local creamery, was the only local Catholic ever to march in a Klan parade. As one version of the story goes (and there are many variations), Brunner had a five-gallon bucket of ice cream in each hand to deliver to a restaurant on the far side of the square. When he reached the near corner, he found his route blocked by a long, single-file Klan march then in progress. Rather than waiting for the parade to pass and his ice cream to melt, Brunner squeezed into line, marched with the Klan around to the other side of the square, and then broke rank when he got to the restaurant.[36]

Roy Mosteller mentioned an anti-Catholic meeting in Churdan, which he recalled as being associated with the Klan in some way. This meeting, however, was open to the public and attracted an audience of forty to fifty, including three or four Catholic men who came to hear the evils of papacy exposed, as the promotions promised. When the speaker described the increases in the Catholic population in the past several decades, "these three or four Catholics all applauded."[37]

Wayne Winey recalled an incident in a nearby town when a Klansman fell and broke his arm during a Klan rally. Taken to the local doctor, the Klansman felt more than a little sheepish when the doctor made him take off the white robe so that he could treat the arm. The doctor was a friend of his—and a Catholic.[38]

An obvious factor that diminished the Klan's appeal locally was that Catholics were already well integrated into the community social structure. They were not theological abstractions; they were friends, neighbors, and business associates. The friendship between the Thomases and the Coynes that prompted the elder Thomas to tear up the *Menace* had its parallels throughout the community. Charles Hird, a Protestant high school student at the time, implied such an integration during an interview. Asked if he remembered the Klan as "scary," he replied:

I don't think it was tense because I don't think anyone was afraid of (them). I just thought, you know . . . why do we need this in the community, like we were fighting Negroes and we didn't have any Negroes. We were fighting the Jews, and we didn't have that many Jews. Then you start to blame . . . the Catholics, (but) then you got all kinds of people that (didn't) want to offend their Catholic friends by saying they thought the Klan was all right. I never did figure out who were the people that would join the Klan.[39]

On the other hand, though tensions never succeeded in polarizing the community, Jefferson was by no means a hotbed of ecumenism either. There were tensions, and the designation of Catholic or Protestant had very real significance. One of the continuing sources of friction was the problem of "mixed" marriages.[40] The Catholic Church would not approve wedding ceremonies performed for its members by civil authorities or Protestant clergy. Especially irritating to Protestants was the Catholic insistence that any children born to the union would be brought up in the Catholic faith. In 1908 the diocese reemphasized its position and instructed priests to enforce it rigidly. The *Bee* printed the Catholic rules on the issue on the front page.[41] Weddings between members of different Protestant denominations occasioned little comment, but couples thought twice before crossing the Catholic-Protestant boundary.

Of course, even here there were exceptions. The way the "rules" were translated into actual practice was always a little more complicated. It was Margaret Minnihan Cudahy's impression that, while the issue was discussed in her home, her father gave his Catholic children considerable latitude. She recalled being told "if we met a Catholic who was a good person, fine and dandy, but if we didn't, he says, 'Who is to say who is better?'" They were not forbidden to date non-Catholics. Her brother Frank did marry a non-Catholic who later joined the church, "but she didn't at the time they were married."[42]

In the end it was the couple who had to decide whether their affection meant more to them than church canon. If it did, they usually figured out some accommodation on the religious question. Kellogg Thomas cited one extreme example. A Presbyterian uncle of his married a Catholic, "one of the Hill sisters." Because neither wished to join the other's church, they selected a new denomination, "and for the rest of their lives were members of the Baptist Church. That didn't happen very often, but it did happen. That's kind of an odd compromise."[43] Odd or not, it does signify that church affiliation was an important factor. The groom could not bring himself to join the Catholic church, and the bride refused to join his.

As the century progressed, Protestant denominations began to worship together more often. Born in 1903, Thomas could not recall even having been in "any other church except the Presbyterian Church until I was maybe somewhere in high school except for maybe an odd funeral or two" and considered his experience fairly typical for Protestant youth of the era. He went to at least one Presbyterian service every week and sometimes two or three. He was not antagonistic toward members of other denominations, but outside school, the Presbyterians were the most significant group of which he was a part. What he did recall about those years, however, was that a "change was coming about," a change from the former strictness. "People would go from church to church a little bit."[44] When pressed, he could not be more specific, but there seemed to be less denominational rigidity, at least among Protestants.

Catholics remained fairly isolated in religious activities. For the most part, Catholics were forbidden to attend services in other churches, a rule that nourished Protestant hostility toward the Catholic hierarchy. Sometimes the prohibition was interpreted to apply even to entering Protestant churches. Roy Mosteller recalled two girls in the same high school class, a Baptist and a Catholic, who were best friends. Neither would even enter the other's church. He explained, "if the Baptist girl would have to go into her church to pick up a song book or something, the Catholic girl would stand on the porch or vice versa."[45]

Yet here again, there were the exceptions. Catholic Pauline Russell often attended Presbyterian and Methodist services with her girl friends. She claimed that Father Peter Murphy was "very easy" on the subject and that the decision was mostly left to Catholic parents. Protestants had no formal restrictions on attending Catholic services although they rarely did except on special occasions. Nevertheless, during the same years that the Klan was holding rallies, the Methodist young people's Epworth League was attending Christmas Eve mass at the Catholic Church. "We didn't feel that they didn't want us there. They were happy that we were there," Gene Melson recalled.[46]

Catholics and Protestants in Jefferson, well aware of the differences between their faiths, had inherited the distrust and suspicions of centuries of antagonism. Yet as they mingled in daily activities, they

ED CAIN LAUNDRY (front and back rooms). Towns offered services which were unavailable to rural households. The crew of the Cain laundry relieved Jefferson housewives of some of the burden of the Monday morning wash. *Courtesy of Greene County Historical Society*

JEFFERSON COLLEGE OF COMMERCE. For a few years prior to the turn of the century, the Iowa College of Commerce offered business courses in several Iowa communities, including Jefferson, Webster City, and Boone. Students could take courses in bookkeeping, commercial law, and secretarial methods, including "the scientific fingering of typewriting." A. L. Garten was principal of the Jefferson College of Commerce. In *Iowa Illustrated*

COUNTY OFFICIALS PORTRAIT COLLECTION. Full beards and imposing mustaches, very popular in the 1890s, are well illustrated in this photo collection of Greene County officials. Clockwise from upper left: J. F. Thompson, sheriff; Owen Lovejoy, county attorney; Lee Davis, auditor; J. W. Fitz, treasurer; W. E. Jenison, superintendent of schools; and J. H. Black, deputy sheriff. In *Iowa Illustrated*

CLASS OF 1899. Graduation was an elegant affair at the turn of the century. The male-female ratio of the Class of 1899 was typical. Women often finished high school in preparation for careers as schoolteachers. *Courtesy of Greene County Historical Society*

BICYCLE CLUBS. Bicycle clubs were popular across Iowa in the 1890s among both women and men. Hobbies, special interests, and athletics drew local residents together across occupation, ethnic, or religious lines. *Courtesy of Iowa State Historical Society*

6   CULTURE CLUB COOK BOOK.

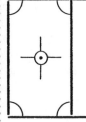

BUCKS JEWELERS. Jewelry, china, eyeglasses—Lincoln Bucks combined a number of services in his Jefferson store.

found it impossible and ludicrous to respond to each other solely in terms of abstract stereotypes. In a small town, one appears simultaneously in a variety of roles, of which the denominational is only one. In Jefferson, with a very small Catholic population and the same school system for all children, the significance of denomination faded as the century progressed.

Another major factor in one's identity in the community was occupation. The 1895 census lists the occupations of Jefferson workers. Professionals and merchants had increased substantially from the 1880s, but there continued to be a strong representation of craftsmen. The diversity of vocation indicates that the small town continued to manufacture many items for itself and the surrounding vicinity and to provide many services.[47] Data from the Iowa census for occupations throughout Greene County are in Table 2.2.

What a man did for a living tended to identify him – and his family – as part of an informal grouping in the community. To a large extent, friendships and socializing patterns followed occupational lines. For example, when the Jefferson Country Club was formed in 1910, it was an organization of the families of merchants and professionals. Its charter roll read like a "who's who in Jefferson." There were thirteen merchants, nine bankers, three lawyers, two judges, four doctors, two dentists, three real estate dealers, two newspaper editors, the owner of the local telephone company, an auto dealer, a druggist, a hotel man-

TABLE 2.2. Categories of occupation, Greene County, 1905–1925

	1905			1915			1925		
	Male	Female	Total	Male	Female	Total	Male	Female	Total
Agricultural	3,005	478[a]	3,483	2,655	30	2,685	2,666	42	2,708
Professional	178	230	408	123	198	321	148	196	344
Domestic and personal	70	89	159	95	156	251	83	3,326[b]	3,409
Trades and transport	500	48	548	692	74	766	558	55	613
Manufacture, mechanical	386	101	487	455	56	511	239	13	252
Unclassified labor	692	7	699	467	–	467	797	55	852

Sources: Census of Iowa, 1905, 1915, 1925.

[a]The 478 figure for Greene County females in agriculture is so inconsistent with those of neighboring counties that it suggests a difference in census procedures. For example, Guthrie County borders Greene on the south and reported only 35 females. Story, two counties to the east, recorded 26. The 1915 figure for Greene County is much more consistent with comparable counties.

[b]The sharp increase in this figure suggests that the 1925 census included housewives in this category while previous surveys did not.

ager, an insurance agent, a traveling salesman, and two retired farmers.[48]

These were the most likely candidates for the school board and the city council. They took the lead in civic projects and community organizations. They were what Atherton describes as that "inner circle" present in every country town "whose own personal interests were so tightly interwoven with those of the community at large that one cannot determine where self-interest ended and public spirit began."[49] If community histories tend to dwell on them more than on others, it is because it was they who left the most abundant records. Their activities became news, and their names appeared more frequently in community annals. On a deeper level, however, they were the ones who had invested most heavily in the community. As Atherton notes, self-interest and public spirit meshed. Theirs was a proprietary attitude. They took compliments or criticisms about the town from outsiders in much the same way that parents react to comments about their children. The term "city fathers" is an apt metaphor.

A second group in town consisted of salaried employees, such as store clerks or courthouse workers. A clerk often worked for a merchant for so long that the clerk too became closely identified with the store, like Fred Derry in McCully and Osgood's general store, Bert Tucker in Gamble's clothing store, or Cleve Barr in Roy Curtis's grocery. Clerks were paid by the week or month, and they put in long hours by the sides of their employers.

"Cap" Lyon worked for twenty years for E. H. Carter in the general store. His daughter, Berniece Raver, remembered the many hours her father spent at work. He was the first one up in the morning because he had to be at work at 7:00 A.M. when the store opened. He came home to dinner at 11:00 A.M. and was back at work when the kids came home at noon. The family had supper together at 5:00 P.M., after which he returned to the store and often worked until 10:00 P.M. "We didn't see much of our father," she recalled.[50]

That was six days a week. In addition, on Saturday night, the stores stayed open as late as midnight as farm families wandered around the square socializing, doing their weekly shopping, and attending the movie theater. In 1918 Jefferson merchants moved up store closing time from 8:00 P.M. to 6:30 P.M. The change was controversial. Some store owners feared that the earlier hour would anger farmers and discourage them from doing errands in town after evening chores. The majority argued that with automobiles, farmers could shop earlier with fewer problems. The main impetus for the 6:30 P.M. closing was that it would permit merchants, clerks, and their families to attend the Thursday evening band concert in the park. The *Bee* maintained that the farmers, who also liked to hear the concerts, would not want to deny the store personnel that opportunity.[51]

A third group were the laborers and mechanics, those who worked with their hands, often out-of-doors. Delivery men, shoe repairmen, auto mechanics, carpenters – they sometimes were salaried but often worked for themselves in small shops or garages. They mixed more freely with the clerks than with the merchants and professionals.

My grandfather's first job in Jefferson was in the Hutchinson Bicycle Shop around the turn of the century. Fred Hutchinson added car dealerships when automakers began developing their national marketing systems, and Grandpa started working on Maxwells, Hupmobiles, Fords, and EMFs ("Every Morning Fixits" as the latter model came to be known by disgusted owners). With the coming of the Model-T, Hutchinson dropped everything but the Ford franchise. Grandpa worked there until he and Pete McLaughlin opened a small garage of their own. In 1932 the new Ford dealer switched to Chevrolet, a vehicle Grandpa detested until his dying day and a major reason he opened his own shop. However, the respect in which he held his first employer, Frederick Hutchinson, was evident when my father, Frederick Morain, was born in 1913.

Grandpa's closest friends were the men with whom he worked – Pete, Earl Raver, Ned Wilson. In the summer, on family camping trips along the Raccoon River, the Morains often camped with the families of Cleve Barr, the grocery clerk; Roy Finch, a shoe repairman; and Mort Wolf, the Ford garage service manager. The men commuted to work while the women and children relaxed and played in camp.

Beyond the city limits lived the farmers, by far the largest single occupational group in the county and among whom there was also a well-understood hierarchy. Distinctions were not made by the type of work they did because, before farm specialization, their daily routines were substantially similar. Distinctions were based on whose land they were farming. At the top of the rural ladder were those who owned their own farms, the owner/operators. The lure of cheap land had brought the pioneer to the prairie. When a farmer could begin with almost as little as a team of horses, a cow, some pigs, chickens, and a plow, a young couple willing to work and save had a good chance of some day owning their own farm. With careful management, a little luck, and someone willing to lend them some money, they could look forward to buying a farm. Historian Joseph Wall characterized the long-term expectations of the typical Iowa farmer this way: "Above all, the farmers wanted to be able at the close of their lives to turn over to one or more of their children their old home places, debt free, better equipped, and more productive than those farms had been when they had acquired them. These expectations seemed to the farmers to make neither unreasonable nor aggressive demands upon society. Most farmers did not expect nor want great wealth. The Carnegie, Rockefeller, Gould dreams of an imperium did not goad Iowa farmers during their waking hours nor disturb their sleep at night."[52]

Ruth Suckow's novel *Country People* details the lives of a young German couple in Iowa whose frugality and willingness to push themselves hard won them their own farm, a comfortable retirement in town, and the respect of their neighbors.[53] Suckow had countless examples in real life on which to model her fictional characters. Some families in Greene County, such as the Thompsons, the Montheis, and the Duffs, were so successful and prolific that they established whole neighborhoods of adjoining farms. One stretch of road southeast of Scranton was called "Duff Road."

Until the widespread use of the tractor after the Second World War, the speed of work horses and the amount of physical labor necessary to run a farm limited the size of most operations to around 160 acres. Census figures recorded that in 1900 the average farm in Greene County was 158 acres, and by 1930 it had grown only to 171 acres. Through the 1930s, therefore, there were often four or five farm units per square mile, maintaining a consistent demand for hired farm labor and small-scale operators. Even if a family owned a whole section, it could not farm it by itself.

However, land prices were rising from the turn of the century through 1920. Intensive drainage removed swamps and small ponds from fertile croplands and allowed farmers to put more of their acres under cultivation. Furthermore, land and life insurance were the two major opportunities for investment for those small town and rural families with some extra money. They did not have ready access to stockbrokers, and not many were willing to gamble on the uncertainties of grain futures.[54] As money went into land, the price went up. The number of tenant farmers rose as it become more expensive to buy a farm. According to the 1900 census, 41 percent of county farms were operated by tenants. By 1930 the figure had climbed to 53 percent. Some rented the farms for a fixed rate, but many took a percentage of the crop and raised livestock. Good tenants might live for years on the same farm. Poor tenants often stayed only a year or two. In hard times security for any tenant was uncertain.

By custom, March 1 was moving day on the farms. Standardizing the day made it more convenient for everyone since those moving out could expect their new homes to become vacant on the same day. Carl Hamilton's *In No Time at All* gives a chilly account of the moves his family made.

Moving was always harder on Mother than anyone else. Frequently it was a case of moving into a house where the other family had "just moved out." It needed a thorough cleaning before moving in but there was not time. Rugs didn't fit; curtains didn't fit; cupboards didn't fit. The floors were bare pine boards with quarter inch cracks and painted around the edges. The rugs seldom matched the unpainted areas.

There was no hot water until the cook stove was set up and going. Each room echoed with a hollow, unwelcome sound. The chill of March was throughout the house. If there was electricity, its evidence was found in a bare bulb casting its glare from a cord in the center of the ceiling.

As I look back on those times, I think of Mother and Dad picking corn by hand in those years when they couldn't afford to hire help. But ranking next to that scene in my mind is Mother's lot at moving time. Throughout her years, the date March 1 was always the subject of some comment on her part for "those poor people who are having to move."[55]

The amount of physical labor necessary to run a farm created a demand for a third group of workers in the farm community, the hired hands. Hired sometimes for spring planting or fall harvest, sometimes through the whole season or even the whole year, they formed an essential labor pool for midwestern agriculture. If they were single (and most were), they moved in with the family. On occasion a married man could find a small house on the farm or near it for his family. Sometimes, farm boys in their older teens would hire out in the neighborhood, but most of the hands seemed to come up from Missouri or elsewhere in the South in search of work. A few local stores like Oppenheimer's Clothing served as an informal labor clearinghouse. Under a sign "Men for Jobs/Jobs for Men," notices put farmers wanting help and men looking for work in touch, and contracts were sealed with a handshake. As Hamilton recalls,

For years, the standard rate of pay was $50 per month plus board and room. No fringe benefits, no bonuses, no social security, no insurance came with it. The man came; he worked. Dad wrote him a check; he left. That was it. He may have added to our lore of stories about hired men, but he didn't clutter up our records. Or the government's.

Once I remember Dad stating flatly at the dinner table that he would *never* pay a man more than $50 a month. One hired man looked at him in a rather peculiar way. But that was all.

Being a hired man, at $50 a month, was supposed to be the first step on the road to farm ownership. Hired man; then a renter; then an owner. It didn't work that way too often.[56]

Although their labor was essential, hired hands had little visibility as individuals in the farm community. They rarely left the farm except on Saturday night and maybe on Sunday morning for church.

Neighbors knew they were there but rarely had contact with them. Where they came from or where they went, no one seemed to know or care. Collectively, however, they were an important component in the rural community. The farms needed their help.

An often overlooked group, originally from the farm, provided an important link between town and country. By the turn of the century most small towns had become the home of retired farm couples who had turned over the operation to their children, to tenants, or to new owners. A couple could live comfortably on the landlord's share of the income from 160 acres or could sell the farm outright and live on the interest. Older couples appreciated the comforts and social opportunities of the town. Suckow's fictional *Country People* described how the old men would find excuses to walk downtown in the morning, to pick up the mail or to buy something, and then congregate at the barber shop or implement dealer to complain about the weather and farm prices and to discuss the crops. The women enjoyed their own social outlets and busied themselves with gardens, sewing projects, and cooking. Their children and grandchildren were often either on the home place or somewhere in the area, and retired couples were an important bridge between the farm and town. They gave their family and former neighbors a place to stay when they visited town and helped keep the towns sensitive to rural needs.

When the Jefferson woman joked that her mother would not let her date "farm kids," she was not implying that farming was not a respectable occupation. Good farmers commanded respect in town as well as in the country. Farming, however, was more than just a man's occupation. It was a way of life for the entire family. Before 1920 rural children were likely to attend one-room schools only through eighth grade. Before rural electrification began in the 1930s most farm homes lacked indoor plumbing, running water, and household appliances that town homes had possessed for two or three decades. Farm wives kept flocks of chickens, raised large gardens, and usually did most of their own baking. The social highlight of the week was the Saturday night trip to town. Poets and politicians may have praised the farmer, but town mothers did not want their daughters to marry and leave the amenities of town life.

One final group of people were residents of neither town nor farm. Their occupational distinction was the absence of occupation. They were "just tramps." Tramps, or hoboes, were not really residents, but at any time, a community was likely to have at least one or two passing through. Before Social Security or expanded welfare programs, these were the nomads of the railroad, grabbing rides in boxcars from town to town where they begged a meal or worked an hour or two for some immediate need. They would appear at the back door, rarely at the front, and ask for food. Sometimes they got it, and sometimes they did not.

Rumor had it that they left signs that only other tramps would recognize to mark homes were there was "an easy touch," so it was unwise to be too generous. There was a report on the signs hoboes supposedly used to identify generous or dangerous homes. A circle crossed by two arrows signaled an unfavorable welcome. A circle around an "X" marked an easy meal. An "X" by a triangle meant that one would be asked to work before getting anything to eat.[57]

Hoboes rarely did any harm, but neither were they invited in to eat at the kitchen table. They seemed more a nuisance than a threat. If a law officer met up with one, he might escort him to the city limits and encourage him to widen his horizons in any direction he chose. In Jefferson tramps often camped around the North Western railroad stockyards on the north edge of town. When times got bad in the cities, more tramps appeared, but their numbers fell off sharply with the Second World War. No one asked their names. Individually, they left almost no permanent mark on the community. They were "just tramps."

For women, whether on the farm or in town, career opportunities were curtailed. In a perverse twist of the language, female human beings who cooked three meals a day over a wood-burning stove, cared for children, sewed, mended, cleaned, canned, washed, and ironed were not considered to be "working." Unless you got paid, you were not working. Boys were encouraged in a variety of career ambitions, but all girls were supposed to become wives and mothers. Those who did not were the exceptions.

There were these exceptions, of course, sometimes by accident but sometimes by deliberate choice. (See Table 2.3) The Harding sisters, Bess and Winifred, remained single and opened a ladies' dress shop on the south side of the square. Bess had taught school for several terms but was happy to give that up to go into business with her sister.

TABLE 2.3.   Women's employment in Greene County by age, 1915

Age	Professional and service	Domestic and personal service
14–17	3	8
18–20	27	27
21–44	157	107
45 and over	11	14

Source: Census of Iowa, 1915.

They bargained with salesmen who stopped in the store, and by the 1930s they were traveling regularly to Omaha to order stock from wholesale dealers. Wilma Downes and Grace Wadsworth taught school for years as married women. May Dunham Rydings continued a memorial stone operation after her husband's death, and Bertha Rutter was for years a secretary/bookkeeper for the Milligan grain business. Minnie Wilson, a former school principal and a frequent lecturer at teaching institutes, worked with her husband in his law office though she had no formal legal training. Eva Bradley did washing and ironing in her home. Normally, however, a young woman worked outside the home for a few years in her late teens and early twenties, quit her job when she married, and left the work force forever. Those who returned normally did so because of financial necessity.[58]

Jefferson had several female physicians. Dr. Gus Grimmell practiced medicine in Jefferson after her graduation from state university medical school. The daughter and granddaughter of doctors, Dr. Gus, as she was called, was a representative of the growing number of female doctors throughout the latter nineteenth century. Dr. Gus married after several years of medical practice and moved with her husband to Minnesota. A local "who's who" published in 1896 described her as a "charming lady, withal popular in the highest social realm" and "a brilliant and interesting conversationalist." According to long-time residents, she could swear like a trooper. As with the Grimmells, medicine was a tradition in the Morden family. Dr. Elizabeth Ann Morden was practicing in 1905 with her son Roy. When her daughter Leone graduated from a Chicago medical school and decided to return to Jefferson to practice, Roy left to open a practice in Des Moines. The census lists 128 female physicians in the state in 1890, 260 in 1900, and 325 by 1910. Most of them, the Jefferson representatives included, had a clientele chiefly of women and children.[59]

The career of Dr. Gus highlights a major deterrent to women's employment in the professions. Many of the legal barriers to education and professional certification had been removed by 1900, but forbidding obstacles still remained. In her 1918 *Legal and Political Status of Women in Iowa*, Ruth Gallaher noted: "Two considerations deter women from preparing themselves for highly specialized professions: the length and difficulty of the training required, and the difficulty of coordinating such work with homemaking and the care of children."[60] Because social custom and household responsibilities required that mothers be at home with their young children, young women considering a professional career usually had to weigh their interest against their desire for a home and family. The combination of career and family open to men was very difficult for a women to achieve.

Therefore, for the young woman seeking work in a small town, the horizons were limited. In most cases the choice in 1900 was among domestic service, teaching school, and clerical positions. According to the 1915 census, seven out of ten working women were employed in either professional service, which included teachers, or domestic and personal service. (See Table 2.2.)

As a domestic servant, one was the "hired girl" who worked in the home. The rambling two- and three-story homes built in Jefferson before World War I frequently contained two staircases, one off the front hall or the living room and a one leading up from the kitchen or pantry. The latter permitted the hired girl to go upstairs to her room or to clean without being observed. Before electrical appliances, maintaining a household required long hours of drudgery, and middle-class women considered some household help a near necessity. The hours were long, the work was hard, and the pay was very low. Working as a hired girl was not an attractive job, but those who needed work had few options. They were not called "maids," a term that smacked too much of aristocracy and class distinctions for the small town. They were more often called "hired help" or just "girls."[61]

Teaching school for a few years between graduation and marriage was a popular career choice for young women and had become identified as women's work, although it had not always been that way. Until the Civil War, men filled a majority of the teaching posts in the state, but due to a combination of factors, the profession underwent a sex change. Men could earn more in other jobs, and women had few options. What really clinched the teaching profession for women was the introduction in the 1880s of teacher certification requirements that mandated attendance at annual teacher institutes or the completion of a teacher training course. A young man might teach in a rural school for a season or two, but the salaries were so low that it did not pay him to invest much time or tuition money to get a teaching certificate. With options, he could afford to leave pedagogy. By 1900 women held 83 percent of the teaching positions in Iowa. When the newspaper listed the names of rural schoolteachers in Greene County in 1917, 119 out of 125 were women.[62]

By modern standards it was easy to become a teacher. At one time, candidates needed only to score well on tests administered by the county superintendent of schools to receive a teaching certificate, but gradually the standards required that they complete some teacher training (normal) courses also. In 1916 the state superintendent of public instruction designated the Jefferson High School to receive $1,000 in state aid for a normal course to prepare teachers for rural schools.[63] Through this program high school students could take

teacher training courses along with the academic subjects and be certified to teach in a rural school upon graduation.

Teacher salaries were low and recognized as such at the time. The
Jefferson school board in 1911 raised wages a little so that teachers
earned from $50 to $70 a month, or $450 to $630 for the nine-month
term. The superintendent, a male at the time although the position was
sometimes held by a woman, got the princely sum of $1,500 for a full
year, $125 a month.

There were separate pay scales for men and women teachers.
Men received more, justified by the theory that they had more expenses and needed to prepare to support their future families. Maxine
Morley wrote a letter to the editor in 1908 objecting to separate pay
scales and urging the formation of a teachers' union to improve salaries. She claimed that women's expenses were just as high as men's.

Though she did not mention it, Morley might also have com-
plained that teachers were held to higher moral standards than other
occupations. Even the whisper of scandal, founded on fact or not,
about those entrusted with the education and moral development of
the future generation could jeopardize their careers.[64]

Because many teachers had come to Jefferson from the outside
and were restricted in evening activities by social conventions, they
did not become involved in civic affairs and rarely had visibility outside
of the schools. Local bachelors, however, took more than a passing
interest in the arrival of new teachers each fall. Many women who
came as teachers stayed in town as wives of local men, but not until
their marriage did they enter fully into the civic and social life of the
community.

Usually, women's teaching careers ended on their wedding day.
Many school districts made it either a formal or informal policy to
prohibit married women from classroom positions. When my mother
came to Jefferson in 1936 to teach music, her contract stated that
marriage would terminate her employment. When she and Dad decided to move up their wedding date from June to Easter Sunday in
1939, she had to get special permission from the school board to continue teaching the remainder of the year as a married woman. (They
were married on Sunday in her parents' home in Lamoni, Iowa, and
she was back in school Monday morning—a deliberate fifteen minutes
early!)

Census figures clearly indicate that for most women, employment
outside the home was not a lifelong condition. It began when they
completed their education and lasted for most until marriage. Reentry
into the work force was the exception.

Part of the resistance to married women as teachers stemmed

from public inhibitions about pregnancy. Women sharply curtailed their outside activities for as many as five months before a birth so that they would not expose themselves as being "in a family way." Another major factor, however, was simply the prevailing notion of propriety: married women were supposed to be at home. "Normal" married women spent their time taking care of their husbands, their children, and their homes. Women who wanted to do something else were not the role models school boards wished to place in front of their children.

Older women were sometimes hired when the prospect of a new little bundle from heaven had diminished and their children no longer required as much attention. Grace Wadsworth taught many years in rural schools, and Wilma Downes continued to teach high school business courses during her marriage to a Jefferson merchant. Mr. and Mrs. Downes ate their meals at McDuffies' boarding house. Still, the ideology of gender made these women the exceptions. Teaching school for most women who tried it was an interlude between their own classwork and marriage.

In addition to normal training, girls could take business classes, which meant preparation for secretarial positions. They learned typing, bookkeeping, and shorthand. Wilma Downes taught these courses for many years. Like the normal course, secretarial training provided the work skills necessary for a young woman to find employment for a few years before she married. It was rarely presented as a lifetime career. The skills necessary for that she learned in home economics.

There were some occupations that could be pursued on either a full- or part-time basis, and sometimes the work could be done at home. The clothing industry provided work for local women at the turn of the century. The 1895 census listed thirty women as dressmakers, four more as seamstresses, and thirteen as milliners. Sometimes as a year-round occupation but sometimes for only a few months, women tailored garments and hats on order. As the women's ready-made clothing industry expanded, producing fashionable items at prices much below what could be sewn by hand, the self-employed seamstress all but disappeared. What remained was an occasional order for alterations, but clothing construction as a home industry sharply declined. The hat industry suffered from the vagaries of fashion, and the locally produced product gradually disappeared.

If you knew these three things about a local resident—ethnic background, religion, and occupation, you could make a pretty good bet about his (or, after 1920, her) political affiliation. The system was not foolproof, but you would be right more often than not. An Irish Catholic railroad hand was a good bet to be a Democrat, and a Scottish Presbyterian lawyer whose grandfathers were both GAR members was an odds-on favorite to be Republican.

Of the three factors, religion was probably the best single indicator, according to Richard Jensen's *Winning of the Midwest*. Jensen maintains that until the Depression and the New Deal of the 1930s, the major political division in the Midwest was a reflection of the religious differences between evangelical Protestants and what he terms the "liturgical" churches, the Catholics, Episcopalians, and Lutherans. He writes: "That bridge linking theology and politics was the demand by (the evangelicals) that government remove the major obstacle to the purification of society through revivalistic Christianity, institutionalized immorality (particularly the liquor industry)."[65]

Local churches were not political organizations and did not formally endorse candidates, nor did ministers hold office or wield much influence in the political party. Still, when there was a clearly defined difference between candidates on an issue like Prohibition or state aid to parochial schools, clergy of neither camp were above preaching on Scriptural texts that made it clear how God would vote if he could have met local residency requirements.

Jensen lists three ways that religion affected politics. Theology defined morality and outlined the proper course of action; churches organized people into groups where peer pressure strengthened the tendency toward a unified outlook; and denominations were channels of information and sometimes agents of collective action. While Jefferson congregations rarely took formal action, state or district denominational conventions sometimes did. In 1916, for example, when Republican gubernatorial candidate William Harding called for substantial liberalization of liquor laws, several major Protestant denominations passed resolutions against him.[66]

The Prohibition issue was perhaps the most obvious instance in which churches flirted with political activism. The insistence of most evangelical Protestant denominations that drinking was a sin influenced (granted, in varying degrees) the individual member's attitudes on the question. It took courage for a Methodist to publicly support a candidate who favored the sale of alcohol.

But such Methodists existed. On a farm at the edge of town lived the Wilcox family – Methodist, nondrinkers, and Democrats. Lumund Wilcox recalled one Sunday morning when the minister was urging his flock to reelect a Republican senator because his opponent opposed Prohibition. It was widely understood that the senator himself would have been miserable if the laws he supported on the chamber floor had been vigorously enforced; his own drinking habits were not nearly as bone-dry as his voting record. That was hypocrisy from the pulpit, according to Nancy Wilcox, Lumund's mother, who walked out of the sermon to register her protest.[67]

On the other hand, there were some Irish-Catholic Republicans. Billy McCormick and A. J. Finn were staunch Republicans. Both were drys. With so few Jefferson Catholics in the first place and some of them Republicans, the proverbial tie between Catholicism and the Democratic party seemed weaker in Jefferson than it was elsewhere around the state.

Whichever party they favored, most people took their political allegiance seriously. J. E. (Pat) Patterson learned the difference between Republicans and Democrats very early. Every year at the family reunion, often right after dinner, Pat's grandfather gathered all the boys and took them behind the barn for a solemn ritual. First, he took off his coat. Then he took off his vest. Finally, he unbuttoned his shirt and pointed to a Civil War wound on his chest. He made it an annual ritual to impress upon their young minds "what those damn Democrats did to your grandfather."[68] The lesson took, and Patterson served several terms as Greene County Republican chairman. Bess Osgood admitted that she had once voted for a Democrat but vowed that she "would never do that again." In her opinion "you aren't voting for just one man, you're voting for a whole regime. When they get in, they bring all their people in with them. Even if I don't like the (Republican) party man, I vote for him."[69]

Party loyalty was a tradition one did not take lightly. The Civil War had firmly planted Iowa in the Republican column, leading Sen. Jonathan Dolliver to quip that "Iowa will go Democratic when hell goes Methodist." The national Democratic party was tagged as a union of white supremacists in the South and immigrant blocs in northern cities. In Iowa, Democrats were concentrated along the Mississippi River and in neighboring Carroll County. The party also contained the remnants of the populist movement of the late nineteenth century, which had peaked with the Bryan campaign in 1896 and, therefore, had a "radical" taint. Democrats tried to tar the Republicans who supported high tariffs as lackeys of eastern financial and manufacturing interests, but they were fighting at a disadvantage. When it was a choice between something as abstract as the tariff or something as real as the scar on your grandfather's chest, Republicans came out on top every time.

Contrary to a popular myth, it was not Iowa farmers who chalked up the highest majorities for the Republicans. It has always been the small town. In Greene County, Democrats often did much better in the rural areas than they did in towns. Irish Catholics in Cedar and Kendrick townships helped to carry those areas for the Democrats though Protestant Grant and Greenbrier townships could often deliver over 70 percent to Republican candidates. The Republican percentage in Jefferson consistently ran higher than the party's percentage countywide. In 1900, for example, Greene County voters favored Republican William McKinley over Democrat William Jennings Bryan by a two to one margin, while in Jefferson alone it was three to one McKinley. In 1904 three out of four voters in the county supported Republican Teddy Roosevelt. In Jefferson it was five out of six.

However one analyzes the data, the obvious conclusion is that Greene County was simply not a fertile Democratic field. When the interviews turned to politics, long-time residents often began naming who the Democrats were—the Wilcoxes, the Cudahys, the Brunners, the Whalens, the Mugans. There were not many in town, in fact so few that their party affiliation distinguished them. Until well into the 1930s, the Democratic party could never put together a strong county organization. Lumund Wilcox, returning to Jefferson from law school in 1934, attended a Democratic county convention. He was one of five people who showed up.[70] The weakness of the party made it difficult to recruit good candidates since the election result was almost a foregone conclusion. The party consistently had difficulty raising money.[71]

The Republican party, by contrast, had a strong organization, and the Republican county chairman had considerable influence. In 1907 the state of Iowa instituted a reform designed to curb the power of local political machines. Rather than nominating all candidates at party conventions, the new law required a primary election in which all party members could vote. The primary changed the rules but by no means eliminated the influence of party organization. The chairman was the man with whom the state or national officials checked when it was time for an appointment. He was also a man to whom candidates for state office paid attention. By the time he was elected chairman, he had worked with local party members enough to win their respect and to have established himself as one who could get something done.[72]

The chairman relied heavily on a few influential party leaders who, by virtue of their occupation or personality, had a strong following, like the Stillmans who edited and published the *Bee,* the only newspaper with a strong countywide circulation. Paul Stillman's popularity put him in the legislature where he became speaker of the house in 1911. The county chairman was normally from Jefferson: farmer and clerk of court John Stevenson, editor Vic Lovejoy, or lawyers Orville Harris and Guy Richardson. Neither the Republicans nor Democrats paid their party officers, but that is not to say that they worked without reward. They satisfied their sense of civic duty, and they took pleasure in the political game.

One final note, however, might help put the role of local politics in proper perspective. There was indeed a love of the "game" of politics that many shared. Throughout the community there was a basic underlying consensus on what the broad ends of the political system should be, and although there might be heated disagreements on how to reach those ends, even political adversaries normally kept things in perspective.

My father recalled an anecdote that illustrates the point well. As a young Democratic attorney and an ardent New Dealer, Lumund Wilcox used to enjoy dropping into the newspaper office to bait Vic Lovejoy. It was not hard. Within a few minutes, Lovejoy would be livid, pounding the desk and castigating Franklin Roosevelt and the whole New Deal program. Quick on the uptake, Wilcox knew how to make Lovejoy's blood pressure soar. When Wilcox left, Lovejoy would lean back in his chair, prop his feet up on his desk, sigh, and tell my father working at the next desk, "Gee, I like that boy."[73]

At the turn of the twentieth century, most Jefferson residents looked at the social order with a sense of satisfaction. People very much like themselves dominated the most important aspects of American life. The major American heroes, like Washington, Jefferson, Franklin, and Lincoln, shared an Anglo-Saxon heritage. The greats of American literature—Irving, Poe, Longfellow, Hawthorne, Melville, and Twain—were in the same tradition. State legislatures, the leading pulpits, and the faculties of major universities likewise were filled with men with whom small town residents felt a cultural kinship. At the local, state, and national level, local residents (at least, the men) saw their own reflection when they looked at those who held power.

Iowa at the turn of the century boasted powerful political figures on the national scene. Republican dominance at home allowed the state's congressional delegation to accumulate seniority, which translated into power. Sen. William Boyd Allison was the senior Republican on the powerful Committee on Appropriations, which reviewed every proposal involving financial support, and was regarded as one of the four most powerful senators in Congress. Iowa's junior senator was Jonathan P. Dolliver of Fort Dodge who had been considered for vice president by both McKinley and Taft. He was widely recognized as an outstanding orator—some said the best in the Senate—and an expert on the tariff question. He was a devout Methodist. Congressman David B. Henderson of Dubuque was speaker of the house from 1899 to 1903, the first representative from west of the Mississippi to hold that office. (Granted, coming from Dubuque, he was not very far west of the Mississippi, but west nevertheless.) Several other Iowa congressmen chaired important House committees. "Tama Jim" Wilson, an Iowa State professor, and Leslie Shaw from Denison served in cabinet positions. Historian Leland Sage writes: "All this Republican power inside Iowa and in its delegation to Congress at the turn of the century was neatly meshed with Republican power in the national administration. It was commonly said to those who wanted something from the federal government, 'Ask Iowa!' "[74] These men were no strangers to local residents. They were "hometown" products whose national influence was a source of self-esteem and comfort to those who worked for their election.

In 1900 even the president of the United States was a product of the small town. William McKinley was eighteen years old when the Civil War broke out. He left his studies at Allegheny College, enlisted in the Union Army, and rose to the rank of major by the end of the fighting. He studied law after the war and began practice in Canton, Ohio. In 1869 he was elected county attorney, and from there to Congress in 1876. He was always a sound-money man and an advocate of a high tariff to promote American industry. He was also a devout Presbyterian respected for his piety.

In 1896 he won the Republican nomination for the presidency. Who was his opponent? It was William Jennings Bryan, another product of the midwestern small town. Born in Salem, Illinois, in 1860, Bryan graduated from Illinois College in Jacksonville where he set up a law practice. In 1887 he moved to Lincoln, Nebraska, and became active in Democratic politics. After two terms in Congress and a defeat in a bid for a Senate seat, he became the editor of the Omaha *World Herald* and began his very successful career as a chautauqua speaker. Also a devoted churchman, Bryan became a champion of biblical fundamentalism and a leader against the teaching of evolution in public schools. Though between the economic policies advocated by Bryan and McKinley there was a world of difference, the two themselves represented the same cultural stream. The question was which Anglo-Saxon evangelical Protestant would occupy the White House.

That, of course, to Jefferson Anglo-Saxon Protestants was the way it should be. In every dimension, America represented the highest evolution among nations and served as a model to those less advanced. America had a special mission among nations. It was indeed "as a city upon a hill." Lincoln referred to the United States as "the last best hope of earth." Democracy had evolved from aristocracy, capitalism from feudalism, and Protestantism from Catholicism. Further progress would come from those on the cutting edge of evolutionary advance.

CHAPTER 3

Gender
Created He Them

Male and female, created He them.
—GENESIS 1:27

LIKE EVERYWHERE ELSE IN AMERICA, Jefferson had very definite rules about what constituted masculine and feminine behavior. Of all the factors contributing to the formation of personal identity, the most fundamental was gender. Democratic and egalitarian ideals undercut distinctions based on race, religion, or occupation, but sex differences were presumed to be rooted in the "natural" order of things. Most residents firmly believed that personality characteristics, intellectual aptitudes, and even a disposition toward morality were innately related to one's sex, that men and women inherently differed in these areas because of how their bodies functioned. As in the case of beliefs about race and religious denominations, individual behavior did not always fit the theory, and local residents made the necessary accommodations.

However, there was a way in which the issue of gender was unlike the race or religion issues for Jefferson residents. No one was seriously challenging the theory of Anglo-Saxon superiority or pushing for racial equality. There was no ecumenical movement to reexamine the reasons for Catholic-Protestant separation in the hopes of bringing about closer relations. There was, however, considerable discussion about what roles men and women should play. The issue even had a name. It was called "the woman question" because the debate most often concerned what women should or should not be doing. The issue was joined most noisily on the question of granting women the right to vote, woman suffrage, which symbolized an official recognition of a new relationship between the sexes. It was not simply a matter of public policy, however. It involved a new understanding of the most intimate of institutions, marriage and the family. During the early twentieth century, traditional prescriptions for masculine and feminine behavior underwent considerable modification, with the predictable anguish that occurs whenever individuals struggle to come to grips with a new image of themselves and those around them.

Some assumptions about the differences between the sexes seemed so obvious that they were simply self-evident. Men were stronger. They were presumed to have more energy, more aggressive characteristics, and hence to be better suited for competitive activities. Because men in this formulation had a stronger sex drive, it was thought they found it more difficult to contain their sexual instincts and needed help from women lest they allow themselves to fall into debilitating excesses. On the other hand, women were weaker. It was presumed that they had a more delicate nervous system and they were more subject to their emotions. Less rational than men, women relied more on intuition. Because these personality differences between the sexes stemmed from differences of structure and function that could not be changed, any attempt to force people into roles for which they were innately unsuited would lead only to personal unhappiness and social discord.[1]

Biological differences between male and female do exist and remain constant from one culture to another. How a culture understands those distinctions, however, varies widely from place to place and from era to era. Expectations of masculine and feminine behavior based on that understanding also vary greatly. In other words, while differences remain constant, understanding of what those differences are and how they affect personality does not.

As elsewhere in America at the turn of the century, Jefferson residents assumed that masculinity and femininity encompassed distinct but complementary spheres of endowments, capacities, interests, and temperaments. The sex act itself was a paradigm of the social relationship. Neither sex could reproduce without the other; it took both. In other human relationships as well it took both the masculine and feminine to produce truly human society. Men were practical while women appreciated aesthetic qualities. Men were competitive, women nurturing. Men were rational; women were intuitive and responded much more to their feelings. The competitive and aggressive qualities of the male that enabled him to survive in the world outside the home made it difficult for him to provide the tenderness and patient nurture that a mother instinctively gave her family within it. Women on the other hand were too tenderhearted and emotional to succeed in business, but they were ideally suited to create a home environment for husbands and children that not only provided comfort from the bruises of the outside world but prepared and inspired their husbands and sons to succeed in it.

While much of the debate focused on the woman question, it necessarily also involved what was expected of men. The code word for the masculine ideal was "character," a term best defined as the sum of a long string of worthy attributes: strong but not overbearing, self-reliant, resolute, resourceful, practical, capable of strong affections but always able to keep emotions under control, and steadfast in support of truth and virtue.

In the obituaries, which summarized and evaluated their lives, men won praise for these qualities. For example, a local man was praised for his "deep, earnest, sincere affection":

He never wore his heart upon his sleeve, as if to claim or covet the attention of those with whom he mingled. It seemed to be his one purpose to stand four square with all the actual requirements and responsibilities of an active, everyday life. The sincerity of this departed friend was one of his shining merits, and that bore fruit in his always doing well what his hands found to do. . . . As a man among men, he always saw to it, sometimes through difficulties, that his word was as good as his bond. His nature was wondrously tolerant and charitable. . . . His family relations were very nearly ideal, for home was the center of his life.[2]

Peter Vest was described as "a man of strong character, of large influence, and of the highest type of sterling honesty":

He had convictions, and he was never afraid to express them. In his religious beliefs, he was Methodist, and he knew the reasons for the faith that was in him and sustained him to the end; in politics he was an uncompromising Democrat, and you always knew where to find him; in all the relations of life, he was a stalwart advocate of what was honorable and just, and was himself an example of that sort of living. He was a great lover of his home and the home circle, and no kindness was too great, no sacrifice too exacting to be exerted for the happiness of those who dwelt within the circle.[3]

Frank Anderson was a "model young man, a son of whom any parent might well feel proud":

He was of exemplary habits, steady and reliable at home or at his work, and was such a man as would meet death at his post of duty. He was his mother's namesake, and his first thought was always of her. He was frugal in his habits, having saved over $800, besides carrying an insurance policy in her favor for nearly $1,500. In every walk of life, his example was on the side of right, and those who came in contact with him can feel that their lives have been better for having known him.[4]

The distinction between home and the outside world was a special problem for the male because it created a dichotomy between occupation and affection. Men were expected to earn a living for their families, and they acquired a considerable measure of their social identity from their occupation, but their greatest love was supposed to be home and family. A career was not an end in itself but the means of providing for one's family. In the Victorian scheme of things home was no less important in the male's affections than in the female's ("His family relations were very nearly ideal, for home was the center of his life"), but men were expected to spend their time away from what they supposedly loved most. This distinction between home and work was not the problem in the small town that it was in the city where father might leave in the morning and not return until night. Farmers and most small town men were home for the noon meal, but store hours were still long and most of that time was spent away from the family.[5]

To support his family the man had to involve himself in things that "really mattered." Some accounts have deleted all references to men's interest in anything but the immediately practical. Lewis Atherton's *Main Street on the Middle Border* claims that literature, music, and art were left entirely to women because it was thought the subjects had nothing to do with reality; "the men were too busy," he writes.[6] Yet, for many years, the Jefferson town band, all male, gathered twice a week to practice and perform. Men sang in church choirs, in glee clubs, and quartets. They were even soloists. J. R. Lindsay "appeared in several old fashioned songs" for a Women's Club performance to a mixed and "appreciative" audience. Four Jefferson couples entertained friends one evening by hiring a "lyric tenor" for a concert in the Baptist Church.[7] The Chautauqua series always included musical talent, appreciated by both men and women.

Yet for the most part the arts were feminine turf. It was acceptable for men to take an interest in literature or music, but it certainly helped if they maintained distinctly masculine interests as well. Thus, when the *Bee* praised a former Jefferson man for the recognition he was receiving for music education in the St. Louis school system, the article hastened to add that he was no effete dandy and that he smoked big, black cigars. One young pianist in Jefferson quit the keyboard at an early age because he just could not suffer through the indignity of performing "The Sweet Violet."[8] Musicians played more often to female or mixed audiences than to all male groups. Most Jefferson parents were more at ease when their sons won recognition as athletes and their daughters as musicians than when the reverse was true.

The assumption of distinct male and female temperaments created particular tensions for the male. One of the problems lay in the ascription to the female of a "higher plane." In a bitter attack on the new custom of women smoking cigarettes, which appeared in the 1920s, Vic Lovejoy clearly articulated his belief in inherent differences between the sexes. "Man is more or less of a 'beast' and for a woman to make a 'beast' of herself because he is does not help the argument one bit. Woman has always been upon a higher plane than man. In fact, if she had traveled upon as low a scale for the past twenty centuries, there would be no civilization today. For a woman to try and crawl down to the plane of a man 'because she has as good a right' presages a sad future for the human race."[9]

The image of the male as "beast" operated on several levels. Sexually, it referred to the belief that a man's sex drive was much stronger than a woman's and, if not controlled by rigid self-discipline (and help from women), would lead to debilitating excesses. Socially, it meant that men's aggressive and competitive tendencies would lead to barbarism if not restrained by the state and tempered by women's nurturing influences. Spiritually, it suggested that women found a state of self-abnegation and piety easier to attain than the strong-willed males did.

The dual standards of behavior to which the dichotomy gave rise allowed men more license and made penalties against them less severe than for women for the same offences. Nevertheless, the Victorian ideal made strenuous demands on men who took it seriously, and by the turn of the century, there is considerable evidence that many men were finding it difficult to live up to it. This is apparently true not only in midwestern small towns but across the nation as well.

Part of the problem was an unsettling ambiguity in the roles men were trying to play. How was a young man to understand what was expected of him? Should he imitate what women did to pull himself up to the "higher plane" they occupied? Certainly not. Survival and progress depended on men's toughness and initiative, and the whole scheme of things was predicated on the two spheres being complementary, not conflicting. Being a "sissy," a man who acted like a woman, was a fate to be avoided at all costs. During a football game against Storm Lake in 1905, a Jefferson back finally broke through for a touchdown in the third quarter, the first time in the whole season that the Storm Lake defense had allowed any opponent to score. The defensive lineman who missed the tackle and allowed that horror to occur "so forgot his manhood" that he cried on the field and earned this derisive write-up in the Jefferson newspaper:

The annals of football contain records of all sorts of casualties, from broken fingers to broken heads; from sprained consciences to sprained backs; but we believe that this is the first incident on record where a game was interrupted owing to a broken heart. . . . It is quite true that Jefferson felt badly when Storm Lake players desecrated and made free with her sacred goal line but the record nowhere shows that any of our players so far forgot his manhood as to creep off and blubber about it like a little girl with a busted dolly. Men engaged in this strenuous sport are supposed to be above hysterics and to reserve their flow of tears for sterner griefs.[10]

Should a man, therefore, yield to his baser tendencies and remain the beast? Absolutely not. He must struggle to overcome them. Success and development of manly character depended on the will-power to overcome the temptation of momentary pleasures. Being tough and controlled was only part of the picture, however. That potential had to be put to high purposes, or it too could become contemptible. Local residents who were reluctant to discuss certain aspects of sex were certainly not reluctant to discuss sexual offenders. A front-page story in 1908 described in detail how a local photographer had deserted his wife and three children to run away with his pregnant secretary:

An exhibition of passion unbridled, a home destroyed, reputation ruined, children disgraced, a faithful hard-working wife struck down with humiliation and shame, and a profitable professional business thrown to the winds. . . . Passion unbridled, character weak, thought of future and its ruin abandoned, a public spectacle, and innocent parties to the disgrace bowed down in everlasting grief and humiliation. All disgusting, exasperating. There ought to be a public whipping post for such men, and enforced labor for the support of the families dependent on them.[11]

One of the factors contributing to the tension in the male role was that morality, especially as it was defined by the churches that dominated small town life, tended to have a feminine aura to it. Religion was part of that "higher plane" on which women naturally felt more at home than men, and worship services often stressed the sentimental and emotional, which was normally forbidden to the adult male. The churches, frankly, had an image problem. They were too closely associated with women and young children.

Bee editor E. B. Stillman described the self-perpetuating dilemma that assured continued feminization of religion.

Women and children pretty nearly make up the rank and file of the Sunday School force. Up to a certain age, the mother may be able to control her boy in the matter of Sabbath observance and attendance at Sunday School. But . . . when that same boy emerges into long pants and conventional ties . . . he naturally looks to his father as an example, and if the latter has absolutely no interest in the Sunday School and apparently allows his family to attend as a matter of sufferance on his part, is it strange that the boy, putting on supposedly manly airs, says, in thought and action: "No Sunday School for father and I if you please." Hence, by imitating his father he shuts his Bible, and the paths of himself and his mother drift each one their own way.[12]

The participation of men in Sunday school work was a "crying need," Stillman declared.

In light of this situation, Protestant ministers had come to occupy a precarious position in the social order. In colonial New England the clergy had been powerful community leaders, but through the nineteenth century, their position had eroded to a pale reflection of what it had once been. They depended on the support, financial and otherwise, of their congregations. Salaries were low in an era when income was a leading indicator of masculine worthiness, and their influence in the community depended on their retaining the good will of those who dominated community life. While Jefferson ministers must have welcomed the editorial support for higher salaries, they probably winced at the case the *Bee* made for it.

Every Christian will admit that good strong men are needed in the pulpits of American churches, but good strong men will never seek a job that is continually held down in the "charity class." A century ago, the minister was the honored leader of his parish. Today, in most instances, he is a sort of "pensioner," a necessary evil. . . . We must honor and dignify the pulpit, give it a prestige, give it an adequate pay, such a compensation that will enable a man to "lay up" for old age the same as he would in any other line of human endeavor.[13]

In such a context, it is not surprising that the most popular evangelist of the day was one who successfully bridged the manly and the moral, who brought to his ministry such indisputably masculine credentials that he could lift religion above suspicions that it was something for women and children only. Billy Sunday was a native of Ames, Iowa, who had earned an impressive reputation as a sprinter and a professional baseball player for the Chicago White Stockings. His sermons were full of anecdotes about his sports career, like the time he won nine hundred dollars in a foot race but gave the money to a church and asked forgiveness for racing on Sunday or how his first prayer had been to ask God to help him catch a deep fly ball to center field. His conversion had begun as he sat on the curb of a Chicago street outside a saloon where he had put away several beers with friends. He listened to the singing of a revival meeting in progress and recognized familiar stanzas he had learned from his mother as a child. He went into the meeting hall, experienced a conversion, and soon quit baseball for the ministry.[14]

Sunday preached with the same vigor with which he played ball. He was not above theatrics, climbing up on chairs and tables to make his points and shouting at his audience, but he knew how to phrase his message to appeal to those who came to hear him. In 1915 Lovejoy's "Seasonable Sermons" identified Sunday as the most potent antiliquor force in the nation and supported the claim by pointing out how liquor publications tried to vilify him. Obviously, Lovejoy noted, "if (Sunday) was an obscure, weak, puny no-account preacher, they would not waste their ammunition on him."[15] What the audience saw in Sunday was an unquestionably masculine figure who clearly knew the ways of the world ("A man once told me I had a tremendous vocabulary, but I told him that I gave up half of it when I was converted") but who denied them for a Christian life. Sunday had achieved that difficult balance: he was at the same time both masculine and moral.

Billy Sunday preached several times in Jefferson, always with a remarkable number of conversions. In 1904 he preached a revival series during which 516 persons claimed conversion. At the afternoon service on the final Sunday he preached to a crowd of 1,500 and won 60 conversions, including the mayor, and that night, to a standing-room-only crowd, he brought 57 souls "down the sawdust trail" at the altar call. The names of the converts were listed in the paper the following week, front page, and the editor praised the series as the greatest blessing that the community had ever experienced. In the next edition the paper reported that there was an "antiswearing" epidemic in Jefferson as a result of the revival.[16] Other evangelists, those "weak, puny no-account preachers" without Sunday's athletic credentials, did not fare as well.

There is other evidence that the masculine role was finding it difficult to accommodate the religion of the times comfortably. The Young Men's Christian Association, a nondenominational Protestant organization, was one way that the churches tried to bridge the gap between the masculine and the moral. Beginning in Jefferson around the turn of the century, the YMCA program combined physical development and athletic competition with Bible study and worship in a deliberate effort to overcome the connotations of religion as effeminate.

A YMCA official made explicit reference to the image problem in a 1908 address on means and ends of the "Y": "You could not hope for success if you approached a young man of this world with a pure and simple religious proposition. He would laugh at you, for his natural inclination is to be skeptical and scoff at religion as being effeminate. But approached through the medium of physical or mental training whereby he can be shown brighter prospects for this life, he is easily attracted, and once in the Association, he is gradually drawn into the religious part of the work."[17]

Greene County organized the first rural YMCA chapter in Iowa, according to Floyd Stevens who was a charter member, with twenty young men southwest of Jefferson. The group called itself "The Dusty YMCA" and with some assistance from the state association, began a program of sports and worship activities.[18]

A similar attempt to develop both manly and moral character was the Boy Scouts movement, which was active in Jefferson by World War I. The Boy Scouts of America was incorporated in 1910 and chartered by Congress in 1916, with the president of the United States as the *ex officio* honorary president of the Scouts. Their handbook described the Scouts as the modern heirs of the heroic tradition begun by medieval knights with their chivalry, personal code of honor, and service to humanity. The tradition had been picked up by the "pioneer knights" who explored and conquered America. Scouts learned first aid, emergency lifesaving techniques, camping, woodlore, and citizenship training. They were expected to conduct themselves at all times in harmony with the highest standards of morality. Scouts memorized a list of a dozen virtues that would produce men of the highest character. A scout promised to be trustworthy, loyal, helpful, friendly, courteous, kind, obedient, cheerful, thrifty, brave, clean, and reverent. Like the YMCA, the purpose of Scouting was higher than simple pleasure or entertainment. It too approached the boy through his natural interests in the outdoors and strenuous recreation but used those interests to develop his character.

Being moral was part of the problem, but apparently being manly also seemed to be more of a task than it once had been. Several historical accounts maintain that as America became more urban, bureaucratic, and technologically advanced, more and more men found themselves cut off from image-enhancing activities. Historian Kathleen Dalton writes:

Men had derived their feelings of maleness from varied sources in the Victorian age – from pride in their self-control and steadfast character, from their toughness and physical prowess, from their freedom to express romantic individualism by creating their own opportunities, from the aggressive conquests in enterprise and on the frontier, from the procreative and sexual roles, or from their dominance over women. As some of these sources of maleness were eroded in the new century – a century characterized by soft city living, beseiged individualism, and feminist cries for the readjustment of the relations between the sexes – many men wondered if their manliness would survive intact.[19]

Manliness as it had previously been defined was more difficult to attain. No matter how successful a local businessman became in Jefferson, his success was insignificant compared to the industrial tycoons of the era – Rockefeller, Morgan, Henry Ford. He no longer protected his family from frontier dangers. The Greene County countryside was settled with reasonably peaceful farmers. Even in athletics, the prowess of local talent paled in comparison to the professionals.

It was to men in this situation in the early 1900s that "a Dakota cowboy, a Rough Rider charging up San Juan Hill, and a big-game hunter standing firm against charging elephants" held an irresistible appeal. When all those images were combined into one and that man also became president of the United States, a hero was in the making. Theodore Roosevelt was indeed a "man among men." He spoke the same language as Billy Sunday, the YMCA, and the Boy Scouts, and he appealed to the public for the same reasons. He condemned the "over-civilized man, who has lost the great fighting masterful virtues." He praised the "stern and virile virtues" that motivated men to highest character.[20]

While Jefferson voters, all male until 1920, often supported progressive candidates, the admiration for Roosevelt clearly went beyond reasoned approval of his policies. Editorials paid him glowing personal tributes. Over and over, the adjectives that described his speeches, his programs, and his presidential style were ones like "forceful and direct," "strenuous," and "vigorous." His demand that football be made less violent (and it was indeed a brutal game at the turn of the century) carried the authority of one who had himself consistently encouraged and participated in competitive strenuous sports. The *Bee* affirmed the president's stand: "Football is certainly in need of reform when the President of the United States feels it worth his while to take up the subject with vigor. . . . He is not squeamish, not at all troubled by a little roughness; he is indeed an enthusiast about football of the strenuous kind."[21]

Likewise, it was news when TR declared his opposition to professional boxing matches. Professionalization encouraged gambling and crime, he maintained. He supported boxing as an amateur sport, however. He himself had boxed as a youth.[22]

The problem, of course, was that the average man in Jefferson was not a baseball star, a big-game hunter, or president of the United States. His daily activities were neither exciting, dangerous, nor, in most cases, physically demanding. Establishing a satisfactory identity was often a problem.

An extreme example of the tension between the moral code and masculine demands occurred in Grand Junction in 1904 in the suicide of twenty-year-old Will Lowery, a Drake University law student. Lowery was charged with intoxication and spent the night in jail after a party with "the boys." His father posted bond the next morning and took him to the family drugstore. The boy, according to later reports, was "in despair." When his father was called out to deliver a prescription, young Lowery "wrote a note stating that he could not stand the disgrace" and took a lethal dose of potassium cyanide from the store supplies.

An editorial two weeks later acknowledged the dilemma the young men of the day faced. Manly behavior was in direct conflict with prevailing morality.

Every little while, some man of good standing in good society succumbs to a "night with the boys" and if he is found in a doorway he is carefully taken to a comfortable place where he is sobered up and in a little while the "boys" are laughing with him over the narrow escape. Not so with the youth. It must be a "lesson to him". He must forsooth be taken to the lock-up and then all his friends, the young girl he admires, perhaps even loves, will know all about it. She will feel the disgrace even more keenly than he does and in this case suicide is the result. . . . Not often does the folly of it have so serious an ending, but it sometimes leaves traces on the heart and brain of the youth that are never effaced.[23]

At the age of twenty, Lowery apparently had internalized the contradictions. Drinking was immoral, but "real men" are not afraid to take a snort. Most young men found a way to live with the contradictions, but the guilt and insecurity that they fostered were very real for many.

The masculine ideal necessarily included the *potential* to go astray. The photographer's passion for his secretary was "manly"; yielding to it was the mistake. The lachrymose lineman's devotion to his team's perfect defensive record was admirable; expressing it through tears was not. It was still a man's world. The husband was regarded as head of the household, even to the extent that the list of babies born each year was published in the newspaper with the names of their *fathers*. Still, opportunities for heroics and other manly pursuits seemed to be becoming more scarce in the face of civilization and progress. What made the male role so difficult to play was that men had to find ways to demonstrate their potential within a set of restrictive moral codes. As historian Peter Filene states the problem in his study of sex roles, how was a man to be both manly and moral at the same time?[24]

Much more has been written about the "woman question" in the twentieth century than about the male role, but the issue necessarily involved both sexes. As long as the community retained the distinction between male and female spheres of activity and prescribed different behaviors and attitudes for each, any change in one necessarily involved a change in the other. Males as well as females had to accommodate their aspirations to what the roles allowed or face the pressures reserved for those who willfully violate community norms.

Compounding the problem of masculine identity was a demand from the female ranks for participation in male activities. The competitive world and the nurturing home had once been metaphors for masculine and feminine spheres of operation, but by the 1890s there were definite signs that women were no longer accepting the front door as the border.

The traditional role that Victorian ideology created for women is well illustrated in a paper delivered in 1904 to a local women's club meeting:

> The home is the fountainhead of civilization. Our laws are made in the home. There are trained the voters who shape the course of the country. Is it not a fact that woman has a great influence over the characters of individuals, over the condition of families, and over the destinies of empires. Many of our noblest patriots, our most profound scholars and our holiest ministers were stimulated to this excellence and usefulness by these holy principles which they received in early years from a pious mother.
>
> The mother in her office holds the key of the soul; and she it is who stamps the coin of character, and makes the being, who would be a savage but for her gentle care, a Christian man.[25]

Not by engaging themselves directly in the struggles that shape the flow of events—that was men's responsibility—but by training those who do, women influence those in power but do not hold that power directly, according to the formula. "Man forms and educates the world, but woman educates the man," Mary Potter, the author of the paper, proclaimed. She was not articulating anything new to her fellow club members. Her audience had been nurtured on these assumptions before they struggled into their first corsets. "To form a beautiful life, many things are needed," Potter continued, "among which are some of them—sacrifice and service; love of duty and find it a pleasure. These duties are clearly defined by our instinct."

Instinct. Innate predispositions were seen to be as inherently a part of the female as her ability to bear children. What so inspired the panegyrics to women was that their sphere was not only different from men's but a higher, more refined one. It was the woman who represented civilization. Men, left to their own tendencies, would never rise above a barbaric struggle for material gain.

Of course, like men, women could fall short of the ideal. The "Fallen Woman" discovered just how high that pedestal was when she looked up from its base. The loathsome subject was often forced to lurk around somewhere beneath a flowery metaphor, but one could catch an occasional glimpse of it. The *Bee* cautioned its female readers: "There is a velvet on the rose petal which is only discernible when it is gone. There is a bloom of innocence on the face of a pure-hearted girl, which is as easily lost as the velvet on the rose petal or the down on the butterfly's wing, and once gone, it can never be regained. It is the heritage of all girls, rich and poor alike, and but a figurative expression of unpleasant facts, that should be read, and thought of, and heeded by some girls in (Jefferson)."[26]

Molding young girls into paragons of virtue was no easy task. Winifred Van Etten, a novelist and professor of literature for many years at Cornell College, spent her girlhood in Emmetsburg, a town about the same size as Jefferson eighty miles to the north. She recalls the restrictions imposed on young girls by a combination of stern Calvinist morality and a late Victorian gentility. Some, she claims, she could comprehend when she became an adult; others she found "totally incomprehensible."

Taboo: A girl must not part her hair on the side. Boys wore theirs that way.

Taboo: Everybody knew about the bad end to which whistling girls came. In some quarters, it was no joke.

Taboo: Legs didn't even get mentioned. Before leaving for church on a Sunday morning, each of us was stood up in front of the east door through which the summer sun sent stabbings of light. If there was the slightest sign of a shadow, back we went to put on another petticoat. I have worn as many as five. . . .

Taboo: Card playing. Whenever cards were mentioned, my mother saw the Devil, horns, hooves, and tail complete.

Taboo: Dancing. There were whispered tales of dissolute girls who checked their corsets in the cloakrooms at the public dance halls in order to "enjoy as much sensual pleasure from the dancing as possible."

Taboo: Looking into the open doors of a blacksmith shop as you went by.

Taboo: Walking on any street where there was a saloon.

Taboo: Walking by a horse doctor's office or the livery stable.

Taboo: Scraping your feet on the sidewalk. I got mud on my shoes one day, and when I tried to scrape it off on the sidewalk, the elders with me fairly snarled reproof.

Taboo: Walking close to a business place in basement quarters. You were to take the outer edge of the sidewalk lest some lascivious male might look up and be filled with glee to discover that you had legs.

Taboo: Owning a dog. No nice girl had a dog of her own. The family dog was all right, but as a piece of personal property, the dog was taboo, especially if it was a female. The owner might as well advertise her profession.[27]

The list may have varied slightly from location to location and family to family, but Jefferson residents at the turn of the century would not have been startled by Van Etten's enumeration.

The decade before 1900 marked the beginning of a transformation in the public dimensions of women's lives. In 1894 the state legislature granted Iowa women the right to vote in school and municipal bond elections. With ratification of the Nineteenth Amendment in 1920, women gained full suffrage, which was not only a political right but a belated affirmation of an already expanded role in the community. In between those two events Jefferson women had begun to petition the city council for community improvements. Through their study clubs, they not only started a local library but applied for and secured a grant from the Andrew Carnegie Foundation for a library building. They pushed for better schools and took an active interest in civic improvements. Many actively campaigned for full suffrage.

To some, these events have been viewed as ushering in a new era in sex roles and an end to Victorian distinctions. In hindsight, however, they appear far less radical. The activities themselves, like organizing and voting, were new for women, but the goals toward which these activities were directed remained traditionally female. Organizing a club, electing officers, and reading papers were something new, but the purpose of the club, to study great works of literature and art, was a conventional pursuit. Petitioning the city council involved women in the political process, but when the issue was the prohibition of prize-fights in the opera house, surely they who had always been the guardians of public morality could justify their unconventional behavior. As historian Filene argues, women at the turn of the century were not starting a revolution so much as "they were merely moving their pedestals to a new location."[28]

The best illustration of the new activity is the early history of the first women's secular organization, the Jefferson Friday Club. On Saturday afternoon, 8 January 1888, eight women gathered in the parlor of Mary Russell at the invitation of her and Elizabeth Stillman to organize the Ladies Reading Circle. They were eminently respectable. All but one were married. Their husbands included a lawyer, the editor of the newspaper, two bankers, a grocer, a butter maker, and the headmaster of the Dunning Academy. Because the club met in their homes, they voted to limit membership to twenty to keep the discussion group to a manageable size. They then drew up a prospective membership list and voted to meet every other Friday from three o'clock until five. At the first full meeting of the club on 21 January, the group selected *Taine's English Literature* to study for the coming year.

A women's reading circle to study English literature sounds harmless today, but it provoked some criticism from contemporaries, perhaps originating among jealous women not invited to join but nevertheless revealing a certain uneasiness with an independent women's organization. Editor Stillman rose to the defense of his wife's club a few months after its organization:

The ladies of the "Reading Circle" have taken solid comfort in this literary research and the social conferrings incident to their weekly meetings; but occasionally they find thorns, with the cruelest of barbs right across their path, like the rest of human folk. But the press bids them be as hopeful as possible under the rankling incisions made by unfeeling sisters. It comes to our knowledge that a lady who wears an expensive "tip" on her hat and passementerie "ad libitum" and who must be refined was heard to say not long since, "Those darn fools in the 'Reading Circle' think they're mighty smart, and don't know any better than to say 'sweet' of rooms when everybody with sense knows it's 'suit' of rooms." A Stunner! We shall expect to hear that the "Circle" is meeting in cellars in sack cloth for their errors.[29]

An interesting dimension to that particular criticism is that the Circle did indeed take errors in pronunciation seriously. Each presentation was followed by a critique that commented on delivery and choice of subject matter. The secretary's minutes of the early meetings included the number of mispronounced words or grammatical errors. Their intent was educational and their demeanor was serious.[30]

By the turn of the century the club adopted as its motto, "Our only greatness is that we aspire." By that time, however, the women had discovered that their aspirations could take on social as well as personal dimensions. For several decades the club minutes chronicled a series of community improvement projects, all logical extensions of their initial interest in things cultural. They considered petitioning the state legislature for a law to establish free public libraries. In 1901 they endorsed a bill before Congress to prohibit the sale of liquor in public buildings and secured a similar endorsement from the Jefferson Culture Club. In 1901 also, they requested that the school board continue the current school superintendent in consideration of the fine job he was doing.

In 1896 Friday Club decided to raise money to purchase a fountain to beautify the courthouse lawn and to provide drinking water. After two years of fund-raising projects they purchased an ornate, multi-tiered affair, and the board of supervisors appropriated $100 to locate it on the square. But who should pay the water bill? The supervisors thought that the city should pick up that expense, but the Jefferson City Council refused. Finally, Capt. Albert Head offered to put up $150 if the fountain were located directly across from his hotel, the Head

TOWN BAND. Although music and the arts were generally considered to be in the feminine sphere of things, the town band was strictly male, probably from their early association with military units. *Courtesy of Greene County Historical Society*

DR. "GUS" GRIMMELL. Because many female patients were reluctant to be examined by a male doctor, the late nineteenth century witnessed a sharp rise in the number of female physicians, like Dr. Grimmell who followed her father and brother into the medical profession. *Courtesy of Greene County Historical Society*

THE LIBRARY. What distinguished the Carnegie Library in Jefferson from similar buildings across the country was the three-tiered fountain in front, the focal point of a battle among club ladies, the city council, and town merchants. *Courtesy of Greene County Historical Society*

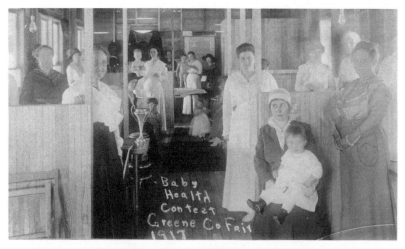

BABY HEALTH CONTEST. If you give blue ribbons to champion calves and lambs, why not to champion babies? The Woman's Club promoted child welfare by sponsoring a baby health contest each year at the county fair. Local doctors gave toddlers free examinations and awarded blue ribbons to the healthiest children. *Courtesy of Iowa State Historical Society*

Do Dubuque Women
Want To Vote?

"NO!"

was the emphatic reply Monday, April third, when **LESS THAN 100 WOMEN** in all Dubuque voted on the bond issue for a swimming pool---a question of taxation!

Men, by your vote June 5th, please do not force the ballot upon women who do not want it and who have just shown you so.

ANTI-SUFFRAGE POSTERS. While there was little organized opposition to women's suffrage in Jefferson, local residents knew that vote tallies in cities like Dubuque and Carroll would register strong resistance to the issue in the 1916 referendum. *Courtesy of Iowa State Historical Society*

P. O. BROWN, BARBER. Often located in the basement levels of corner buildings on the square, barbershops were, like livery stables, a male domain where women rarely intruded.   SHUEY'S DRUG STORE. Shuey's Drug Store became a landmark on the north side of the square, selling a broad range of medicines and housewares for seven decades.

House, on the south side of the square. This infuriated merchants on the other three sides of the square, and progress on locating the fountain reached a standstill. In 1899 the club formally presented the fountain to the city council with the request that the city assume responsibility for it, but the council took no action. The fountain was then stored in a barn where it lay undisturbed for several years.

Friday Club found itself petitioning the city council on a second issue in 1899. In January there had been a prizefight in the opera house, an event club members found extremely distasteful. The club formally requested that the council prohibit such matches, branding them "a menace to the good name of our city, corrupting to the morals of the youth, brutalizing to all beholding it and an outrage to society." According to one history of the club, there has never been a prizefight in Jefferson since.[31]

Shortly after that, the club returned to the subject of city beautification with the purchase of a trash can for each corner of the courthouse square. Trash and rubbish on the sidewalks and streets had long been an eyesore and a nuisance to long skirts. The club even hired boys to pick up trash and put it in the cans, but the idea never took with the public and gradually the cans disappeared. As a club history tactfully phrased the real issue in days of horse-drawn vehicles, project sponsors "had not realized that the most objectionable litter around the square was not the kind to be put in trash cans." The club also petitioned the council for the removal of hitching posts, a request that met solid opposition from store owners, farmers, and the council itself.

In 1899 Friday Club joined with three other Jefferson women's clubs in an ambitious program to provide a library for the community. They sponsored a variety of projects to raise funds, including a "book social" to which admission was one book. They collected 450 books, which became the nucleus of a library collection. In January 1901 a committee from the clubs donated $327 and their book collection to the city council, and this time, the council accepted. The city rented two rooms off the northeast corner of the square, and the town opened a public library.[32]

In 1904 with funds from the Andrew Carnegie Foundation, Jefferson erected a small but stately building and provided a permanent funding source to promote the intellectual and cultural life of the community through the library. The basement of the building provided a small meeting room for clubs. And, in what must have been a sweet victory for the Friday Club, the library board accepted the donation of the ill-fated fountain, which had lain in storage since the deadlock over its location. The fountain soon graced the front lawn of the library, and water cascaded gracefully from tier to tier.

Though their record in these projects sometimes fell short of unqualified success, it nevertheless reveals that the club was taking an active interest and role in community affairs. It also shows that this involvement was consistently on aesthetic, cultural, or moral issues. The women were not stepping out of their traditional spheres as much as they were using the organizations to expand those spheres into a public dimension. The clubs were pressure groups that lobbied on educational and cultural issues; they represented the politics of aesthetics.

Friday Club was but the first of several women's study clubs. Culture Club had organized in 1891, and the Margaret Fuller Club appeared in 1900. The Ingleside Club and PEO, both devoted to literary and cultural topics, came into being in the next few years. A 1910 newspaper roster of club membership in Jefferson listed over 150 women in these groups.[33]

While almost every one of the clubs justified itself by claiming some worthy purpose, there was an exception. Bess Osgood and Theo Houston organized the Delta Kappas as a purely social organization, with no higher goal than its members' pleasure. Nearly eighty years later, Mrs. Osgood still took pride in the unaspiring ends of the organization: "I'll tell you and I'm not ashamed of this. (Delta Kappa) is a club that didn't do anything to benefit ourselves or anybody else. And we bragged about it. We didn't try to educate ourselves and we were not philanthropic."[34]

Since the clubs usually met in members' homes or the small club room in the basement of the library, their memberships were necessarily restricted by space considerations. Until 1914 twenty-five was about the upper limit. In that year, however, at a meeting in the basement of the Baptist Church, Jefferson women organized an ambitious new club to overcome these size limitations and to provide a club experience for every interested woman.

They called it the Jefferson Woman's Club. Club sponsors systematically canvassed the entire town to sign up members. They deliberately kept dues within reach of every woman, one dollar per year. Some men joined the club initially, although most of the meetings were held during the day when they were at work. Their dollar dues were welcomed, but in a few years, their names disappeared from the rolls. Membership in the Jefferson Woman's Club reached nearly four hundred at one time. Through a variety of fund-raising projects, the club was able in 1925 to purchase a large house, which they converted into a permanent home. Until then, they had met in Protestant churches.

The organization maintained six departments of study: art, literature, and travel; music and drama; home and garden; parent teacher;

current events; and Bible study. Members could attend meetings in any or all departments. In addition to the study departments, however, all members automatically belonged to the Civic Department, the community outreach division of the club. Through the next two decades, the Civic, as it was known, lobbied for street lights, purchased materials for the school, paid part of the salary of a county welfare worker, distributed Christmas baskets and clothing, and supported Red Cross projects. Through the Civic, the Woman's Club became a powerful lobby for social action on issues of importance to local women. The Civic symbolized the expanding scope of local club women, from personal enrichment to social improvement.[35]

However, what this chronology of club life also suggests is that while Jefferson women did take a more active part in public life after the turn of the century, the public issues in which they were involved were consistently feminine topics according to the traditional Victorian division. The culture that held up the arts, morality, and nurturance as the highest ideals toward which women could aspire witnessed women beginning to organize and, with increasing political clout, to seek active community support for these aspirations. They understood themselves to be not so much challenging their traditional sex roles as aggressively seeking to fulfill them.

It was this abiding conviction that women and men occupy different spheres in the eternal order of things that complicated one of the major political issues of the era, the question of women's right to vote. The Iowa Constitution originally limited suffrage to "white male citizens" but after the Civil War, an amendment eliminated the word "white" to extend voting rights to black men. For over sixty years Iowa women (and men) petitioned session after session of the legislature to submit an amendment to the electorate, but not until 1916 did the voters of the state, all male, have a chance to express their opinion directly.

Like most political issues, women's suffrage never stood alone. It became entangled in a web of conflicting interests and perspectives. The Catholic church and some Protestant denominations opposed it on Scriptural bases and claimed that it was a threat to the family. Some European immigrant groups with strong patriarchal patterns opposed it. Wets opposed it because they feared women would vote for Prohibition. Strongly responsive to these constituencies, the Democratic party tended to oppose suffrage.

Republicans were divided. Dry forces favored it because they too believed women would vote against liquor and a host of similar vices. Resenting the ease with which illiterate immigrant men could secure a privilege denied to even the most educated native-born women, old-line American groups favored suffrage as a way of preserving "American" superiority over rapidly increasing immigrant blocs. But the issue was never simply a political pawn. It raised questions of genuine and deep-seated concern about the proper role for women and the natural social and political relationships between the sexes.

Though they may have arrived at different conclusions, prosuffrage and antisuffrage forces often began with the same conviction that the physical differences between the sexes accounted for far-reaching differences in personality, aptitudes, and predispositions and that men and women were ordained to play different roles in society. The two groups differed on what those roles should be.

The bedrock of most antisuffrage arguments was the assumption that woman's place was in the home. It was the role of wife and mother that she was best suited to play. The husband represented the family in the political world just as he did in the economic. He spoke in the family's best interest, and his vote represented the family as a unit. Sometimes, opponents of suffrage argued that women were too emotional or uninformed to make competent voters, that the political system would suffer, but more often, they saw it as a threat to social stability and to women themselves. Women would debase themselves by participating in the political process.

Lowrie Smith, newspaper editor in neighboring Scranton and an opponent of women's suffrage, argued that women were morally superior to men, with "greater refinement and higher ideals." This was true, he explained, because "men stand at the rough edges and the moral precipices all through the pathways of life guarding and shielding their mothers, wives, and sisters from even the appearance of evil."[36] Women performed their primary function within the family, not society in general. Political participation and the wider association with the world beyond would pull women down into sordid activity.

Prosuffrage forces were certainly not claiming that the sexes were identical either. They too staunchly believed in natural gender distinctions. Lovejoy, however, attacked Smith's premise that women were morally superior because they were protected. "Women's high refinement and loftier ideals," wrote the *Bee* editor, "are God-given. They are as deep as human nature. They cannot be changed, though their beneficent operation may be impeded, as now, by man-made limitations."[37] In his opinion female superiority was divinely determined and unalterable. Hence, women could participate in politics without losing their "loftier ideals."

Prosuffrage writers chronicled the improvements that women would surely effect: Prohibition, better schools, stronger penalties for immorality, and an end to government corruption. The reformers assumed, of course, that women would not vote the same as men, that candidates would have to appeal to a powerful new constituency committed to social and spiritual improvement. To deny women the vote was to deprive the political system of their moral strength.

Jefferson readers were treated to a spoof of antisuffrage arguments with a reprint of a *New York Times* editorial entitled "Why We Oppose Pockets for Women."

1. Because pockets are not a natural right.

2. Because the great majority of women do not want pockets. If they did, they would have them.

3. Because whenever women have had pockets, they have not used them.

4. Because women are expected to carry enough things as it is without the additional burden of pockets.

5. Because it would make dissention between husband and wife as to whose pockets were to be filled.

6. Because it would destroy man's chivalry toward women if he did not have to carry all her things in his pockets.

7. Because men are men and women are women. We must not fly in the face of nature.

8. Because pockets have been used by men to carry tobacco, pipes, whiskey, flasks, chewing gum and compromising letters. We see no reason to suppose that women would use them more wisely.[38]

While some of the objections to suffrage seem ludicrous in hindsight, the fears of its consequences were very real at the time. Suffrage symbolized a fundamental change in the relationship between the sexes. Women's clubs could push for specific improvements at the local level without threatening social disorder, but full political equality for all women was more abstract, a public commitment to a new relationship which seemed to challenge the traditional–natural–order.

In 1894 prosuffrage forces won a partial victory when the state legislature granted women the right to vote in town and school district referenda to levy taxes, borrow money, or issue bonds.[39] The law required different ballots for men and women and exempted women from voter registration. While legislators were probably not thinking foremost about future historians (they so rarely do), they nevertheless required separate voting boxes and separate tallies of men's and women's ballots, a great boon to those later looking back and wondering if men and women voted differently.

The record does indeed show a difference. On the question of a new Jefferson high school building in 1915, women favored it 194–137 while men opposed it by a 234–327 total. Reports from other towns showed similar trends. A bonding issue in Bagley to improve the electric and water systems was approved by both men and women, the former, 57–32, and the latter, 18–8. When Harlan voters were asked to approve $120,000 for a new high school and grade school, 412 men and 412 women voted in favor. Opposed were 114 men but only 38 women. A school bond issue in Aplington passed by a 134–25 margin. All the votes against it came from men; women favored it 45–0. The election results Jefferson voters were reading showed women consistently supporting local expenditures for improvements in health, safety, and education, issues that related directly to their roles as caretakers of the home.

Opponents pointed to the results of local referenda and charged that suffrage would bring higher taxes. A banner headline for a full-page ad in the *Iowa Homestead* screamed, "Women Suffrage Means Higher Taxes." Below was a comparison of tax rates in suffrage and nonsuffrage states showing the former to be substantially higher. The ad cautioned farmers that women's suffrage would mean a doubling of the city vote with no material increase in the farm vote: "It is not your wife and daughter who will vote, but the women of towns and cities who have easy access to the polls and axes to grind."[40]

In 1916 the legislature submitted to the electors of the state–all male–a constitutional amendment to strike the word "male" from the requirements for full suffrage. Many local women's groups expressed their support. As part of one Jefferson Woman's Club program, "upwards of a dozen well-known Jefferson ladies took part in a production of the Charge of the Catt Brigade," in honor of Carrie Chapman Catt, Iowa-born leader of the national women's suffrage organization. At a May Fete extravaganza written and directed by Minnie Wilson and performed at the fairgrounds by a cast of over nine hundred, one of the floats in the Iowa Progress parade was an automobile carrying several prominent Jefferson women dressed all in white and waving women's suffrage signs and banners. A suffrage tea at the home of Jessie Sayers raised money to cover expenses of the local suffrage organization, of which the *Bee*'s society editor, Mary Cook, was president.[41] What is obvious from even these scattered references is that supporting women's suffrage put one in respectable company. Note well–anything this respectable could hardly have been understood by these women as a serious threat to established order.

There was little local organized opposition to women's suffrage in Jefferson. There is an obvious difficulty in trying to organize women when the cause is opposition to women's political activity. There were state and national organizations opposed to suffrage. Lovejoy informed his readers that he was refusing to print news releases from antisuffrage groups because of their "dog in the manger" attitude: "We have no special quarrel with women who do not care to vote. It is their privilege to hold such opinions as please them: that is their business and the business of nobody else. But when they meddle and interfere with the efforts of their more ambitious and progressive sisters, they are absolutely wrong, and are exhibiting, to state it mildly, a phase of character which is both unlovely and unwomanly."[42]

There was opposition, of course. Judge E. G. Albert staunchly maintained that women were not meant to engage themselves in politics, an opinion that did not change with the ratification of the Nineteenth Amendment. When women became voters and therefore potential jurors, Albert made it a practice to excuse them from jury duty for the slightest pretext. He accepted almost no excuses from men who sought to escape this near-sacred duty. This tradition in district court continued so long that after a while women were no longer even summoned.[43]

One difficulty with actively opposing suffrage was that it put one in some rather unsavory company. The liquor interests around the state were the most outspoken opponents and the largest source of financial support for antisuffrage forces. For some, like the *Bee* editor who claimed that "booze is the greatest moral issues of our times," women's suffrage was justified if for no other reason than that it would secure victory for the drys. While Lovejoy admitted that not every man who opposed suffrage was "on the side of booze," he still insisted that "the backbone, liver, gizzard, and guts of the opposition to woman suffrage is bound up in the corporosity of the liquor interests."[44]

When the constitutional amendment came to a vote in 1916 at the June primary, the county supported a losing cause. Greene County men favored granting women full voting rights by a substantial 1692–1018 margin, but Iowa men as a whole turned thumbs down. Predictably, those counties that were Catholic, Democratic, and wet chalked up the biggest "no" vote, while Protestant, Republican, dry territory like Greene gave it its strongest support. But in between there were enough men who were either fearful of the unknown or committed to a tradition that demanded a clear separation of gender roles to defeat the amendment.[45]

The vote in the county showed Jefferson precincts supporting suffrage by about 70 percent. Grand Junction, with a substantial Catholic minority, barely passed it, 160–155. In Cedar Township, with some rural Irish Catholic neighborhoods, the issue split 40–40. Only Scranton and Willow townships, in the far southwestern corner of the county, opposed it. Lovejoy credited the Scranton editor with the victory for the "anti" forces.[46]

Though suffrage lost the battle on the amendment, it was winning the war. In 1918 Congress submitted the Nineteenth Amendment to the states, prohibiting the denial of suffrage rights on the basis of sex, and the Republican majority in the Iowa legislature quickly ratified it. In August 1920 Tennessee became the thirty-sixth state to ratify it, making the amendment an official part of the United States Constitution. In November Jefferson women went to the polls for the first time and did their part to elect President Warren G. Harding.

In several interviews with Jefferson women old enough to vote in 1920, I asked if they remembered any special thrill about voting that year. Surprisingly, none of them did. After all the struggle that had gone into winning the vote for women, these women did not recall their first election as anything special. Yet, perhaps in an ironic way, this was the true victory for women's suffrage. By the time the political battles had been won, the larger controversy had already been decided in favor of an expanded role for women. When women did go to the polls, they were not doing anything daring, challenging social conventions, or risking their reputations for an ideal. They were merely voting, a responsibility incumbent on all citizens. Many had voted on local issues earlier, blunting the novelty of the 1920 ballot. Had the right to vote been achieved sooner before public sentiment had accepted it as inevitable, many might have been less comfortable exercising their new privilege.

There is a footnote to the suffrage battle. Even after the U.S. Constitution granted women the vote, the state constitution denied them the right to be elected to the legislature. In 1926 the voters went to the polls to approve an amendment removing that restriction. The issue passed easily. In Greene County the vote was 721–222. Still, the size of the "no" vote testifies to the persisting assumption, even after women's suffrage had been a fact for six years, that men and women were not the same, that each had a natural sphere for which he or she was innately better suited. The victory for women's suffrage was a victory for those who believed that women's sphere should be equally represented in the political process, not that suffrage would eliminate the distinction. "Women's high refinement and loftier ideals are God-given," Lovejoy had written. "They cannot be changed." In the long run, of course, suffrage did much to undermine the "separate but equal" approach to gender, but that was not the intention of local supporters at the time.

Clearly, the feminine sphere was expanding. What is also obvious is that women's drive to expand their activities was not altogether altruistic. From their club activities, their projects, and their personal associations with each other, Jefferson women derived tremendous personal satisfaction. Just how satisfying these activities were is best

illustrated by observing how desperately women who were denied
them longed for such opportunities.

Not every woman found her own horizons expanding. Farm
women in particular found little opportunity for these types of social or
cultural activities. What was sometimes called the "woman's movement" or the "woman question" in town had its counterpart on the
farm, but because many observers failed to identify that the source of
farm discontent lay primarily in the frustrations of farm women, they
failed to associate changing women's roles in town with the rural dissatisfaction of the early twentieth century. But there is evidence to
make a case that rural discontent was the women's movement of the
farm wife.

Between residents of the town and country, there was a recognized though seldom formally acknowledged distinction. Farm families
resented suggestions that they were unsophisticated rustics, "hay-
seeds," "yokels," or "just farmers." Men and women who grew up on the
farm vividly remembered how the farm was regarded: "One of my best
friends and I had a kind of bond because we came into town school a
while before we were much accepted. We started in the seventh grade.
There weren't many people who came into high school if they hadn't
been in before. His people were big land holders even then. At the end
of his sophomore year, they yanked him out of school. There was work
to do on the farm, and he had plenty of education. He was (just) going
to be a farmer."[47]

When the daughter of a Jefferson lawyer married a local farm boy,
well-meaning friends expressed their sympathy to her mother: "I graduated from college about ten days before (the wedding), and the main
thing that people told my mother (was) they just thought it was a
shame that I spent four years in college and was wasting it by getting
married and moving out into the country."[48]

Alice Ann Andrew grew up south of town and attended school in
Cooper before transferring to the Jefferson schools. She recalled what
she termed "a tremendous discrimination" against rural children.
"Some people thought we were socially below them." Discrimination
extended beyond Jefferson in her memory. When she went to the University of Iowa, "there was one sorority that told me they couldn't rush
me because I was from the farm, the Alpha Chi's no less."[49]

Farm families felt betrayed. Farming was supposed to be the most
noble vocation, and farm life superior to life in the city.[50] Not only was
being close to nature supposedly more pleasant, but farms were reputed to be the cradle of virtue when compared with the corrupt cities.

An Iowa farm editor expressed this typical theme as he warned that the declining farm population foretold a demise of the nation's greatness: "Unless we can maintain a farm life in which the greatness of American life can flower, the armies of progress will suffer that decadence which comes to the host of all nations when they come from pavements, instead of from meadows and plowed fields."[51]

While there was nothing new in such rhetoric, by the turn of the century, it was beginning to have a hollow ring. Whatever the farm's potential for developing virtue or character, there was a growing recognition in town and on the farm alike that town residents enjoyed some amenities of life that were beyond the reach of even the most well-to-do farm families. The problem went deeper than economics; it was a concern of rich families as well as of poorer ones. Fundamentally it was that life on the farm by the early twentieth century was becoming less and less appealing, not because farm life was growing worse but because, in comparison, life in urban homes seemed to be improving so much more rapidly.

In 1908 President Theodore Roosevelt appointed a Country Life Commission to study the condition of American farm life, and its report was far from complacent. It drew attention to the isolation of farm families from cultural resources, to the inadequate and often poorly taught curriculum of the rural schools, and to the absence of institutions working for improvements. For most Greene County farm families in 1907, electricity was still thirty or forty years away. By comparison, during the same year, Jefferson women were enjoying the rapidly expanding social and educational opportunities of club life, the marvels of electric lights and appliances, running water and indoor plumbing.

In the area of education town children clearly enjoyed a considerable advantage. The Country Life Commission report was substantiated at the local level when Greene County school superintendent H. C. Roelofsz cited statistics from a state report: "In our towns and cities, 30 per cent of the pupils reach the high schools, and only 5 per cent of the pupils of our rural communities ever get far in the work. Yet the rural and urban populations of our state are approximately equal."[52]

The Country Life Commission report especially emphasized the plight of the farm wife who normally lacked modern household conveniences and domestic help. Roosevelt seems to have taken to heart the recommendations of the report. In 1910, on a whistle-stop tour across the Midwest, the former president made a two-and-a-half minute speech in Jefferson. He commended farmers for surrounding themselves with "all the modern appliances for saving labor" and maintained that the farm wife was also entitled to the same sort of laborsaving equipment in her work. However, Roosevelt spent most of the whistle-stop appearance praising farm life. He noted how pleased he was to be in Iowa "which he felt tempted to say was the best place in the union" and how fortunate Iowa was that her prosperity rested chiefly on agriculture, with "life on the farm . . . after all the heart and center of it." "Such was a good life," said the ex-president.[53]

The basis of the distinction between farm and town was ultimately not an economic one. Farmers with economic grievances in the latter nineteenth century had organized agrarian reform movements like the Populist party, but economics was not what this problem was about and protest organizations did not appear. In fact, agricultural historians cite the first two decades of the twentieth century as among the best economic years midwestern farmers ever had. The period was so good that farm economists would use conditions existing during the years 1909 to 1914 as the standard for "parity," that mythical equation that supposedly yields the farmer a return on capital and labor equal to a similar investment in other sectors of the economy.

Then what *was* the problem? A penetrating analysis appeared in a 1913 *Good Housekeeping* article by Iowa author, farm editor, and politician, Herbert Quick. In "Women on the Farms," Quick discussed the causes behind "the drift to the cities," that phenomenon of declining farm population generating considerable national comment at the time. His concern, however, was not only for the statistical decrease but for the increasing "spiritual drift" among rural families who *wanted* to leave the farm for an urban home whether they actually did or not. What distinguished Quick's article was his insight that identified farm *women* in particular as the major source of the growing discontent with farm life.

> The "drift to the cities" has been largely a woman movement. I have found the men on farms much more contented and happy than the women. My mother wanted my father to leave the farm, and move to a college town where the children could have a "better chance." He did not accede to her wishes; and one bit of spiritual drift was checked. But just to the degree that farmers have reached the plane of letting the wife and daughter vote on the future of the family, they have been pushed toward the city. . . . I have found the men and boys filled with the traditional joy of open spaces and the freedom of spirit which goes with it; and in many, many cases, their women were pining for neighbors, for domestic help, for pretty clothes, for schools, music, art, and the things they saw when the magazines came in.[54]

Quick also saw the problem going beyond economics. "The present woman movement on the farm is toward a higher plane than the economic one," he wrote.

Henry A. Wallace offered a similar analysis of the discontent of farm wives. In 1927 he wrote that he was beginning to think of the farm problem as "a problem of the farm wife" as much as anything else. "Of the families that leave the farm," Wallace maintained, "I suspect that women are responsible for the departure of more than half."[55]

Jefferson residents supported these contentions that it was the farm wife who felt the inequities between farm and town life most keenly. Things like household conveniences, running water, indoor plumbing, educational opportunities, social outlets, and cultural resources were of greater importance for the farm wife than they were for her husband, who could measure himself in terms of the economic prosperity of the farm operation. The coming of telephone lines in the decade before 1900 meant more to the farm woman than to the man, Barbara Hamilton recalled, "because (she was) no longer isolated in the house without anyone to talk to. Men got out and worked together but you are in the house by yourself." After reading a newspaper article on the history of electricity, a Jefferson lawyer who had been born on a farm stopped me on the street to explain that he understood his mother's dreams for her children much better once he realized that farm women went without electricity for forty years longer than town women.[56]

Poignant illustrations of the frustrations of farm women Quick identified surfaced in an interview with a woman born on a farm outside Jefferson in the 1920s. Even as a child she was aware of her mother's discontent. Edited into a narrative but still in her own words, the transcript is an especially moving commentary on the lot of the farm wife.

I never went to a rural school. I lived in town with relatives when I was in grade school. When we moved to the farm between Jefferson and Grand Junction, I rode the school bus into the consolidated school in Grand Junction so I had the experience of being the farm child who comes into town, but I never went to an actual rural school. Don't ask me why I was living in town when my parents were on the farm. I really don't know except it may have been more convenient for them or they thought the educational opportunities were better. I would guess that it was possibly the latter because I never thought that they were trying to get rid of me. It was very unusual for a small child to live away from home. I don't think my parents were atypical in the intensity of their desire for education for their children but maybe in their willingness to go that far to make it possible. I can't say if most farm families were that intense about education, but the people my parents knew were. There were three ahead of me in my family, two brothers and a sister, and they all went to college, and that was unusual.

When I was living back on the farm and going to school in Grand Junction, I hated riding the bus. Everybody else on the bus, of course, was in the same circumstance, but I hated it. We spent an hour in the morning and an hour at night. There was still a distinction between farm and town kids even though it was a very small town. We still had the feeling of being somehow different and outsiders. I can't give you any concrete example. It was a feeling.

I think my stronger memory is being the only girl who was on the honor roll and that was really being an outsider. And that had nothing to do with farm or town. It was just something that was not a "respected" kind of thing to do. Girls were not to excel academically. The other girls didn't approve. I got less approval from the other girls. I felt it very strongly, and maybe it was just that particular group. But I remember that I really felt terribly outside. My interests weren't the same. I was coming in from the farm to town. I was not athletic or interested in anything. I was a good student, and that was a terrible thing. It was not nearly so much that way in Jefferson later.

I always knew I was going to college, but we had a little bit of a confrontation with Dad when it was time for me to go into high school. He was a little reluctant at that time for me to go ahead and Mother said flatly I was going to go, whatever it took. And it took transportation. It took somebody to drive me in and pick me up in the afternoon, and to take me back for play practices or extracurricular activities. It was quite an endeavor for sort of middle-aged parents at that time.

When there was a question of whether or not I was to go ahead, Mother was the one who said, "Absolutely." In my family, both boys and girls went on to school, but one of the questions my father and mother confronted was whether it was necessary for a girl to go on. But it was also a question for the boys. I think Dad was very reluctant to give up their farm labor. It was very valuable to the family and to our particular circumstances. The women did not do the farm work as many other farm wives and daughters did.

I admired my older sister very much—her strength, her involvement in education, her intelligence, for making her own way in many respects. I think those were the aspects I most admired.

My feelings for my mother were such a mixed kind of thing. I guess I felt sorry for her because I could see she wanted a different kind of life. Her life was so restricted. She had no opportunities to really do some of the things she wanted to do and be. She wanted more education and more opportunity to be involved with people. Mother belonged to the woman's group at church and a club of the girls that was basically a social activity. It was very important to her. She had more social needs than Dad, and that was one way of satisfying them in the restricted sense that was possible for her.

She wanted to have more independence and say in her own life structure and life-style and family finances. She had no input on finances, and that was just the way it was. That was very typical of then. The egg money she earned was the only questionable area. Everything else was Dad's. He was not unkind on his part. That is simply the way they functioned.

I also felt sorry for her because she always had physical ailments but never had adequate medical care. She told me in later years when she could bring herself to speak of such things, that between the time my oldest brother and I were born – a period of fifteen years – she had twelve miscarriages. That's in addition to the four of us children. And she had seven major operations. They simply operated for whatever it was with no prior treatment. My mother was so tired most of the time.

We often had a young girl from Mitchellville in transition from being at that facility and going out into the world. As my mother explained it, these were not bad girls. They were from homes where they hadn't been given any care. They were considered part of the family. They ate with us and went to church with us. Mother would share our meager resources by buying clothes for them. Of course, they didn't get much wages for the week. They were an extension of the family and they did help Mother with some of the great deal of work, because, as I said, she was basically a frail woman.

I was aware of feeling sorry for her even when I was growing up, but I didn't know why. It was at least by late high school or early college years when I tried to evaluate my feelings of sympathy for her because I really loved Dad more. Dad and I were very close, but Mother was the one who was the disciplinarian and the one who instructed me on the rules of how it was to be a proper young girl growing up. Mother/son and father/daughter relationships were very close. When Dad wanted my sister or me reprimanded or scolded for something, he'd tell Mother and she did it. He didn't do it directly. He was really quite a harsh disciplinarian with my older brothers. They were the ones that were going to carry forward the family tradition and be the people who must have strength and the people with control.

Mom and Dad accepted their lot, whether or not they were contented with it. I'm sure Mother was never contented, but they accepted their lot and they did their duty. They worked extremely hard, but they had aspirations for their children far beyond what they themselves experienced or could probably even have defined. The giving up of children so the children could have a better life is part of the heroism that I see with my family. They let my brother go to the Naval Academy when he was eighteen, knowing that they would really never see him as part of the family again, which was true. They lost him in a sense, but he went on to a different life. They allowed me to go to Washington to work while I was still quite young. Could I do that with my children? I'm not sure. I admire that so tremendously. Mother was always concerned that what she had known of farm life was not to be my life.[57]

The narrative and Quick's insight illuminate the disparities between urban and rural life that were felt so keenly by women on the farm. Town women were finding new satisfactions in their club activities and associations outside the home. Their lives were expanding and becoming more interesting as they worked to bring cultural opportunities to the community and to provide better educational resources for themselves and their children. Farm women were keenly aware of what they lacked both in household conveniences and in social and educational opportunities. Farm women no less than city women knew what aspiring meant, but rural circumstances made it almost impossible for them to participate in the new roles.

By World War I, however, there were stirrings of improvement. Transportation had always been a major problem in rural areas. With the widespread adoption of the automobile after 1910 came new opportunities for farm families, and they were quick to take advantage of them. Within ten years several townships in Greene County had effected school consolidations, complete with bus service, to replace one-room schools and to provide high schools for advanced work. Scranton and Cooper area residents consolidated in 1919, and Paton and Dana followed in 1920.

In 1915 the *Bee* noted with satisfaction that social life in rural areas was improving.

There has been a revolution in farm life in the past twenty-five years. The rural telephone has done wonders to promote acquaintanceship and better neighborly intercourse. Automobiles and better roads are the newer things that are building up the social side of country life, and giving to them the advantages now enjoyed by residents of town. A family "living to itself" is not in an envious position. . . . The towns have moved out along such lines in the past, and there is every reason why the country should do so. Jefferson has its commercial club, its country club, and its women's clubs. Some people think we are "over clubbed", but this is hardly a proper claim. There seems to have been a valid demand for each and every organization here, and if there has been, the demand for social life in the country is all the more emphasized. Association with our fellow creatures "knocks off the rough edges" and gives us a better perspective of what life should be to all humanity.[58]

What inspired this tribute to rural associations was the appearance of neighborhood or township associations called community clubs. In 1916 *Wallaces' Farmer* ran a long and flattering feature on the activities of Greene County community clubs. At that time there were ten such clubs with an average membership of around sixty-five, although Greenbrier meetings sometimes drew over two hundred and others were nearly as large. The forerunners of the Farm Bureau, these organizations met in members' homes, often on the lawns in the summer or at rural churches for both social and educational purposes. Charles Davis, county agricultural agent, was instrumental in promoting the community clubs and sometimes arranged for a speaker on agriculture from Iowa State College. Davis arranged for each club to spend a day touring Iowa State to encourage parents to consider its educational potential and to acquaint them with its research and outreach facilities.

Wallaces' Farmer praised the clubs for their social and cultural dimensions.

In country communities, farm boys and girls have little opportunity to develop special talents, and in many cases, the older folks are simply existing from one day to the next. At these club meetings, some training is given in speaking before an audience, and those who take part get to feel more at ease when they happen to be called on to make a talk. Those who can sing are given an opportunity to develop their talent before an audience, and the same is true with those who can read, play the violin, piano, or other musical instrument. The musical features help to relieve the monotony that might make a strictly educational program tiresome. Each club arranges its meetings to suit itself, and it plans its own programs.[59]

Some clubs even experimented with cooperative purchases of coal and discussed the possibilities of cooperative marketing of livestock, although no group developed very far along these lines.

Because farm families did not have access to the public library in town, an important officer in several of the clubs was the librarian, who secured books on loan from a traveling library sponsored by the state. The only expense to the club was the actual cost of shipping the books to and from its Des Moines headquarters. The books provided reading material for some homes where, as one school teacher put it, "there was scarcely a book or paper to be seen."[60]

Furthermore, the clubs fostered ties not only among members but to other rural organizations and to town and school groups as well. A county federation board included the president of each community club, the secretary of the commercial clubs of town businessmen (forerunners of chambers of commerce), and the superintendent of each school. Minnie Wilson was elected president of the federation board in 1916, extension agent Charles Wilson, vice-president, and county school superintendent H. C. Roelofsz, secretary-treasurer. Under Wilson's direction, the federation sponsored a gala May Fete, a grand and patriotic pageant at the fairgrounds with a cast of over nine hundred persons on the general theme of how great it was to live in Greene County.[61]

During World War I, the community clubs evolved into the Farm Bureau as that organization emerged and its ties to Iowa State College were strengthened. In the 1920s the Greene County Farm Bureau added a home economist to assist farm women and the response once again demonstrated how much farm women craved social and educational opportunities. Alice Ann Andrew recalled the early work of the home economics specialist who came out with "all kinds of great inspirational things" for the women to do. Classes were enthusiastically received for they carried with them the opportunity for an aspiring woman to take action.

They'd send an Extension Service person over and then she'd have leaders from the different townships come in [for instruction] and they'd go back to their neighborhood. I'll never forget one session with dress forms. It was a hot old August day, and they were pasting all this stuff over a so-called T-shirt. About half of them fainted with the heat, but that was how eager women were to learn to create their own clothes. *They were almost as spiffy as the town ladies* (emphasis added).[62]

On another occasion, nearly 150 women attended an extension workshop on hat making. There was more to that meeting than just an interest in the whims of millinery fashion. These were women who were frustrated by years of being "almost as spiffy as the town ladies."

In 1923 James Hilton, later to serve as president of Iowa State College, replaced Charles Martin as Greene County extension agent and inherited Martin's carefully cultivated network of rural associations. It was Hilton's assessment that one of the most valuable and lasting contributions of the community clubs and, later, their Farm Bureau counterparts, was bringing town and farm people together.[63] For the first time, there were organizations other than the churches promoting the interaction of farm and town residents. Hilton cited merchants Ed and Fred Gamble, some local bankers, the owners of the grain elevator, and a few other Jefferson businessmen as leaders in promoting the farm and town exchanges. Until that time, according to Hilton, there had been little formal contact between the two groups.

The coming of the automobile and electricity did much to eliminate the differences between homes in town and countryside, but the social distinctions persisted long after the original causes had disappeared. While they persisted, the distinctions created a very painful dilemma for the farm family. Quick summarized the problem succinctly: "There is a woman here and a woman there who sees that the whole scheme of family life falls to ruin if the (farm) home suffers in comparison with homes of those friends and relatives who live on wages in the towns. She and her husband begin to realize that it does not pay to build the farm into a profitable property which is despised by the very children for whom they are giving their lives."[64] The dilemma was that farm parents who wanted a better life for their children sometimes had to be willing to see their children move into town or to the city to become part of a different society than what the parents represented. "The giving up of children so the children could have a better life is part of the heroism that I see with my family."

Quick identified rural discontent as "the woman movement on the farm." To call it a movement may be misleading. Farm women rarely took the initial steps to organize in their own behalf. Their organizations usually began as auxiliaries of other associations. There were no calls for sweeping legislative reforms or redefinitions of social relationships as there had been in the drive for women's suffrage. There were no marches or public demonstrations.

Nevertheless, Quick's insight is astute. The features of rural life that were most frequently cited as deficient were "feminine" issues— education and cultural opportunities. What made farm life seem inadequate was the tremendous improvement in precisely these areas that town women were experiencing. To understand rural discontent through the first third of the twentieth century, one needs to see it first through the eyes of the farm wife aware of new opportunities for town women and frustrated by her inability to participate in them. In no small part this was the root of "flight from the farm."

Changes in traditional sex role patterns were unsettling for many people. When my grandmother came home one day with her hair bobbed, her young son went off to his room and cried his eyes out. His mother—with her hair bobbed! She was just not "that kind of woman." Only naughty women had their hair bobbed. He was certain that she was not that kind of woman, but if she was not, why had she done it? What would people think? Somehow, unlike Samson, grandmother did not lose her strength or her reputation when she got her hair cut, and somehow too, my father adjusted. Likewise, most people adjusted to the new ways. The catastrophes prophesied for those who tampered with the "eternal laws of nature" failed to materialize. Civilization did not cease, the family did not fall apart, and Jefferson did not descend into barbarism, at least not immediately.

CHAPTER 4

Technology
Rise Up as Eagles

They shall mount up with wings as eagles;
they shall run and not be weary.
— ISAIAH 40:31

RAPID ADVANCES IN TECHNOLOGY during the first third of the twentieth century brought about substantial improvements in the standard of living for Greene County residents. New inventions sparked, charged, fired, heated, lighted, pumped, agitated, rinsed, ironed, vacuumed, projected, transmitted, and broadcast a revolution in daily routines. The marvels of the age meant freedom from former limitations of time and space, centuries-old drudgeries, and old perceptions of individual opportunity. Necessarily, these changes also altered institutional structures—the family, local government, schools, the church, and the business community. Jefferson offers an excellent example of these changes as community residents rapidly adopted the new technology.

Changes in transportation brought about by the automobile were of particular significance. To appreciate the revolution that automobiles introduced, one needs to understand something of what the "buggy world" was. Like the bull's-eye of a target, Jefferson is located in the center of the county twenty-four miles long on each side. Organized when horse and buggy was the standard mode of transportation, county lines were drawn to insure that even the most distant citizens could drive to the courthouse, conduct their business, and return home in a single day. From the corners of the county, that trip took a full day.

Transportation limitations made traveling even a short distance a memorable occasion. Growing up on a farm north of Scranton, Roy Mosteller made the ten-mile trip into Jefferson four or five times a year and recalled it as quite an event. His father hitched up the team after an early breakfast, and Roy and his mother drove three miles into Scranton where they left the rig in a livery stable. They caught the eastbound train for Jefferson and arrived there fifteen or twenty minutes later. They shopped and visited relatives for the day, returning to Scranton around 5:00 P.M. where they picked up the buggy, drove out to the farm, and arrived in time for a late supper. Even with the train, the effort was enough to limit the trip to a seasonal event. When they made that effort, they stayed the full day. Roy's father could not afford to take off the whole day from the farm, but Roy and his mother enjoyed it.[1]

At the same time, Dr. J. K. Johnson, Sr., was using the train to provide service to his patients. The Jefferson osteopath had a local practice but also saw patients in Grand Junction and Rippey, setting appointments according to the rail schedules. But newborns rarely checked with the depot, and emergencies were not always adjacent to the tracks. Many infants were greeted into the county by a neighboring farm wife because doctors did not arrive in time, particularly in the winter.[2]

Walking was the mode of transportation for most city dwellers. Some Jefferson residents kept their own teams of horses in small stables behind their houses, but most rented a horse from the local livery when the need arose. Those who had frequent calls for out-of-town travel could justify the maintenance of a team, but in town, people walked.

The first automobiles in the county appeared around the turn of the century. These machines were by no means among the first of their kind. By 1900 there were 13,824 automobiles registered in the United States.[3] It was in that year that the local editor took his first ride in one of the new contraptions, a quick spin around the square, and he thoroughly enjoyed it. By 1905, the *Bee* reported, there were 1,573 registered automobiles in Iowa, of which Jefferson had five "which carry numbers and are counted in the totals." In addition, Jefferson had two motorcycles. Since not all machines were registered and "carried numbers," official figures were somewhat below the actual number in operation, but the figures offer a rough estimate. "The automobile flourishes," the article commented, with their popularity greatest among "country doctors, merchants, and especially bankers in the small towns. It is this use of the automobile in the small towns that makes the total so large." Des Moines was reported to have had 125 vehicles.[4]

The automobile was still a curiosity, however. It was basically a plaything of the rich—"and not merely the rich, but the somewhat adventurous and sporting rich: people who enjoyed taking their chances with an unpredictable machine that might at any moment wreck them," wrote historian Frederick Louis Allen.[5] A 1906 article in the *Journal of the American Medical Association* bemoaned the fact that there was no automobile of sufficient economy, durability, simplicity of construction, power, and compactness to meet the needs of rural physicians.[6] Of what *practical* use was the automobile, asked farmers and townsfolk with tighter budgets and more utilitarian concerns?

In addition to its uncertain utility, three other factors discouraged people from buying early automobiles.[7] One deterrent was their unreliability. Bess McCully Osgood was a small child at the turn of the century when her father, a local merchant, bought what she described as one of the first "lemons" of the American auto industry. It was a Sterling, "a big, beautiful, red seven-passenger car." The family loved to drive it in the countryside on Sunday afternoons, but each week brought a new adventure: "It got stuck every time we went any place. We didn't keep it very long because it wasn't satisfactory. . . . (The Sterling) was a lemon, you know, like you get every once in a while."[8] The McCullys' huge Sterling lumbering through the countryside probably did little to encourage farmers to make a similar investment.

Road conditions were another negative factor. All too often, country roads turned into a black gumbo, which successfully mired even the best automobile. Even though the county had a reputation for relatively good roads, "boils" appeared when the frost went out in the spring, and unwary drivers could find themselves in a seemingly bottomless pond of black mud. One woman remembered a boil near her family's farm north of Grand Junction. The road between Jefferson and Scranton had several, and a bad spot between Jefferson and Farlin was still claiming victims as late as the late 1930s. A horse and wagon could navigate dirt roads far better than heavy automobiles, a critical factor in discouraging rural residents from making the investment in the latter.[9]

That investment itself was a fourth factor. Early automobiles were expensive. They were playthings of the rich because only the rich could afford them. It was the country doctors, merchants, and especially bankers who purchased the early cars. An article in *Leslie's Monthly* magazine reviewed many models available in 1904, listing their specifications and price. Nearly one-fourth of those described sold for over $4,000. Eight cost over $6,000. In 1900 when an average acre of Greene County farmland sold for $36, one could buy an entire 160 acre farm for $6,000. Among local residents with $6,000 who had to choose between an Apperson Touring Car (four-cylinder, forty-horse power, cellular radiator, four speeds with reverse, 2,800 pounds, seating for six, complete with electric lights and top) and a 160-acre farm, the desire to sow wild oats was rarely as strong as the desire to harvest the domestic varieties. The *Leslie* review also noted several makes that cost under $1,000, including an $850 Ford, an Oldsmobile, and a Cadillac. There was even a motorized buckboard for $450. Still, that was a lot to spend for something as impractical and unreliable as an automobile.[10]

Of course, in the great age of the entrepreneur there were those who were willing to provide automobiles to residents who did not care to own one. Thinking of the car literally as a horseless carriage, one enterprising local man planned an "automobile livery" to rent out the new machines just as horse-drawn vehicles had been. The *Bee* reported that Charles Louk had rented a building on the east side of the square "for livery headquarters and has ordered some machines which are expected to arrive within a few days. Of course, no machines will be sent out except in care of a competent chauffeur. The official name for an automobile livery is a Garage, pronounced Garazj, with an accent on the first syllable."[11]

In the beginning the automobile created friction between town and country residents. As long as it remained primarily an amusement for the well-to-do, farmers tended to view the auto with justifiable hostility. Early automobile owners, overwhelmingly town residents, drove into the countryside for pleasure outings, but farms were not recreation areas to those who lived there.[12] Automobiles frightened livestock and horses and made the roads unsafe. Country roads were where drivers went to "open it wide up" and to see how fast their cars could go, a practice that did little to endear them to the farmer.

This is not to say that no farmers saw potential good in the new machines. Acquainted with steam and stationary gasoline engines, some farmers very early caught a glimpse of what the automobile could mean for isolated rural residents.[13] Nevertheless, until a reliable and dependable model became available, farmers viewed the intruding machines suspiciously.

In 1904 speed limits in the country were set at twenty miles per hour. In heavily populated areas of town the maximum was ten miles per hour. If a buggy driver held up his or her hand the driver of an auto was required to stop and even to help quiet the horses if necessary. The potential for mishaps caused by terrified horses was so great that the rural-dominated Iowa legislature passed a law requiring the traveling motorist to "telephone ahead to the next town of his coming, so that the owners of nervous horses may be warned in advance."[14]

In August 1905 the *Bee* reported that an Illinois judge ruled that automobile rights on the highway were subordinate to those of other travelers and that "the automobile must carry the burden of taking every precaution against damage to others who use the roads." The defense had argued that requiring special care from auto drivers was class legislation discriminating against them and that automobiles should have equal rights on public highways. Farmers who depended on horses resented the automobile driver's position since it was the farm family in the wagon who was threatened with injury from frightened teams, not the town family in its heavy touring car.[15]

Accidents continued to occur. Two months later the *Bee* reported the story of a 68-year-old man near Newburg, Iowa, whose horse had been frightened by the approach of an automobile carrying five passengers. The car did not stop, and the horse bolted, climbed an embankment, upset the buggy, and dragged the old man underneath. Again, the court ruled against the automobile.[16]

Throughout the Midwest, in isolated outbursts, farmers expressed their anger over what seemed to be "an invasion of the countryside by pleasure-seekers from the towns." In Minnesota farmers near Rochester plowed up roads, which made them impassable for auto travel but still usable for horse and buggy. In Ohio a group of farmers threatened a boycott of any merchant who purchased a car. When an Illinois woman on a country road was injured by an automobile, angry farmers attacked automobiles and pushed them into the ditch.[17]

Closer to home, sixty miles to the west in Denison, seventy-five farmers met in 1906 to discuss their irritations with the automobile. One speaker, the *Bee* reported, claimed that farmers could no longer send their wives and children to town on errands since autos had made buggy travel hazardous. Another advocated a farmer boycott of all merchants who owned automobiles. He favored giving those who owned cars a reasonable time to sell them before the boycott went into effect.[18]

Aside from safety concerns, drivers created other inconveniences for farmers. Bad roads and the primitive mechanical design of the cars often sent the driver looking for a tow. Farmers who lived near a bad stretch in the road were frequently interrupted by requests for assistance. Each farmer had his own fee for hitching his team to the mired machine. One report mentioned one dollar, while two brothers living along a bad stretch of the Lincoln Highway kept a team of horses in the spring ready for business and charged two dollars per retrieval.

Chester Oppenheimer, a local clothing merchant, once found himself begging the assistance of a farmer. On a Sunday drive with another couple the Oppenheimers' car became hopelessly bogged in a mud hole. The farmer who was asked to interrupt his Sunday afternoon to hitch up his team and drag them out charged $2.50. Oppenheimer objected. "Two fifty? The charge has always been a dollar." The farmer said nothing. He simply backed his team and let the car roll back into the mud. "Next time," he said calmly, "it's going to be five dollars." Oppenheimer paid, but the story does not end there. Shortly after the incident, Oppenheimer saw the farmer in Jefferson and signaled him to come over to the store. "I want you to come in and pick out any hat you want, free of charge," Oppenheimer told the farmer. "You taught me a valuable lesson."[19] While many motorists learned the same lesson, few learned it with the dignity of Chester Oppenheimer.

While these isolated examples must not be read to suggest an organized protest by farmers against the automobile, they do indicate resentment. That drivers were nearly always from the town or city reinforced the farmers' view of the automobile as something disruptive and alien. Sensitive to potential friction, several towns banned automobiles from chautauqua grounds during the summer season.[20] Similar incidents across the nation prompted Woodrow Wilson, president of Princeton University in 1906, to remark that "nothing has spread socialistic feeling in this country more than the automobile. To the countryman, they are a picture of the arrogance of wealth, with all its independence and carelessness."[21]

What did much to eliminate rural antagonism to the automobile was a vehicle that served the needs of the average farm and town family. It was produced by a Detroit manufacturer. Its wheels were tall enough to keep it above the mud. It was simple to operate but reliable. It was affordable by the family of moderate means. The manufacturer was Henry Ford. The car was the Model-T.

It was Ford's dream to build a "perfect automobile" and then make millions of copies of it. Standardization was the key. "The way to make automobiles," he declared as early as 1903, "is to make one automobile like another automobile, to make them all alike."[22] It was Ford who first applied the assembly line to the manufacture of automobiles with stupendous success. Each operation was broken into small components. Constructing the ignition system, for example, was reduced from a twenty-minute operation to one requiring only five minutes. The chassis had once taken twelve and a half hours. Ford reduced that to one and a half hours. Not only the finished product, but the assembly-line process itself fascinated local residents. In 1915 the *Bee* reported that a completed Model-T rolled off the assembly line every forty-nine seconds. It was this standardization that overcame the major obstacle to widespread auto use, its cost. In 1909 a new Model-T sold for $950. From then on the cost dropped from $780 to $690 to $600 to $550 and so on until by 1926, a Model-T cost only about one-third of what it had in 1913.[23]

Another important factor in the popularity of the Model-T was the simplicity of its maintenance and operation. It was not difficult to drive, although some found it more challenging than others. James Dillavou on a farm north of Scranton did not inform his wife that he planned to buy a car when he went into town. He intended to drive one back to surprise her. Surprise her he did. When she ran out into the yard to see it, he yelled at her to get out of the way because he was not sure how to stop it. She just stood there staring, and he hit her. He was not going fast and she was not hurt, but it was still more of a surprise than he had planned.[24] Several people mentioned how fathers or uncles occasionally hollered "whoa" and pulled back on the wheel during some of their first runs. Most families, however, managed a more suave transition than the Dillavous.

The Model-T was not only affordable and easy to operate; it was reliable. It was never fancy, but it could usually get its passengers where they wanted to go. In fact, according to the wisdom of the times, the Tin Lizzie (as it was called) could go "anywhere except into society."[25] It did not require a mechanical genius to keep it going. My grandfather claimed you could fix a Ford engine "with baling twine and chewing gum." That was an exaggeration, of course, but others reported their own curatives. If the radiator leaked, crack in an egg. It cooked and sealed the leak. To keep the radiator from freezing up in the winter, cover it with horse blankets while it is still warm and drain it when finished for the day. The gas tank under the front seat fed down into the engine by gravity. If the car headed up a steep hill, the tank was lower than the engine, and the car "ran out of gas." That was no problem for enterprising drivers. They backed up the hill to keep the tank higher than the engine. In fact, the Model-T was even more than transportation. On Monday mornings one farm family drove the vehicle into the yard, jacked up the rear end, and ran its washing machine off the rear axle.

Tires were a special problem. An experienced driver rarely left home without the materials to fix a flat. Carl Hamilton had his share of flats. He recalled that "everybody carried patching material. You roughed up the inner tube, put some sticky goo around the hole, put on a patch, and then, if possible, immersed the whole thing in the water tank to see if it was really airtight."[26] On one excursion, a high school boy and three friends found themselves in the country with no spare and with one very flat tire. They begged enough oats from a nearby farmer to pack the tire full and limped back into town.

The problem of flats became especially acute during World War I when the rubber shortage made new tires difficult to acquire. The Osgoods put off buying a new set of tires until wartime rationing made them unavailable. As a result, the car never left Jefferson for the entire duration of the war because they felt they could not risk a flat.

The Model-T was not the only reliable make with a price within reach of the middle class, but it was by far the most popular. It was the Model-T that came to symbolize a countryside on wheels. By 1914 over four out of every ten cars in Greene County was a Ford, while the remaining 60 percent was divided by seventy-five other auto makers. By 1917 Ford was capturing 57 percent of new car sales, outdistancing its nearest rivals, Buick and Overland, by over seven to one. In 1920 registrations listed 1,512 Fords to 282 Overlands, 223 Buicks, and 218 Chevrolets. The next most popular model, the Oakland, was a distant fifth at 86.[27]

As the automobile became available to the average family, it was adopted very rapidly. A 1916 report stated that Iowa led the nation in per capita automobile registrations and that eight of the top nine car states were in the Midwest. Iowans registered one car for every sixteen persons in the state.[28]

Greene County illustrates the trend. From five cars reported in 1905, registrations rose to around 160 in 1910. In that year, the *Bee* estimated that there was one car for every one hundred people in the county. By 1914 car registrations permitted a more reliable calculation and placed the ratio at one car per seventeen persons. In that year, auto registrations reached one thousand, and the *Bee,* considering car ownership still to be a noteworthy fact, listed the names of all car owners.[29]

While town residents bought the first cars, rural families were quick to take advantage of the new vehicle once it became moderately priced and dependable. According to one source, farmers purchased one-half of all new automobiles sold in Iowa in 1910. *Collier's Magazine* reported that 1 Iowa farmer out of every 34 owned a car in 1909, compared with only 1 owner out of each 190 families in New York City.[30] Of the 278 Greene County car owners on the 1914 list whose mailing address was Jefferson, only 123 lived within the city limits. The remaining 155 were farmers on Jefferson rural routes. For the county as a whole, auto ownership in 1914 stood at about one car for every 5 males over the age of twenty-one. For Jefferson alone the ratio was one car for every 7.5 males. By 1920 according to local sources, there was one automobile for every 5 Greene County residents. Clearly, farmers were not slow in taking advantage of a faster mode of transportation when the cost came down.

There are several other reasons for the rise of auto use in the Midwest at the time. The population was heavily rural, located on the farms and numerous small towns spaced five or ten miles apart. Unlike the cities with their trolley lines and taxis, small town and rural residents had to supply their own transportation, a demand that could never be met by an "auto livery" service. In addition, farm income was high, which spelled prosperity for the small towns as well. This prosperity financed not only the autos themselves, but miles of road improvements and even some early paving.

By the first world war, the attitude toward the automobile had changed dramatically. No longer was it a plaything of the rich. It was well on its way to becoming a necessity for town and farm families alike.[31]

In the early years automobile travel from one town to another was complicated by the absence of an adequate system of marking highways. Rail lines handled the bulk of traffic traveling from one community to another, and country routes leading from these lines were familiar only to those who lived in the area. No highways as such were numbered or marked. Local folk knew how to get from here to there, and few others ever had need to know.

However, as families began to explore the countryside, they had to learn which roads to take and where to turn. The American Automobile Association, organized to promote auto travel, published one of the first road guides with just such information. The book was designed for long-distance travel. Communities lying off what were designated as the major routes between larger cities were omitted. In Greene County the guide marked only one route, an east-west road connecting Scranton, Jefferson, and Grand Junction.

Getting travelers from one town to another before any standardized system (or any system for that matter) of road marking had been developed was a complicated task. The *AAA Blue Book* assigned each road two route numbers. One number was for motorists traveling in one direction, and the other number was for those going the opposite way. For example, motorists driving from Council Bluffs to Marshalltown passed through Jefferson on Route 505. From Marshalltown to Council Bluffs the route was 199. Indexed to each route number was a detailed description of how to navigate from one town to the next. Since the instructions had to describe landmarks in the order in which the driver encountered them, every road had to have two sets of instructions, one for those eastbound and one for those westbound. The necessity for the dual numbering system was obvious when one turned to the written instructions. To get from Jefferson to Grand Junction in 1915, one confronted the following:

mileage
        0 = Omaha, start of route
    136.3 = mileage from Omaha to Jefferson
    136.3 = Jefferson, Main and Cherry Sts., park on left. Straight thru. Cross
            RR. 136.7
    140.2 = End of road, turn left with poles.
    143.6 = End of road, turn left with poles.
    143.8 = Right-hand road, turn right with poles.
    143.9 = 4-corners; turn left, leaving poles.
    144.3 = 4-corners; turn right with traffic across RR, into
    144.5 = GRAND JUNCTION.

Theoretically, a driver starting in Grand Junction could read those instructions backward and arrive in Jefferson, but the AAA was trying to *promote* motoring. Therefore, the *Blue Book* published reverse directions with their own instructions for Route 199, Marshalltown to Omaha.[32]

The AAA and the Iowa Highway Commission pushed hard for a uniform system of highway numbering and marking, but even before such a program became a reality, Jefferson families were venturing far from home in their automobiles. One family traveled back to see their relatives in New Hampshire. Another went to see a brother in South Dakota. Getting all the way to Spencer on the first day was an accomplishment. Several families began annual vacations to Colorado and the Rockies, camping along the way and cooking their meals by the roadside or staying in the newly opened "tourist cabins" that sprang up along the major routes. The lengthy summer vacation had once been limited to the well-to-do, but inexpensive camping facilities or roadside cabins made trips easier for those of more modest means. A study in 1927 revealed that twice as many farm families were visiting national parks "as families associated with any other professional class."[33]

The automobile also hastened a reorganization of local government. Road maintenance had long been a point of controversy, but for automobile enthusiasts, the issue became a passion. Rural residents too had a deep concern for they were often isolated when heavy rains or spring thaws turned mud roads into sloughs. However, farm families also felt the tax bite most keenly and sought a system of road finance that avoided costly construction and maintenance at their expense. Until the imposition of a tax on gasoline in the 1920s, road funds came primarily from assessments against property, which fell most heavily on farmers. Naturally, farmers insisted that supervision be kept in their hands as a guarantee that rural interests would be given due regard.

Early state laws delegated responsibility for road maintenance to the most local level possible. Townships were subdivided into road districts. Rural residents paid a road tax, but they were allowed to work out that assessment by hauling gravel or dragging a stretch of road assigned them by the district road supervisor. In a heavily rural state the arrangement meant in practice that farm families took responsibility for the roads close to their homes. There was a logic to the system: people got what they paid for. In an era when few but farmers used country roads, those who worked hard benefited most directly. Even so, the quality of the roads left much to be desired.

In 1883 delegates to a state road convention met in Iowa City to discuss economic, political, and engineering dimensions of the situation. They endorsed resolutions that required payment of road taxes in money rather than labor; called for the appointment of a township road master for at least part of the year, thus eliminating the district and making the township the basic unit of responsibility; and advocated the establishment of a county road fund. The latter resolution proposed a new role for the county in an era when many viewed even the courthouse as too distant and removed to be effective in something as important as the roads in front of their homes.

In 1884 the state legislature approved a measure that permitted – but did not require – counties and townships to implement several of these proposals. The new law allowed the board of supervisors to levy a tax to create a county road fund and permitted township trustees to consolidate districts and require that road taxes be paid in money. The changes, however, were optional.

Where the new arrangements were implemented, they worked well. In 1894 the legislature required each county to establish a county road fund. In 1902 most of the other local option provisions in the 1884 law became mandatory: districts were consolidated into one township unit and all district revenues were pooled into a common fund. Taxes were to be paid in money. Thus, the township, not the smaller road district, assumed major maintenance responsibility.

Battle lines in the legislature solidified between those who wanted to return to the most local control possible and those who pushed for larger units that could command greater resources, including engineering expertise. Automobile travel had begun to spotlight the need for better roads, but auto use was still minimal and limited primarily to a recreational activity of city and town residents. In 1904 Iowa lawmakers defeated a bill to repeal the 1902 reforms and went on to establish a state highway commission to collect information on road conditions and to give advice when asked.[34]

The State Highway Commission was originally under the direction of the deans of colleges of engineering and agriculture at Iowa State College. It began collecting information and comparing data about local expenditures. It soon issued an alarming report.

A system of inadequate government control and questionable contracting had developed in the construction of bridges and culverts. Companies supplying the materials for bridges and culverts had divided the state among themselves, the report claimed, each monopolizing sales within its own district. Furthermore, most local officials had no knowledge of the market value or standards of quality of building materials. Prices and quality varied markedly. The commission called it a "vicious system" and accused the companies of "little less than blackmail schemes for controlling the bridge and culvert funds of the State."[35] According to commission figures, bridges and culverts were consuming over half of all road funds, sometimes for shoddy materials, and diverting far too much from legitimate road work.

Not surprisingly, the supply companies lobbied hard against the commission and its proposals. Also aligned against the commission were rural forces who continued to fear that losing control of road maintenance authority would mean higher property taxes and less emphasis on the secondary roads upon which they depended.[36]

However, there were also those who advocated a more efficient approach, even if it threatened local control. Several Greene County men became recognized statewide as knowledgeable leaders of the "good roads" forces. J. W. Holden, a farmer from Scranton who served six terms on the county board of supervisors after eleven years as township trustee, was thoroughly familiar with the problems of maintaining passable roads. Holden was elected president of the Association of State Supervisors, which made him familiar with county matters across the state. In 1913 Holden was appointed to the three-man board that directed the activities of the State Highway Commission.

In that year also the highway commission received substantially expanded powers. The legislature dealt a severe blow to the supply companies' comfortable arrangement by giving the commission the authority to "disseminate information and instruction" to county supervisors and township officers on road matters, including data on prices, and to investigate and report to the attorney general any "violation of duty, either omission or commission." County officials still had responsibility for local maintenance, but increasingly they operated under guidelines from a state authority.

The conditions of roads varied widely across the state. Even before widespread use of the automobile, Greene County had established for itself an enviable reputation for good roads. In 1904 it became one of the first counties in the state to receive rural mail delivery because the relatively good condition of its roads made such service possible. In 1907 a report by the State Highway Commission cited Greene as *the* leading county in the state for good roads, based on the miles of graveled roadways and the number of cement bridges.[37]

The county had the advantage of substantial deposits of gravel, a gift from receding glaciers thousands of years earlier. Gravel pits along the Raccoon River and the Spring Lake quarry supplied tons of cheap surface material. Loaded into wagons a shovelful at a time in the early days, the gravel filled mud holes and mixed in with road surfaces to provide solid road beds. Even so, travel in rainy seasons was risky. As late as 1919, motorists were warned to expect difficulty on even the best route across the state until after 10 June.

While local roads were the farmers' main concern, a group of Iowans was working to establish a route across the state as part of a major highway connecting the east and west coasts. The Iowa Transcontinental Road Association was the idea of a Denison postmaster, Will Myers, who with the help of the Denison Commercial Club organized a convention in Boone with delegates from towns along the Chicago and North Western line.

In May 1910 the organization assembled and elected Jefferson banker Henry Haag as president. Haag was also a champion of better roads through wiser expenditure of road fund money. Under the old system, when farmers would "work out" their road tax by spending a day dragging a section of road assigned them by the township road supervisor, road work was often done in the fall when demands of a farm were lighter. However, it was in spring when roads were soft that they needed attention, Haag pointed out in a 1910 speech to township officials. "Our standard of citizenship is measured by the kind of highways we keep," Haag declared.[38] So devoted was he to good roads that he himself, a local bank president, often drove a team around the square to drag the streets after heavy rains to keep them from becoming too rutted or developing mud holes where water might collect. He served with J. W. Holden on the board of supervisors and studied the road issue extensively.

The purpose of the association was to promote one route as a thoroughfare across the state and to see that it was adequately maintained. In each township through which it passed, a township inspector reported on the condition of the route. In Greene County the highway passed through Grand Junction, Jefferson, and Scranton. Haag assured the public that the association did not advocate higher taxes for road improvements. He insisted that, wisely spent, the existing levy of twenty-five dollars per mile of country road could adequately maintain the twenty-seven miles of the route in the county.

In June the association announced that it was marking the route across the entire state with white signs at each section corner. Every mile, a telephone pole was painted white and a white sign, eight inches tall and twenty-four inches wide, was nailed at least eight feet in the air. Large black letters proclaimed "Iowa Official Trans-Continental Route." When a stretch of the route became impassable in wet weather, red flags at the preceding section corner warned motorists of the danger.[39]

Haag's untimely death in August of 1910 was viewed as a tremendous loss. His obituary cited him as "Greene County's greatest asset."[40] Though he died before the project was finished, Haag had helped to create an organization of great significance to the community. In 1913 the Lincoln Highway Association was formed with representatives of twelve states. It incorporated the route of the Iowa Transcontinental Road Association, thus placing Jefferson on the proposed coast-to-coast thoroughfare.

The 1916 gubernatorial contest threw the spotlight on the good roads issue. While some national Republican leaders were demanding increased military expenditures to protect the United States from the European war then in progress, the *Bee* frequently pointed out how much better the same money could be spent on highways. On 5 May, Stillman blasted Teddy Roosevelt's call for a $1.5 billion military budget, arguing instead that good roads were more essential to American defense than a large army. The $625 million spent on American military preparedness could have built twelve national highways coast to coast. As late as 13 December, the *Bee* was maintaining that Greene County's $25,000 share of the military budget ought to be going for local roads.

The campaign was complicated by a bizarre twist in the Prohibition issue. The two parties had switched their traditional perspectives on the topic. The Republican candidate, William Harding of Sioux City who favored liberalized liquor sales, had won a bitterly fought primary against a split field of Prohibition candidates. The Democratic nominee, E. T. Meredith of Des Moines, favored Prohibition. Furthermore,

Harding opposed expanded funding for roads and a greater role of the state in the supervision of road work while Meredith supported both. Harding was a bitter pill for many Republicans to swallow, and some refused to make the effort. Jefferson editor Paul Stillman, former state representative, speaker of the Iowa House, and a significant figure in state GOP circles, bolted the ticket, primarily on the issue of Prohibition. However, the roads issue was also critical, and the *Bee* kept up a steady call for increased road expenditures.[41]

Though Harding won the election, Iowa continued to support a substantial road improvement program. The war stimulated interest in road building, as troop and supply transport taxed American railways severely. Champions of better roads were quick to point to the potential of trucks and buses, if there were adequate highways. The *Bee* published a state-by-state comparison of road expenditures in 1917 and 1918 that placed Iowa at the top of the list. Even in the face of federal deficits and rising taxes, road building increased substantially (Table 4.1).

TABLE 4.1. Expenditures on road building by state, 1917–1918: federal, state, and local government

	1917	1918
Iowa	$ 15,140,000	$ 15,500,000
West Virginia	8,000,000	14,000,000
Louisiana	8,000,000	5,300,000
New York	7,000,000	10,000,000
Kansas	6,500,000	10,500,000
Indiana	6,000,000	17,380,000
Illinois	5,500,000	17,000,000
Texas	5,000,000	25,000,000
All states	$144,298,860	$263,096,610

Source: *Jefferson Bee*, 20 March 1918; the list was compiled by the Goodrich Tire Company.

In the months immediately following World War I, American military officials called attention to the need for a transcontinental highway to facilitate faster transport of men and materials in emergencies. The four major transcontinental railways had been strained to capacity to move troops and supplies to the East Coast. In cooperation with the Lincoln Highway Association, army officials promoted a convoy that traveled from Zero Milestone near the White House in Washington, D.C., to the West Coast following for the most part the route designated as the Lincoln Highway. Des Moines and Davenport led a group of central Iowa cities trying to pull the route through Iowa to the south, but the decade of organizational groundwork by the Iowa Transcontinental Road Association paid off for the towns along the Chicago and North Western line.[42]

Camping overnight at the county fairgrounds in Jefferson, the three hundred men were served a special supper at the country club by the Woman's Club and the Red Cross. Tanks that had seen combat in the recent European war were on display with the convoy and attracted considerable local interest. Army and Lincoln Highway officials used such opportunities to give speeches on the need for federal and local support to establish a hard-surface road across the country. Thirty years later the commander of one of those tanks, Dwight David Eisenhower, would himself attract considerable interest among local residents, but when he toured Jefferson with the convoy, he was just another young army officer.[43]

The preceding April Greene County had become the first county in the state to receive federal funds for paving. Money had been approved to provide hard surface on stretches four miles east and west of Jefferson and two miles north. The State Highway Commission approved the application once the portions of the road had been graded and prepared for paving with county funds. The work, however, had not begun by the convoy's arrival in July.[44]

Nevertheless, the convoy passed through at a critical time. A new state law permitted counties to pave roads if a majority of voters approved. A referendum to pave the remainder of the Lincoln Highway across the county, the portion not included in the original funding, was slated for a vote three days after the convoy left Jefferson. Paving advocates were not certain how the vote would go. Story and Tama County voters had rejected similar proposals in the spring. Only urban counties like Clinton had given approval to paving projects under the new law. Greene County voters, however, approved the measure by over three to one, and the county became the first in the state to complete paving on the Lincoln Highway from county line to county line.[45]

Farmers whose land lay within one and one-half miles of the paving were assessed 25 percent of the costs. It was assumed that the route substantially improved the value of their land. In some cases that assumption was less valid than in others. Part of Floyd Stevens's farm lay north of the Raccoon River within "assessment distance" of the highway, but his home and the larger portion lay to the south. To get to the highway from his house he had to travel two miles to the Jackson bridge and then a mile and a half north. But the rule held, and he paid the assessment.[46]

A highway named for President Lincoln appealed to many local residents. E. B. Wilson, a Jefferson lawyer and western state district consul for the Lincoln Highway Association, and his wife donated a statue of Lincoln, which stands on the south side of the courthouse along the original Lincoln Highway route. Two markers with emblems of Lincoln were placed along the highway by an admiring Scranton farmer. In 1921 J. E. Moss, a local officer in the association, wrote a short note with his five dollars to renew his membership for the fourth year. It read: "I am glad to pay it as the Lincoln Highway will be the greatest memorial in the world in memory of one of our greatest citizens, and of the greatest world power. I am one of the Civil War soldiers. Lost a foot at Mission Ridge – glad to yet be alive. Will be one, if not the heaviest, tax payer towards paving the Lincoln Highway, having two miles of the route through my farm in Greene County, Iowa."[47]

Both local roads and primary highways became an issue with increased auto traffic. Steadily, power and responsibility had shifted from a neighborhood unit to the county and the state. Keeping a heavily traveled roadway in good condition was a major responsibility, too large to be left in the hands of amateurs in a makeshift system. In 1925 the powers of the highway commission were again expanded to include general authority over all primary roads outside of cities and towns. With passage in the 1920s of state gasoline taxes earmarked to finance construction and upkeep of roads, an old political issue took on important new dimensions. How should the tax money be divided between primary highways connecting major cities and secondary roads to get farmers and their produce to markets? Representatives from urban areas favored expanding funds to the primary system while rural forces were adamant on keeping farmers out of the mud. The issue was (and continues to be) a hot one.[48]

Long-distance travel was one area of dramatic change, but more significant were the everyday innovations that the automobile brought to family life, retailing practices, education, and religion. The new machines sometimes required adjustments in traditional family patterns. For example, the father normally drove, as he had the buggy, but a factor complicating the traditional pattern was that the automobile was a new experience for everyone. Fathers did not have more experience than their children, and in some cases, they soon had considerably less. In the Bowley family on a farm northeast of Jefferson the father turned over all maintenance to his teenage son who was routinely driving back and forth to school. "He wanted it ready for him when he wanted to use it, with gas and oil in it," Burdette Bowley recalled. "But beyond that, he expected me to keep it running and didn't want to be bothered by it." Burdette's father drove the family to the state fair, but he refused to drive in Des Moines traffic. That responsibility he turned over to his son who had logged far more road time on his daily trips to and from school.[49]

Furthermore, the question of access to the family car was not the same as access to the horses. The automobile did not need to rest after a day in the fields as the horses did. Cars transformed the relationship between field work and social life on the farm. As Floyd Stevens pointed out, Sunday was a day of rest for the horses as well as for the farm family, and good farmers were careful not to tire out the horses they planned to use on Monday with a long Sunday trip.[50] But that was not a consideration with the automobile, a fact that forced families to reconsider who could or could not go where and for how long. In her novel *Country People* Ruth Suckow describes how the family car subtly changed the relationship between parents and children: "August had kept his hands on other things, but he couldn't keep the boys from using the car. When they took their girls, it wasn't an all-day occasion, as when Frank had gotten his grandpa's old buggy to drive Lottie to the fair. They went out on Sunday afternoons when they felt like it. August would go out and find the car gone again. It was no use trying to stop them. Emma thought it was dreadful for the boys to 'pleasure-drive on Sunday' . . . but both she and August got used to it. All young people seemed to do it."[51] It was the democracy of the driver's seat that caused so many families to face new decisions.

Driving patterns for women showed considerable diversity. Town women who were married before their parents had purchased the family's first car were often slow to get behind the wheel. Many had not driven buggies, primarily because they had encountered few situations to do so. In town they walked. When they went into the country, they were almost always accompanied by a husband, son, or father. Consequently, their need to drive was minimal. Jessie Sayers, according to her daughter, drove a car only twice in her life. On her first try she backed through a handsome Russian olive hedge as she was trying to get the car out of the garage. On her second and final performance she cut a right corner too closely and damaged the fender. That was it. Two for two, she abandoned the driver's seat forever.[52] Marge Dillavou recalled that her older sister also renounced driving after a few early mishaps. Their experiences were not especially traumatic. They simply preferred walking or riding, as they had always done, to taking the wheel themselves, and they found it just as easy to do so. However, other women learned to drive right along with their husbands. They drove the car uptown for shopping or wherever they wanted to go. Grace Gamble and Ida Hamilton often took off for small towns in the county just for the fun of the trip.[53]

RURAL MAIL CARRIER. Because the roads were generally in good condition, Greene County had some of the first rural mail carriers in automobiles. *Courtesy of Greene County Historical Society*

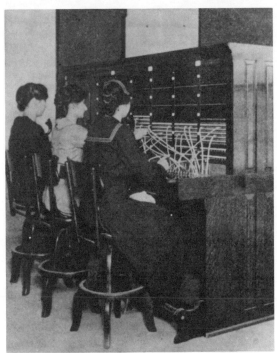

SWITCHBOARD. "Number please" became a household phrase with the introduction of the telephone switchboard. The "Central" lady not only connected calls but also located the doctor in emergencies, gave the correct time of day, and sometimes passed on important information like the location of fires or the announcement of births. Here at the Citizens' Mutual switchboard are operators (left to right) Pearl Thornton (Raver); Maude Reese (Peacock); and Lucille Berry (McVicar). *Courtesy of Greene County Historical Society*

HENRY HAAG. Local banker and first president of the Lincoln Highway Association, Henry Haag was a champion of the good roads movement. *Courtesy of Greene County Historical Society*

REFRIGERATOR. Though its capacity was small by modern standards, the electric refrigerator was a great boon to the household. It spelled the demise of the ice wagon that delivered large blocks of ice to Jefferson homes and delighted local children by making available small chunks on hot summer days. *Courtesy of Iowa State Historical Society*

MUDDY ROADS. Many drivers allowed their optimism and confidence to get the better of their common sense. Spring thaws seriously limited travel, and "Get Iowa out of the mud" became a rallying cry for the good roads movement. *Courtesy of Iowa State Historical Society*

MAYTAG AD. This advertisement from a 1916 edition of *Successful Farming* was targeted at rural families who longed for the conveniences available in the city but who lacked the electric lines that made them possible. *Courtesy of Iowa State Historical Society*

CHAS. BOFINK. The kitchen stove was the heart of the home in the days
before electrical appliances. It cooked meals, baked bread, dried socks and
mittens, heated bath water and laundry water, and helped make homework
at the kitchen table a little more bearable.

Farm women, more familiar with teams and buggies, also learned to operate the new machines—and had much greater reason to do so. Town women could walk to stores, to church, or to club meetings. Farm women could not. One of the greatest sources of discontent among farm women was their isolation, their difficulty in getting to group activities or to anything to break the daily routines around the farm home. For them the car was a godsend.

Arvilla Long was living with her husband on a farm south of Glidden in the 1920s. She vividly remembered her first "solo flight." Her husband was busy, but she had to get to town. The Model-T was in the barn, which meant that she would have to back it out, and backing up a Model-T was no simple operation in the days of gear pedals on the floor. Going forward was easy, but navigating in reverse was an art. She did it, however, a feat she recalled with unmistakable pride nearly sixty years later. Once she learned how to back it up, she gained for herself an independence she had never before experienced. She could go into town when *she* wanted to go.[54]

Children born after the turn of the century, both sons and daughters, were growing up in the automobile era, and many learned to drive at surprisingly early ages. Before state legislation established minimum age requirements, some Jefferson youth drove before they were teenagers. Lumund Wilcox drove the family car on the morning route to deliver milk when he was eleven. Gene Melson drove up and down the street one evening when he was twelve while he waited for his uncle to finish some business.

By their teenage years many Jefferson children had had experience behind the wheel. High school children on the farm often drove into class, particularly in Jefferson since the school district did not provide bus service until the 1940s. Roy Mosteller, as a high school student at Churdan, rode a pony to class through his first three years, but as a senior, drove the family car in from the farm. On Wednesday night he often attended a movie in Churdan or Jefferson (with a car he had his choice) or sometimes went to the Gobblers' Nob dance hall north of Scranton.[55]

In at least one instance four high school students pooled their resources to purchase an old car of their own. It was nothing fancy, but it served its purpose, most of the time. Coming home from a trip to Des Moines, they drove north to Boone to catch the Lincoln Highway west into Jefferson. When they turned left at the intersection, the right rear wheel came off and rolled away down the street. The four lifted the axle, slipped the wheel back on, secured it with a new cotter pin, and returned home in good shape. In another situation two high school couples double-dating to the Cooper senior class play noticed a fire burning beneath the floor boards. They stopped, lifted the hood, and dumped gravel on the flames. They then changed a spark plug and continued on their way.[56]

As these and countless other examples illustrate, the machines were simple enough for men, women, and children to operate but not as powerful as they shortly would become. "Cars didn't go so fast and there weren't so many of them on the road. Your car had a top speed of thirty and it took you two blocks to get it that high," explained Lumund Wilcox who confessed to a little experimenting with "top speeds" on those milk runs while most Jefferson residents were still sleeping.[57]

Some families found that traditional routines were easier with the automobile, while others discovered with the ease of travel that they now could do things that they had never done before. This was particularly true for women for whom the home was the center of activity. Several town residents recollected that their mothers went downtown only once or twice in an average week. When they went, they walked and carried their purchases home. In some cases fathers who managed stores or worked around the square did most of the family shopping, and the women rarely had occasion to be around the square at all.[58] With the automobile those patterns began to change as women appeared downtown more often. Gradually, shopping became a routine in their lives to a degree that it had not been before, and they increased their contacts with life around the square.

With this development came a change in the nature of retailing, which is best illustrated in the grocery business. Until the 1920s retail food stores were small family-owned operations that bought commodities in bulk and packaged them as customers ordered. As late as 1925, an advertisement for the local bakery listed eleven groceries in Jefferson at which its bread could be purchased. For a town of thirty-one hundred persons and the surrounding farm community, eleven groceries, plus separate meat markets, a creamery, and independent dairies represented a widely diversified retail food business.

Most of the groceries maintained free delivery service. Customers telephoned their orders, and the store delivered to the home at no charge. Walt Stidwell, whose father ran a grocery and meat market, could even recall delivering to rural customers in the winter and when the farm family had a special order, like meat for the threshing crew, though rural deliveries were not common. Most families became regular customers of one or two stores. Meat could be ordered from the grocery or from one of the two or three butcher shops in town. When a meat order was placed with a grocery store, the grocer purchased the meat from the butcher and delivered it along with the groceries, adding the price to the grocery bill but not charging directly for the service.[59]

Milk and dairy products were retailed through a similar but separate system. Before the days of electric refrigeration small ice-boxes held enough milk and other dairy products for a few days at most. These products arrived at the home on a regular basis from a dairy close to town. The Wilcox family loaded milk cans in the morning to serve their regular customers. George Gallup did service on the same milk route in his youth.

Major changes in the grocery business occurred at the same time the automobile began to be used to go shopping. One change was the introduction of brand names and subsequent retail price competition. When crackers or pickles were sold from a box or barrel, when oatmeal was weighed out from a large bin, or when lard was scooped into a cardboard container, it was difficult to compare prices because the quality of the products varied. They often came from different suppliers. With brand names, however, the product was standardized so that the Tone's Old Golden Coffee sold at Briardale Grocery was the same sold at Square Deal. Only the price varied.

Before the war, grocery ads were staid pronouncements on reliability and quality. During the 1920s, however, grocery stores not only began to stock more brand-name items, but also began to feature these products in their advertising. Price specials began to creep in. By the end of the decade ads routinely announced weekly specials. The A & P grocery chain invaded Jefferson with its complete line of brand-name products, including the company's own, and carried specials on Heinz, Post, Swift, and Del Monte goods. Other groceries followed suit.[60]

Specials on selected prices attracted customers to the store. The merchant could afford to take a loss on the special if that item attracted enough customers to the store who purchased the rest of the items on their grocery lists at full price. Getting the customer to the store, therefore, was a critical factor.

The automobile made it possible for shoppers to get there.[61] No longer did the housewife rely on the grocer to select her items for her. She could drive to the store, survey the available stocks, compare prices, and make her own selections. While many families continued to give most of their business to one store, the lure of specials elsewhere could entice them into another grocery. The automobile did not by itself cause a revolution in the grocery business, but those changes probably could not have happened as they did without it.

Since the 1920s, the number of groceries declined as the larger operations claimed a greater and greater share of the business. Although delivery service continued into the 1950s from at least one Jefferson grocery, most stores had abandoned routine delivery service by World War II. With their customers as mobile as they were the grocers concentrated on luring them into the store rather than on home delivery. In an effort to become a "one-stop" center, stores began providing their own meat counters and dairy cases and eventually forced out the independent meat market and even the creamery.

Customer mobility was a critical factor for merchants in several retail areas. Just as the mail-order catalog had once threatened to steal local customers, big city department stores now began to seduce the rural and small town shoppers. Trips to Des Moines or to Fort Dodge were no longer all-day affairs dependent on railroad schedules. However, as several studies have indicated, the county seat towns like Jefferson for the most part held their own with the coming of automobiles. What they lost in retail sales to larger cities, they picked up from the smaller towns around the county. Those who lost most heavily by the introduction of automobile travel were merchants in the smaller communities like Cooper or Farlin who could not compete in variety or price with big city offerings. The automobile dealt a fatal blow to the ability of very small towns to retain the rural shopper.[62]

Another area in which the automobile had a profound effect was the educational system. At the turn of the century each township was dotted with country schools, often one every two miles, so that a township six miles square might have as many as nine country schools. The rural school was within walking distance of farm children and taught the equivalent of the first eight grades.

To arrive on time in the morning teachers of country schools had to live close to their buildings. In 1903 Bess Harding was teaching a rural school southeast of Jefferson. Although her family lived in town only three miles away, she boarded with a country family because the trip was too far for her to make on a daily basis. Her father drove her out to her school in the family car on Monday morning and picked her up on Friday afternoon. Through the week she walked to a nearby farm.[63] Wilma Downes grew up on a farm a mile west of Cooper. Her older sister was fortunate to get a classroom assignment close enough to permit her to live at home and walk to school. She walked nearly two miles to school every morning. She "saw the sun come up twice," once when she left home and a second time as she came up over the top of a small hill just outside of Cooper.[64] Grace Wadsworth commuted about six miles one way to teach school a decade later, but this was the longest distance the interviews encountered. She recollected the time she had hitched up her team and left them standing while she finished some of her preparations. The team, knowing the route only too well, began without her and was intercepted by neighbors a half-mile down the road. For the most part, however, teachers lived near their schools, boarding with neighboring families. Teachers were frequently isolated from others their own age who shared similar interests, and the turnover among rural teachers was great.

For most rural children in 1900 the one-room school was the extent of their formal education. To continue study a farm child often had to board in town through the week and pay the town district tuition. Myrtle Dillavou lived with a family in Jefferson and helped with domestic chores in exchange for room and board while she attended high school. Her family lived on a farm in Kendrick Township, and only by "going away to school" in her midteens could she continue her education. Until a state law in 1911 required school districts that did not maintain a high school to pay the tuition of any of their students who attended classes outside the district, tuition expenses were another deterrent to farm children. In addition, particularly for farm boys, attending school meant the loss of valuable farm labor. Consequently, many farm families could not justify the expense of high school education. In 1916, according to a state report, the chance of a town child enrolling in high school was six times greater than that of a rural child. While town schools were offering twelve years of graded curricula and expanded academic and extracurricular attractions, rural schools did not have enough students to justify a basic program beyond elementary levels.[65]

Consolidation was the key for the rural district. To duplicate an expanded educational program in every one-room school was impossible and impractical, but if all the children were taught at one location, the increased size of the student body would permit an expanded curriculum. With the automobile consolidation became an option. Students could live at home, commute to school, help with morning and evening chores, and continue to be an integral part of family life through their teen years.

Support for consolidation developed slowly. Bristol Township voted down a 1917 referendum on consolidation, 94–95. In 1919 however, Franklin Township voters approved the consolidation of nine rural schools and the Cooper town school into one new centrally located building in Cooper. The district purchased and operated school buses to transport rural students. Scranton Township closed its rural schools in 1919, began the construction of a new building in Scranton, and purchased buses. Voters around Dana in the northeast approved a

consolidation measure in 1920 and construction of a new building began immediately.[66] One of the most important benefits of consolidation
was that the new district began or expanded a high school program,
greatly increasing the opportunity for rural children to take advanced
course work.

Rural districts provided transportation for many of their students.
Bus service to Cooper and Scranton began with consolidation. Three of
Scranton's first buses were Model-T adaptions while the remaining
four were horse-drawn. Wooden walls enclosed the passenger section
and protected the students in cold weather. Riders sat on long benches
along each side and faced each other.

The situation of farm students attending Jefferson was different
because Jefferson was an independent district, not part of any township school district. Townships surrounding Jefferson continued to operate their own country schools through eighth grade and paid tuition
for their high school students. Jefferson, however, did not provide
transportation for these outlying students. Therefore, rural students
who attended Jefferson were left to their own resources, and families
frequently pooled driving responsibilities.

Busing students became a business for some. A Jefferson man,
C. W. Coler, began a private bus service for rural Jefferson students in
the 1920s. In the early 1930s a Farlin man began a private bus service
for that area. George Taylor, who lived in Farlin but operated a service
station in Jefferson, purchased a bus that held around twenty-five passengers. Since he drove to and from Jefferson every day anyway, he
began driving the bus, charging each rider one dollar per week. As a
special service he even ran back into town on Friday night, at a charge
of ten cents per rider, to permit students to attend football games. The
service was inexpensive and relatively dependable, although Ken
Kinsman could recall occasionally getting stuck north of town in the
spring mud and having to hike around three miles to the school.[67]

The car made it possible to get country students into town but
once there they faced another problem—a social one. There was a
social barrier between farm and town to which farm children especially
were sensitive. Farm children at first felt awkward and out of place in
the unfamiliar surroundings. They felt that town children considered
them socially inferior. The earlier the farm student was introduced into
the town school, the more likely he or she was to consider continuing
on to high school. While the country schools were not high schools and
did not compete with the towns for students, their closing indirectly
helped to increase high school enrollment. Students who came into
town before they reached the secondary level made that painful adjust-
ment before they considered the high school option. The Jim Dillavous

deliberately sent their daughter Beryl into Jefferson for her eighth grade year so that she would be accustomed to the system when she began high school, "when grades really counted." It worked. She was elected president of her senior class and graduated valedictorian. The closing of rural schools sent large numbers of children to town where they could make the transition early.[68]

Grace Wadsworth, longtime teacher in the rural school, noted a more subtle way in which autos affected high school enrollments. In the years immediately following the war, she recalled, people seemed to realize that a one-room school was no longer an adequate preparation for a child. The world was becoming more complex. The automobile widened one's horizons beyond the narrow confines of the local neighborhood, and one had to deal with a more complicated society than before. The automobile made it possible to travel longer distances to school, and that same automobile was making it necessary to know something about the world beyond one's own locality. Parochialism was breaking down, bringing with it a dissatisfaction with the system of numerous, small one-room schools.[69]

Whatever the difficulties or incentives, Jefferson high school enrollments began to increase around the first world war. The size of the freshman class could vary sharply from year to year, but overall, enrollments in the 1920s were substantially greater than they had been a decade earlier. In 1910 there were thirty-eight freshmen. In 1915 the figure stood at thirty. In 1920 there were sixty-six freshmen, and by 1922 there were seventy-three. One factor attracting students to Jefferson was that it had the only normal training course in the county that could certify its graduates to teach in Iowa's elementary classrooms. Nevertheless, there was solid growth outside the normal department as well.

In addition to its role in transporting children to and from school, the automobile had a significant impact on student life. Farm children were normally the only students with cars at school. Over the noon hour these students had four distinct social advantages—wheels. Although the high school was located only two blocks off the square, students sometimes found it necessary to drive uptown for lunch or to circle the courthouse square during the noon lunch hour. Among the more adventurous there was racing over the Seven Hills road south of town, a mile and a half stretch over some precipitous hills, or around a track laid out on some wooded land southwest of town.

The automobile also transported crowds to school events, particularly to football games. In its first years the Jefferson team was only indirectly associated with the school. Many of its players were of high school age and several were enrolled in class, but the school had only an informal tie with the team. By the first world war players were still buying much of their own equipment, including their uniforms and gear, which came in assorted colors and materials, but the team was definitely billed as a school team.[70]

There were rules governing eligibility that required all players to be enrolled in classes.[71] In 1919 Jefferson dropped a 101–0 disaster to Denison when the latter permitted returning World War I veterans to play on the high school team while Jefferson did not. Jefferson cleared the bench, Kellogg Thomas recalled, and everyone played "as long as he could still walk." By 1920 a faculty member of the high school assumed formal coaching responsibilities. Before that a volunteer from the community, normally an alumnus of the team, had coached the players after school.[72]

When Jefferson played Carroll each year on Thanksgiving Day, the town gave the team its full support. By the 1920s nearly two thousand Jefferson fans drove the thirty miles to Carroll to watch the game. Carroll fans were no less loyal on the return matches. Jefferson maintained a strong football tradition and the automobile helped make following the team a major community event. Support for girls' athletics never became popular in Jefferson. The girls' basketball team in the 1920s still traveled by train to its games, and crowds were much smaller.

By any measure the automobile had a significant impact on education. It broadened the world in which students grew up but enabled them to live at home while they learned about it. It made possible larger schools that could offer greater opportunities, and it facilitated interscholastic competition.[73]

The trend toward consolidation in education was paralleled in religion. Like country schools, rural churches were located close to the homes of those in the congregation and served as neighborhood centers where families gathered for worship and social exchange. Before 1900 there were nearly twenty rural churches in the county, but by 1930 the number had declined sharply. As with the school situation, the declining rural population was one factor. As farms began growing larger, the number of farm families declined. Rural congregations found it hard to secure and maintain a regular pastor, and they often had to share a preacher on Sunday morning.

A greater problem was that rural churches were losing members who preferred to drive to worship with the larger town congregations. An article in the *Christian Century* in 1923 pointed out that "the town church, with its resident pastor, graded Sunday school and young peoples' organizations, invites attendance by offering more adequate religious training."[74]

Furthermore, those who had attended the nearby rural congregation primarily because of its proximity could now, with the automobile, attend a church of their own denominational preference. Presbyterians who had attended a Methodist Church in the neighborhood could drive to the Presbyterian congregation in town if they desired. Denominational lines asserted themselves. If a denomination had a congregation in town, the rural churches normally closed and their members drove into town on Sunday morning. Several rural Methodist churches that had shared pastors closed their doors in the 1920s as their groups were absorbed by town congregations.

However, when a denomination had only one congregation in the area and that church was located in the country, there was no great rush to close it and move into town. There were two congregations of Friends, one north of Scranton and the other west of Paton. Neither closed because there was no town congregation with which to consolidate.

An interesting instance in which a congregation accommodated itself to changing circumstances occurred with the rural Church of Christ in Jackson Township west of Jefferson. In this case, the automobile helped the congregation to continue worshiping together. By the 1920s a number of older members had retired from farming and moved to town, leaving the operations to their children. The families of the second generation, now owning cars, preferred to drive into Jefferson for Sunday services rather than to have their parents drive out to the rural church. Therefore, the church building was dismantled and rebuilt in town where the transplanted congregation continued to hold weekly services.[75]

As in most changes there were both advantages and disadvantages. Rural families found the worship services of a better quality but they often missed the tightly knit social circle that the rural congregation had provided. However, the consolidation brought rural and town people together and provided new acquaintances in an era when there was often little other structured interaction between the two groups. Rural children found the transition to town school easier when they had classmates whom they first knew through their church associations.[76]

In countless ways the automobile was transforming local life. Greater mobility allowed individuals more options. It allowed people greater choice among activities in which they wished to participate. No longer did the local community or rural neighborhood establish the boundary for daily activities. A Greene County band practiced on Monday night and gave summer concerts on the courthouse square on Thursday evening through the summer. Band members drove in from as far away as Bagley and Gowrie, towns twenty and thirty miles away.[77] The adjustments necessary to accommodate the new technology transformed such basic units of community life as the family, local government, retailing, the schools, and the churches. "The world was bigger than it had been," Grace Wadsworth recalled. Whether or not one liked that new world, there was no way to return to the old.

During the same period when the automobile was drastically altering Greene County life, a second technological advance compounded the rate of change. Shortly before the turn of the century, Iowans began to enjoy the invisible, silent, almost magical power of electricity. Few persons understood what it was or how it worked, but soon everyone began to appreciate what it could do.

At the Centennial Exposition in Philadelphia in 1876, Alexander Graham Bell displayed a machine that could transmit a voice over a long distance. The telephone was a curiosity, but it quickly gained popularity. Only six years later, the Milligan grain elevator, located on the Chicago and North Western tracks on the north edge of town, strung a wire to its mill on the Raccoon River south of town and added a small generator and two telephones. The wires looped from tree to tree, or whatever was handy, to keep them off the ground. Workers could actually talk to each other even though they were one and a half miles apart! Elmer Milligan described the amazement this produced: "Even after they had talked over these telephones, (people) still swore that it was impossible to converse from the elevator to the mill."[78] The company rented the two telephones for $12.50 a year and continued the line until 1889 when the mill was torn down.

According to a 1942 recollection by Charles Rhodes, the first toll-line service was extended by the Bell system along the Chicago and North Western route to Council Bluffs around 1888. Even in perfect weather conditions, the system was unsatisfactory. Only the telephones along the railroad could use the long-distance line, and calls to and from Des Moines took a long time to make connections. Rhodes recounted the story of a Jefferson businessman who called on the toll phone for the first time: "He had never seen or used the pesky contraption. He was brave, however, and willing to do or die in a good cause. Entering the telephone booth, he took the receiver firmly in his left hand, then holding it at full arm's length, he shouted at the top of his voice, 'I'm here!' "[79]

Several local residents became intrigued with the new invention.

As a boy, F. M. Dean constructed a homemade set of telephones and strung a line between his parents' home on East Lincolnway and a neighbor's residence across the street. Jefferson druggist E. W. Foy, impressed with the possibilities of the new technology, wanted a telephone from his store to his home so that he could talk with his wife through the day. Since Foy knew nothing about telephones, he asked Charles Cockerill, then a local jeweler, to rig up the system. Cockerill had worked for a short time in the west for his brother's telephone business and was enthusiastic about the new invention.

Actually, according to his own account, Cockerill's experience with telephones went back even farther. As a boy in Villisca, Iowa, he had experimented with a set of "talking machines." He recalled it as "made up of two tin cans with a dry bladder stretched over one of the open ends and with a hole punched in the center, a string attached to the bottom and then stretched to the barn some two hundred feet away."[80]

Others asked for the service. George Eagleson operated the bus barn, a "busy and popular industry at the time." Passengers arriving in Jefferson with luggage wanted a ride to their homes or hotel and paid a quarter for the bus service. However, since drivers in the bus barn never knew if the trains were on time or if there were passengers wanting their services, they wasted a lot of time driving back and forth between the barn and the depot. Eagleson realized the potential of the telephone for his business and persuaded Cockerill to install a line between the barn and the train station.[81]

In 1891 the city council passed a resolution granting the Cockerill Telephone Company the right to "use the streets and alleys to erect poles." The first lines connected only the telephones on each end. Foy could call home but nowhere else. Eagleson could call the depot but not Foy's drugstore. However, as more customers asked for service, Cockerill installed a fifty-line switchboard that brought all the phones into an integrated system, and shortly, as business increased, replaced that with a hundred-line board.

E. B. Wilson, an early subscriber, wrote an interesting account of phone service in those first years:

In 1889, the telephone office was in the small room now used by the Charles Jewelry Shop (on West State Street). The switchboard looked like an ordinary roll-top desk. I do not believe that there were more than forty or fifty subscribers.

When you wanted to talk with somebody, you went to the instrument on the wall, turned a little crank which ran a little mill in a box, took the receiver off the hook, and heard the operator say, "Hello." Then you said, "Give me John Smith's store."

The operator was Hattie Anderson, a quick-minded, very likable girl, who did her work well. Hattie had all the names and numbers in her head and knew them instantly. She used to tell me she knew who I was better by hearing my voice over the phone than by looking at me.[82]

In 1893 Cockerill built his first long-distance lines within the county, to Farlin, Scranton, and Churdan, and extended service to farm families along the routes. These were among the first farm lines in the state.[83] By 1895 every town in the county had a line to Jefferson. When the expansion went to Grand Junction, Cockerill asked for a town franchise, but the proposal was voted down. Furthermore, a fire destroyed the building in which the exchange was housed, and the Cockerill's Grand Junction venture was a total loss.

Expansion continued, however. In cooperation with the Hawkeye Telephone Company in Perry, Cockerill negotiated an agreement with the Mutual Telephone Company of Des Moines for long-distance service to the capital. Telephone subscriptions increased rapidly. In 1899 the local directory carried 125 names. The next year, the number had grown to 178.

Cockerill changed the name to the Jefferson Telephone Company. In March 1902 it was reorganized as the Greene County Telephone Company with a capitalization of one hundred thousand dollars. The intention was to consolidate all the telephone interests in the county into one large exchange so that "no matter where located every telephone subscriber may call up and talk to his most removed neighbor in any distant corner of the county without paying any toll service whatever."[84]

The dream never materialized. Early phone service had been limited primarily to the towns because of the expense of stringing wires from one farm home to another. Farm families, however, also wanted the service. In 1902 farmers initiated construction of a second telephone exchange under mutual ownership. They had discovered that simple telephone lines could be built very cheaply. With wires, poles, and telephones, Farmers Mutual strung up service to the neighborhood on a cooperative plan. There were no full-time employees at first, but the service, though limited, seemed satisfactory. By 1903 they ordered a switchboard of their own. The Greene County company offered to provide services to Mutual subscribers for five dollars a month, but the offer was turned down.

The Farmers Mutual incorporated and expanded. They operated two branch lines at first, one south and one southeast of Jefferson. In 1905 and 1906 several small rural systems combined with the Mutual, and by 1910 the Citizens Mutual, as it was then called, operated 236 exchanges and 219 rural telephones. It paid switchboard operators four hundred dollars a year, and in 1915 purchased a lot in Jefferson, constructed a building, and installed a new switchboard. While the quality of connections on the Mutual was often not as clear as the Jefferson system, its appeal was its free service to surrounding communities, something the other did not offer.

Two separate telephone companies in the community created an inconvenience. Subscribers on one line could not speak with persons on the other. Businesses had to maintain both lines in order to have contact with all customers. Advertisements listed both telephone numbers. In 1912 after some shifts in local ownership, the Greene County Telephone Company, which had been renamed the New Telephone Company, sold out to the Bell Telephone Company, the giant national firm. The Mutual continued, however, and the community endured the two separate systems into the 1930s.

Despite the minor inconveniences telephone service was a great boon to farm families. Barbara Hamilton recalled what a wonderful thing it was for the farm wife for it let her talk to her neighbors when her work did not permit her to leave the house. It provided instant contact with doctors and emergency service. Telephone operators took messages for local physicians when they could not be reached. In one case, when a doctor could not get to a farmhouse in time to help with a delivery, the father took instructions over the telephone and relayed them in to a neighbor serving as midwife. A baby girl arrived in fine shape.[85] Soon, it was hardly more difficult to talk to the East or West Coast than it was to speak to someone across the room. It cost more, and patrons reserved long distance service for special occasions, but the potential was there.

The telephone was but the first of the marvelous changes brought about by electricity. No one had to sell the idea of electricity to Jefferson; its benefits were too obvious to ignore. In 1882 Thomas Edison built the first generating plant in the United States in New York City. Only twelve years later, in 1894, Jefferson installed its first generator, the showpiece of the Jefferson Light, Heat, Power, and Water Company. In the grandiose rhetoric of the era the *Bee* chronicled the event: "The first electric light that ever shone in Jefferson struggled into existence down at the power house not far from nine o'clock last night and threw a strong radiance all about the premises that showed its intimate acquaintance with the Grand Master Workman of all light — the sun."[86] The following week, the newspaper noted that "the chandeliers, brackets, and other fixtures which accompany the introduction of electricity are being properly attached and set in order this week, preparatory to starting this circuit at the earliest possible moment."[87]

By 1896 the plant was equipped with "the finest machinery known to electrical appliances and contrivances" and had "a capacity of 1,500, 32-candle power incandescents and 40 2,000-candle power arc lights."[88] A Jefferson hotel installed electric bells to ring for desk service. An evening lawn party of the Baptist Church was illuminated by lanterns *and* electric lights. The improvements began to show up in many new places.

As the demand for electricity grew, the power company increased its output. In 1907 the company announced that it would provide all-night service. The following year, the company distributed electric irons to Jefferson housewives on a trial basis and asked them to compare them with their heavy, stove-heated ones. The new models were an unqualified success, and sales skyrocketed. My grandmother claimed that the electric iron was the greatest drudgery-saver ever invented, a statement perhaps fully appreciated only by those who have stood for hours near a hot stove in a hot kitchen on a hot summer day lugging a hot heavy iron back and forth. In addition, because nearly all women ironed on Tuesday ("Monday washday, Tuesday ironing") and because the irons pulled so much more current than the normal load, the electric company promised to furnish the extra electricity needed on ironing day, one of the first instances of "peak demand" on the power plant. The *Bee* commented: "It is to be hoped that Jefferson will shortly be favored with an all-day service. For the present, electricity will be furnished on Tuesday and Wednesday forenoons of each week for the flatiron service."[89]

Nowhere were the improvements effected by electricity more noticeable than in the home. Electric irons were but the first conveniences. Toasters, vacuum cleaners, mixers, fans, and hot water heaters quickly followed. Refrigerators became popular in the 1920s. The landscape was changing, too. A photograph of the west side of the square at the turn of the century shows hitching posts and a watering trough in front of a corner drugstore. A 1930 shot from the same angle shows the same drugstore, but in front of it were cars parked diagonally on a paved street and a whole row of electric lights.

As marvelous as the new electric technology was, however, it spread its blessings unevenly. Unlike automobiles and telephones, which served both town and farm needs, power lines ran only short distances into the country, and few farm families enjoyed the new conveniences. Unequal access to electricity was a major factor in creating a social distance between the town and rural home. A 1920 study showed that urban women, the majority of whom lived in homes with electricity, spent the equivalent of a full twenty working days per year less on laundry than did farm women who were without electric washers. One 1919 USDA study reported that rural families spent over ten hours a week just pumping water and carrying it to the kitchen.[90]

In 1920 the federal census asked for the first time how many farms were using electricity. The surveys showed that out of six million farms, only 7 percent had electric power. Only 11 percent had running water, and these tended to be concentrated in New England or the Far West where private companies could extend services to rural areas more easily. Well into the 1930s, nine out of ten rural homes in America were without electricity.[91] The Iowa census of 1925 reported that 265 Greene County farms enjoyed lights, heat, and indoor plumbing, out of a total of nearly 2,000 farm households. The number was rising, but painfully slowly for the remaining families.

In a few instances some farmers installed their own generating units and wired their homes and barns for lights. The Delco Light Company manufactured a farm generator unit and advertised it extensively in the rural press. A gasoline-powered engine charged a battery that stored electricity for home needs. At a cost of less than a cheap auto, the Delco ad proclaimed, a farm home could have "its own light and power for washing machines, water pumps, vacuum sweepers and lights." In reality the capacity of the system was limited, and it usually strained to provide power for much more than lights.

Dorothy Bowley, a daughter of a prominent Jefferson lawyer, was given a Delco system for a wedding present when she married a Hardin Township farmer and prepared to move to the farm. She was the exception in two ways. First, most farm families did not have Delco systems, either because of the expense or the inconvenience of maintaining their own generating plants. Second, most town girls of her era managed to fall in love with town boys who had no interest in nor prospect of moving to a farm. The thought of moving from homes with electrical conveniences to ones without lights, indoor plumbing, or even running water made even the most love-smitten stop and think over the proposition carefully.[92]

Why was there such a long time between urban and rural electrification? The fundamental problem was the initial cost of installing the lines. Since there had been too few cases of rural lines in operation to calculate the actual costs, even the experts had to rely on estimates, which sometimes ran as high as $2,000 per mile. A report by the Wisconsin Electric Association, a private trade guild, placed the figure at $1,225 per mile for a line that might serve fewer than five homes, and this at the time was regarded as a low estimate.[93]

The question was who should pay for the installation. At first there seemed to be three possibilities. The stockholders of the utility companies could have taken a cut in dividends to expand the lines. A second option was the consumer, including both urban and rural customers. To keep profits at the same level while absorbing the considerable expenses of rural installations, company income would have had to increase, meaning higher rates for urban homes. The third possibility was the farm customer alone. To both the stockholder and the urban resident there was a comfortable logic to this choice. Those who wanted the service should pay for it. Why should either investors or urban residents subsidize rural electrification? If farmers wanted electricity, so the argument went, they should pay for it. And since urban customers and stockholders had much more influence with private utilities than farmers, their perspective carried the day. It was not a conspiracy against farmers; it was capitalist economics.

A fourth possibility, government subsidy of rural lines, developed in the 1930s. In 1936 Congress created the Rural Electric Administration to provide low-cost loans to associations who would build and operate rural electric systems. Greene County was one of the first in the state to organize and apply for the funds.[94] Rural electrification would not become a reality in Greene County until the late 1930s. What is more significant in this study is that many farm families remained "in the dark" for nearly a half century after town families began enjoying the new technology. There were personal and social costs in the delay.

In addition to all the changes during the period that did occur, it is necessary to point out some changes that did not. The shiny new machines simply arrived by train or truck from somewhere else. Jefferson residents enjoyed them without enduring the soot of tall factory smokestacks, the ugliness of labor strikes, or the problems of the urban poor. For several decades rural residents enjoyed the fruits of industrialization without having to confront the social problems that industrialization creates. When the new machines arrived, however, they greatly expanded the options available to Jefferson residents. Simple conveniences made life more pleasant, and electrical appliances relieved people of numbing drudgery. The automobile and the telephone did much to end rural isolation. Beginning around the turn of the century, daily life in the small town underwent a rapid transformation. It was the pace of change that was astounding. Those who grew up with the new technology quickly learned to take it for granted, but to those who had grown up before the new machines became commonplace, it was a whole new world.

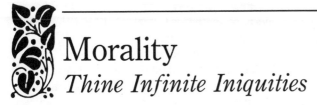

CHAPTER 5

Morality
Thine Infinite Iniquities

Is not thy wickedness great? and thine iniquities infinite?

—JOB 22:5

JEFFERSON YOUTH WHO CAME OF AGE in the decade following the Armistice grew up in a different environment than their parents once knew. There was a new sense of what life was all about. The catch words describing the decade are caricatures—the Roaring Twenties, "flaming youth," flappers, the lost generation, the jazz age—but they all point in the same direction to energy, movement, and change.

Those witnessing the changes brought about by new technology were also watching a change in community standards of behavior. Through the first third of the twentieth century there came to be a new standard of conduct, a new definition of what activities were or were not proper, acceptable, and encouraged. In 1900, activities the major Protestant churches considered sinful were largely absent from *public* events in Jefferson. Drinking, card playing, Sunday recreation, suggestive entertainments—these were forbidden either by legal decree or social convention. As historian Sidney Mead put it, Protestantism had come to dominate American culture through the latter half of the nineteenth century, "setting the prevailing mores and moral standards by which personal and public, individual and group conduct was judged."[1] In Jefferson, when one worried what "they" would think or if "they" would approve, "they" were Protestants. The Protestant minister may or may not have been invited to the most important social events of the year, but what went on there in 1900 was generally in keeping with what he preached on Sunday morning.

By 1930 a definite change had occurred. Methodist women formed bridge clubs, and the junior-senior prom was a school-spon-

147

sored dance. Even though Prohibition was the law of the land, many showed much greater tolerance of the use of alcohol, and the "wets" were less concerned about pulling their shades.

Significantly, what had not occurred during the period was an official overhaul in the Protestant moral code. The churches still recited the same list of "don'ts," and members still nodded their heads in agreement–in church. As a result, there came to be in effect two moral codes, occasionally contradicting each other but more often maintaining a wary coexistence. Some things were not acceptable in church or when the preacher was present or in school (where the traditional codes still predominated) but were acceptable anywhere else. For example, dancing had lost some of its social stigma, but as late as the 1950s, some Methodists strongly objected to a young people's folk dance *in the church basement.* Protestant women who were willing to admit that there was probably nothing really wrong with card playing still raised their eyebrows at the Catholic women regularly playing cards at their church group meetings. The authority of the Protestant code had suffered considerable erosion. What was once sinful had been demoted to "sinful-in-church."

One of the clearest examples of declining support for traditional Protestant standards is the contrast between 1900 and 1930 in the activities permitted on Sunday. At the turn of the century, Protestants took very seriously the fourth commandment, "Remember the Sabbath and keep it holy." They had written their definition of Sunday holiness into a set of restrictive blue laws for the entire state. Section 5040 of the Iowa code declared: "If any person be found on the first day of the week, commonly called Sunday, engaged in carrying firearms, dancing, hunting, shooting, horse racing, or in any way disturbing a worshipping assembly or private family, or in buying or selling property of any kind, or in labor except that of necessity or charity, he shall be fined."

Gradually at first but rapidly after the war, the traditional restrictions began to give way. The question of Sunday baseball games was an issue in Greene County in the summer of 1916. The Rippey club wanted the larger crowds that Sunday games would attract, and with the automobile, the potential audience for the games had increased considerably. When an ordinance to allow Sunday baseball was defeated by the city council, Lovejoy cheered: "The *Bee* thinks that friends of baseball and of the Fair Association are making a mistake in trying to force Sunday ball in Jefferson. It will hurt the interest mentioned. It may work in the big cities – and in Carroll – but the consensus in Jefferson is against it."[2]

With the eight-hour day, Lovejoy argued, the "laboring man" did not need a special day of recreation; what he really needed was the "poise of mind" to permit him to enjoy the Sabbath "as God commanded." While Lovejoy admitted he was not prepared to evaluate how much of a "crime" it was to play ball on Sunday, he was definitely suspicious: "If anything in the line of sport disturbs a considerable number of people, either mentally or otherwise, the chances are there is something wrong about it."[3]

In the county and around the state, however, there was a growing restlessness with the restrictive statutes. The restrictions that were being debated in Greene County had already been virtually nullified in the larger cities and less Protestant rural areas of the state. Nevertheless, with their disproportionate representation in the Iowa legislature, rural Protestants still had the power to codify their own definition of righteousness. Section 5040 was on the books. However lax its enforcement, the Sunday blue law was a symbol that the godly were still writing the laws, and the godly saw no reason to accept anything less.

Legislative attempts to modify the statute met with little success. In 1917 the House considered a bill to legalize Sunday baseball, concerts, theaters, and numerous business activities, with the provision that permitted towns under ten thousand to prohibit such activities. In other words, sin would be legal in the cities but only optional in small towns. Rural Protestants refused to give license to libertines anywhere, and the House soundly defeated the measure, 25–79.[4]

An analysis of the vote clearly shows a rural-urban division on the measure. Of 104 representatives voting, 25 came from counties that had cities of at least ten thousand persons, those in which the Sunday ordinances would have been repealed. Of these "urban" representatives, 15 voted in favor of repeal and 10 voted against it. Of the remaining 79 representatives, the "rural" legislators who had no city of more than ten thousand in their districts, only 10 favored it while 69 opposed it.

That did not end the controversy, of course. In the previous election Iowans had chosen a new attorney general, Horace Havner, who campaigned on a promise to enforce *all* the laws. Havner favored substantial modification of the Sunday laws and was disappointed when the general assembly defeated the proposed revisions. To spur the legislature to action in the next session, Havner announced that his office would vigorously enforce the law as it appeared on the books. To this end he drafted a long letter to county attorneys with a ruling on what was and what was not legal on Sunday.

E. G. Graham, the local county attorney, duly published Havner's construction of the Sabbath ordinance. Amateur sports were permitted if no admission were charged and if they did not disturb the worship of either a public assembly or a private family. Public utilities, newspapers, and liveries could operate. Garages could sell gas and oil and assist motorists with car trouble. Hotels, bakeries, and meat markets were permitted their usual operations, and druggists could sell medicine.

Forbidden under the ruling were amateur sports where admission was charged, Sunday baseball, shoe shine parlors, barbershops, all kinds of work "except that of necessity or charity," and the sale of all kinds of merchandise and property. Lest someone still manage a measure of pleasure, Havner specifically prohibited the sale of ice cream, soft drinks, fruits, vegetables, cigars, tobacco, candy, and confections, including popcorn and peanuts. However, ice cream and soft drinks could be included with meals sold in a restaurant if there were no additional charge for them.[5]

Lovejoy's "Seasonable Sermons" opened fire on the attorney general's methods and motive. "The laws are perfectly good," Lovejoy declared, "and should stand as a menace to all evil doers." Havner was ignoring the real disturbances and coming down on minor infractions only to get the law repealed altogether. Lovejoy fumed: "The railways continue to conduct all lines of their business, autos chase about with noise and disturbance, picnicking, fishing, street corner loafing, open post office, and dozens of other things are continually indulged in that have far more of the disturbing element in them than buying a cigar."[6] Ice cream and cigars? Did their sale violate the letter of the law? Did their sale violate the *spirit* of the law, "to preserve and maintain a proper observance of the holy Sabbath day"?

The owner of a popular candy store and ice cream parlor became a test case of how the law would be enforced in Jefferson. Charged with selling ice cream on Sunday, Louis Tronchetti was found not guilty by Justice A. D. Howard. In a decision more distinguished for the reasonableness of its conclusion than for the logic employed to arrive thereat, Howard found Tronchetti not guilty because ice cream has "food value" and hence came under the category of a necessity: "There is no question as to the food value of ice cream which under our statute must contain at least 12 percent of weight of milk fat. Under the present day conditions, ice cream is recognized as a food by physicians and is considered an absolute necessity in some cases of sickness. Numerous persons, especially in hot weather, do not care for anything for their lunch or evening meal except ice cream. To deprive them of this would be a hardship."[7]

Howard's ruling went on to promulgate his own list of activities that did or did not violate state law. In most cases his list coincided with Havner's although he forbade Sunday gasoline sales to local residents and permitted "worthy" entertainments like Sunday chautauquas even if they charged admission. As long as they were sponsored by nonprofit organizations promoting the moral improvement of the community, they came under the category of "charitable activity," Howard stated. The *Bee* applauded Howard's ruling as " 'safe and sound' in accordance with the spirit of modern times, and the habits and usages of the present age."[8]

In 1919 the Iowa legislature again defeated an attempt to modify the Sunday ordinances. This time, the bill would have permitted a popular referendum on the measure in towns from five hundred to five thousand and allowed cities over five thousand to set their own standards. The Senate approved the measure, 33–13, but the House was striking no deals with Satan and buried it, 24–77.[9]

The blue laws were not modified for nearly forty years, but regardless of what the statute read, the twenties was a decade of much less somber Sabbath observance. By 1925 the *Bee* was displaying several ads for Sunday amusements. Nic-O-Let, a private park near Boone, offered summer patrons a baseball game and band concert on Sunday afternoon, for a slight charge. Closer to home, seven miles northeast of Jefferson at Spring Lake, ball games and evening concerts were also standard fare for a summer Sunday afternoon.[10] Since neither site was within the limits of a city or town, they were subject only to county law enforcement officials. Neither the Boone nor Greene County sheriff was anxious to add to his responsibilities a vigorous and unpopular enforcement of the blue laws.

By 1926 the Rialto Theatre in Scranton was advertising Sunday movies. The Strand and New State theaters in Jefferson, under common ownership, continued their never-on-Sunday policy until 1929, but this too gave way. Without fanfare they began showing Sunday movies. By that time the change seems to have generated little controversy. Sunday afternoon matinees, with reduced adult tickets, replaced the traditional Saturday afternoon showing.[11]

Not until 1933 would a bill again be introduced in the state legislature to remove the Sabbath restrictions, but even though it failed again, its title provided a revealing insight. House File 446, a bill for the "repealing of unenforced Sunday blue laws . . . (which have never been enforced and (have) been openly violated by the state)," failed to pass.[12] It was not true that the law had never been enforced, but it was clear that by 1933 it was openly violated. Not until 1955 did the Iowa legislature finally remove the Sabbath statute from the code, a remarkable testimony to its value as a symbol of the dominance of the righteous.

Violation of the Sabbath, however, was only a minor infraction on the Protestant checklist of evils in comparison with one of the truly deadly sins, the use of alcohol. Ratification of the Eighteenth Amendment in 1919 prohibiting the manufacture and sale of alcoholic beverages culminated a Protestant crusade of nearly a century. In an ethic that stressed the value of self-restraint, alcohol was an obvious vice of the first rank. The intoxicated lost their reason and inhibitions, and a drink in any form, went the standard temperance line, could be the fatal first step down the road to depravity. Temperance sermons painted vivid images of the terrible ends that awaited those who yielded to the temptation of "demon rum."

Yet, what must also be understood is that however negative their rhetoric denouncing drinking, evangelical Protestants firmly believed that the sinner had a soul that could be saved. Reformed alcoholics, particularly those who became devout Christians, were the pride of the temperance movement. When a Jefferson lawyer reached a stage in his alcoholism that threatened to destroy his practice and livelihood, concerned community associates took up a collection to send him away for treatment. He returned, a reformed alcoholic, and "never touched another drop." A few years later, he was invited to address the senior class at its commencement ceremonies, and the community took pride in his rehabilitation. As it had been with their Yankee predecessors two generations earlier, it was a sense of responsibility for the welfare of those about them that fueled the fervor of the temperance forces.[13]

The villains of the temperance scenario were not the drinkers but those who exploited the weakness of others for their own profit—the saloon owner, the bootlegger, and the brewer and distiller. Liquor laws reflected this. While public intoxication was a misdemeanor punishable by a fine, the person supplying the alcohol was, by a 1915 statute, made responsible for damages the drinker might commit under its effect. In 1917, even more to the point, the person who supplied alcohol was liable *to the drinker* for any damage the drinker might do to himself or herself while under its influence.[14] Who was responsible for the murder of a drunk who was killed when he attacked another? Billy Sunday, that most flamboyant of all temperance lecturers, maintained that the real murderer was the one who sold the drunk the booze.[15] In a defensive move the liquor industry claimed that liquor license fees contributed to the public welfare, but it garnered little sympathy. Said the *Bee*: "Any fool knows that the liquor tax is not, and never was, paid by the liquor interests. They pay a tax, of course, but it is added to the price of the booze, and paid always by the poor devil who drinks the stuff, just exactly as the (purchase) of dry goods and groceries pays a proportion of rent, clerk hire, and proprietary profit. The stuff they send the *Bee* makes no mention whatever of the big fines, and jail sentences, paid by poor devils who cannot leave the booze alone."[16]

Liquor interests were understood to be behind the political machines of the cities, working to support corrupt city government and untiring in their efforts to prevent restrictions of liquor operations. Not only was their product itself a social menace, but their practices were equally disreputable. Applauding the tougher regulations, Lovejoy accused the liquor establishments of having brought them on themselves by adulterating their products, selling to habitual drunkards, robbing patrons in their establishments, and other dishonorable practices.[17]

More was involved than personal morality, however. In fact, temperance advocates understood there to be a close relationship between alcohol and many social ills. This relationship was what generated so much of the motivating energy behind the temperance drive. Prohibition would bring about social progress. An impressive body of statistics pointed out the contribution of alcohol to a myriad of evils. A 1917 "Seasonable Sermon" typified the perspective:

Nine-tenths of the criminals in America are brought to that state of outlawry either directly or indirectly by the use of intoxicating liquors. Nine-tenths of the crimes of murder, arson, larceny and white slavery are due, directly or indirectly, to the use and sale of intoxicating liquor. Nine-tenths of the men and women who inhabit our penitentiaries and houses of correction, trace their downfall, directly or indirectly, to the use of booze. Nine-tenths of our poverty-stricken people, nine-tenths of the occupants of our orphan's homes, nine-tenths of the inmates of our homes for the feeble-minded, can trace their unfortunate condition back to the flowing neck of a whiskey bottle. Everybody admits these facts, nobody denies them, no one can disprove the assertions.[18]

Prohibition protected "the decent, the respectable, and the weak," the latter being the drinker who lacked the necessary self-restraint to resist. Nor were the positive benefits of temperance overlooked. A Sioux City newspaper reported that with the introduction of a tougher prohibitory measure and the closing of saloons, one bank opened 350 new savings accounts.[19]

This relationship of abstention to stability, success, and respectability on one hand and of drinking to crime, poverty, and social ostracism on the other was crucial. Town loafers and ne'er-do-wells who hung around the livery stable and called out obscenities to local women who passed within earshot actually provided a valuable community function. They were living proof of what happens to drinkers. Temperance tracts and sermons cited examples of young men from good homes whose first step on the road to ruin was the fatal glass of beer or whiskey.

Atherton notes in *Main Street on the Middle Border* that some larger communities had a small upper-class elite who by virtue of "varying combinations of wealth, length of residence, occupation, and breeding" stood apart from the "God-fearing, middle-class people devoted to church and lodge."[20] The upper class, often Episcopalian or Unitarian in eastern cities, might or might not conform to middle-class temperance norms.

At the turn of the century, Jefferson, however, had no such stratum. Local bankers and professionals, like Henry Haag and W. G. McDuffie, belonged to mainline Protestant denominations. The community was without a visible element who openly violated the temperance norms without the predicted results. On the surface at least the formula seemed to hold true. Drinkers (or at least those publicly identified as such) tended to be found among the improvident and shiftless, those who lacked the character to make respectable citizens of themselves. Given the limited number of contacts that local residents had with the outside world, the absence of role models who ignored the code but escaped its forecasted consequences was important in maintaining the temperance ideology.

One measure of the community's commitment to the temperance standard was its support for laws curtailing the sale of alcohol. In 1893 the state legislature passed the Mulct Act, which allowed counties to license saloons if a majority of voters favored it. Greene County remained dry. In 1917 Iowa voters (still an all-male club) were confronted with an October referendum on the Prohibition issue. On the ballot was a proposed constitutional amendment making the sale of alcohol in Iowa illegal. Congress was debating a similar addition to the federal constitution (and would pass it in December), and interest in the Iowa ballot was high.

For the first time since 1882 Greene County voters had the opportunity to express themselves directly on the liquor issue. There were no political party labels and no candidates. Greene County men voted almost five to three in favor of Prohibition, 2,201–1,305. The state vote, however, ran the other way. The amendment was narrowly defeated, 213,747 to 214,636, a 50.1 percent majority against it.

The returns followed predictable patterns. Protestant and Re-

publican townships voted dry while Catholic, Democratic neighborhoods voted wet. Also expected was the close correlation with the 1916
referendum on women's suffrage. Not only in Greene County but
around the state, most Prohibition strongholds in the 1917 referendum
had turned in strong support for women's suffrage the previous year.[21]

The defeat of the Iowa Prohibition amendment soon became moot
with congressional passage of the Eighteenth Amendment to the
United States Constitution in December 1917. Ratification by the necessary thirty-six states took only one year, and on 16 January 1919 national Prohibition went into effect. Victory at last had come to the drys.

Ironically, however, it was not until the decade of national Prohibition that drinking began to lose some of its social stigma in Jefferson.
Drinking was still a private activity after the war, something one did at
home or in a friend's home, and above all, only with those who did not
consider drinking offensive. After all, it was now against the law. What
seems to have been the rule was that an occasion was dry unless all
those present clearly understood that alcohol would be served. Nondrinkers were not invited to wet functions, and along the alcohol line,
an acknowledged social division existed.

What was important, however, was that a "new wet" element
emerged that did not fit the stereotype that temperance advocates had
outlined. The new wets were not the lower classes who frequented
saloons. They were not dirty, smelly, impoverished social outcasts.
They did not swagger around the streets insulting women and picking
fights. Some of them were, in fact, from among well-to-do community
families. It was not cheap beer that they wanted. They preferred cock-
tails before dinner. As Frederick Allen noted, the twenties witnessed
increasing popularity of distilled liquors, not fermented ones. It was
the cocktail glass and not the beer mug that symbolized the new wets.
The saloon had been distinctly masculine turf, but the cocktail party
normally included couples. "Under the new regime," as Allen put it,
"not only the drinks were mixed, but the company as well."[22]

A few families in the business community became known
drinkers. The Head brothers, local bankers and members of one of the
wealthiest families in town, hosted parties that, at least by reputation,
were notorious by Jefferson standards. Further augmenting the ranks
of the wets were students who went to college and returned home with
more liberal views toward drinking.

The pipeline quenching this thirst was an informal underground
distribution network. Neighboring Carroll County established a national reputation for quality during Prohibition. The little German
Catholic community of Templeton became famous for its "Templeton
Rye," supposedly the only product of the decade that one requested *by*

name. At least in local mythology, Templeton was a major supplier of Al Capone's speakeasy empire in Chicago. Cars and trucks allegedly carried the contraband to urban distributors who made contacts with individual customers.[23]

One Jefferson man recalled his own career during Prohibition. As a teenage son in a poor family, he found that Prohibition made possible a good source of income. He was paid fifty cents to hide a bottle at a designated pickup point. The tall grass by a certain fence post at the fairgrounds was a common spot, but there were others around town. Suppliers became known to customers by word of mouth, and when someone placed an order, the supplier found a boy who would deliver the liquor to the designated spot. For this runner there had been no moral dilemma involved. Prohibition meant economic opportunity. Nor was he particularly concerned about arrest. He claimed that the local sheriff was not after the small fry like himself delivering a bottle or two. They set up roadblocks when they suspected a large shipment going through but "looked the other way" at minor purchases.

As some prosperous and respectable couples and college-educated youth began to reject the traditional norms, the temperance mythology began to show some signs of distress. These people did not lose their families, commit crimes, or ruin their health. (Or when they failed in business, as did the Head brothers, the failures were not usually chalked up as a direct result of their alcoholic indulgence.) In the old formula it was the responsibility of the abstainer to save the weak, but it began to grow unclear precisely from what the weak were to be saved.

By an overwhelming majority most active Protestant church members by the end of the 1920s still frowned on the use of alcohol (as did several Jefferson Catholic families), and there remained in the community a division between those who drank and those who did not. The Protestant churches continued to preach against it, and by and large, their congregations, particularly the older members, continued to abstain. The *Bee* continued its staunch support of the law. The fact that it was not enforced in the cities was no reason to repeal it, Lovejoy argued, any more than laws against murder should be repealed because murders continue.

In 1933 national reaction against bootlegging and its attendant vices led to congressional passage of the Twenty-first Amendment repealing Prohibition. A referendum on ratification came before Greene County voters in June. The vote was remarkably consistent with the 1917 tally on the same issue, 63 percent dry, while the state compiled a slim wet majority. (In one Carroll County precinct the vote was 400–2 in favor of repeal.)²⁴ Local townships followed general patterns established in the women's suffrage and 1917 referenda (Table 5.1).

By 1933 however, and the repeal of national Prohibition, drinking no longer carried the social stigma it had two decades earlier. The moral fervor to save the intemperate from their weakness had diminished. Gradually, despite the official position of the major Protestant churches, which continued to condemn the use of alcoholic beverages in any form, community sentiment moved toward defining drinking to excess as the sin, not simply drinking.²⁵

Perhaps the changing moral climate can best be observed in new attitudes toward minor articles of the traditional canon. Dancing and card playing were once forbidden activities among the major Protestant denominations. Blanche McWilliam recalled that her grandmother, Jeannette Sutton, warned that "the Devil *lives* in a deck of cards," and she firmly believed it.²⁶ Card playing was gambling, and not only was the activity itself sinful, but the habit it cultivated might lead one to those hellholes where the wicked congregated, to the saloons, dance halls, and pool halls.

Nevertheless, there was a codicil to this condemnation of card

TABLE 5.1. Voter patterns in women's suffrage and Prohibition referenda, 1916–1933

Township	For women's suffrage %	For Prohibition %	Against repeal of Prohibition %
Bristol	67	80	71
Cedar	50	48	45
Dawson	56	61	70
Franklin	70	71	61
Grant	70	62	79
Greenbrier	79	79	89
Hardin	69	57	72
Highland	68	66	67
Jackson	54	55	58
Jefferson #1	72	63	58
Jefferson #2	72	55	51
Jefferson #3	73	70	67
Junction #1	51	55	38
Junction #2	67	63	57
Kendrick	59	63	57
Paton	65	67	84
Scranton	43	65	66
Washington	62	58	63
Willow	40	54	38

Source: *Iowa Official Register, 1917–1918,* 469; *Jefferson Bee,* Oct. 1917, 20 June 1933.

playing. Not all card games were forbidden, only those using the standard poker deck. Games like Rook, Somerset, and Authors played with their own special decks were different. These were not gamblers' games. Even toward games like cribbage, which used the standard poker deck, attitudes were ambiguous. The S. J. Melsons were devoted Methodists, but their son could not recall a time when he was not playing cribbage with his father. Yes, they knew the church's stand on card playing, but they experienced no tension in violating the official ecclesiastical pronouncements.[27]

Bridge also became popular during the 1920s. There was a daily radio show from WHO in Des Moines on the game. Some women formed bridge clubs, which met on a regular basis. Although the game would occasionally draw wrath from the pulpit, bridge clubs became an accepted form of casual entertaining. It was becoming increasingly difficult, furthermore, to single out card games for censure when other social activities of a similar nature were accepted.[28]

Dancing was similarly suspect although, like card playing, the case was not airtight. That it brought into close proximity live bodies of the opposite sex made it an obviously dangerous entertainment. Not only was the activity itself questionable, but dance halls were not a fit environment for the righteous. Dance halls existed in Carroll, but then, this hardly surprised Greene County Protestants who expected such from the papist citadel of western Iowa. By the 1920s, there were dance halls closer to home. North of Scranton, Gobblers' Nob dance hall attracted crowds not only on weekends but on an occasional weeknight as well. On the north beach of Spring Lake was probably the best known dance hall in the county, and it featured some of the big name bands of the decade. Lawrence Welk and Jan Garber played Spring Lake![29]

An unmistakable sign that the old norms were passing came in 1930 when the high school sponsored a dance. Public schools had always reflected the official morality. Teachers were expected to subscribe to the highest moral codes since they were models for the young. Since democracy requires high standards of morality and civic responsibility as well as an educated electorate, the reasoning went, public schools were expected to promote morality and citizenship as well as basic education.[30] That officials allowed school sponsorship of a dance clearly points to a changed community standard on the subject. In 1929 the junior class held its spring banquet at the Lincoln Hotel and followed the traditional format: a formal dinner and a few short entertainments. In 1930 however, they held a junior-senior prom at the Jefferson Country Club and danced. Alice Ann Andrew, a member of the senior class, remembered that "Bill Hamilton's sister was a great dancer" and gave them all a quick course in ballroom dancing prior to the big evening. The girls wore long dresses. After that, school dances became a tradition.[31]

Fred Morain was a high school junior in 1930, and it was his responsibility to contact the president of the country club to request permission to use the facilities for the school dance. The president that year was Chester Oppenheimer, who was Jewish. While there is no way of knowing how other men might have responded had they been in Oppenheimer's position, Dad remembers that he had been glad that it was Oppenheimer and not, as he put it, "an old guard Methodist or Baptist." For official school functions traditional codes were often applied more strictly for fear that "they" would object.

While the simplicity we are tempted to ascribe to previous generations is one of which they were probably unaware, there nevertheless appears to have been at the turn of the century an underlying ethic that integrated several dimensions of community life. According to William H. Whyte, this common thread provided "a degree of unity between the way people wanted to behave and the way they thought they *ought* to behave."[32] Things eternal and things temporal meshed more easily than they would thirty years later.

For example, economics and religion shared a common formula for success. In each, life was a struggle, a test of character. In 1915, the *Bee* reprinted an article from *Leslie's Magazine* entitled "The Young Man's Capital." What a young man needs to rise in the world is health, character, intelligence, industry, and politeness, the article stated. These are far better than inherited wealth. "The most successful captains of industry in the country came into the world as poor as you are, but they had plenty of capital of the best kind."[33]

The same formula applied to morality. Developing character was a test of will power. More than anything else, the foundation of the old moral code was a firm faith in the virtue of self-control. Do not spend your resources on immediate pleasure; invest them to bring greater satisfactions in the future. Work hard. Use your time and money wisely. Goodness and frugality are eventually rewarded; evil and sloth will be punished. At the turn of the century, according to Joseph Gusfield, "self-control, impulse renunciation, discipline, and sobriety (were) hallowed virtues."[34]

Even sexuality was understood in a capitalist vocabulary. By the turn of the century most marriage manuals preached that sex was a debilitating activity, particularly for the male. Overindulgence drained the body of energy necessary to ward off disease and to achieve one's full mental potential. It is no coincidence that a nineteenth century term for the sex act described the male as "spending" himself. Since women were assumed to have a subdued sex drive, it became their responsibility to restrict sexual activity (for the males' good as well as their own), and marriage to a good woman was one of the best things that could happen to a man—in the long run. The disciplined man was the one who could face the world with all his resources at his command.

Just as saving and investing were not the ultimate goal of the capitalist, however, self-denial was never an end in itself. The payoff came in the future. Self-denial on earth earned rich rewards in eternity. Those who laid up their treasures in heaven by resisting earthly temptations invested their lives wisely. Sinners drank liquor, gambled, succumbed to sexual temptations, or combined a host of petty dissipations to waste their substance in riotous living. The righteous denied themselves these transient pleasures, "keeping oil in their lamps for the bridegroom's coming." The reward of self-denial was future happiness in terms of financial success, community respect, and ultimately heaven itself. America was indeed a land of opportunity for those who could marshall their physical, economic, and moral resources wisely. Those who could not had themselves to blame. In the old formula the personal qualities that propelled you to success in your professional and personal affairs also looked good on your Judgment Day resumé. That comfortable resonance between present and future, between here and eternity, once sustained the confidence of small town Protestants in themselves and the social order they had created.

By the twenties, however, that bond was less solid. The churches still had a monopoly on the vocabulary and affairs of eternal life, but fewer people seemed to be investing quite so heavily in the futures market. Other activities offered greater immediate dividends, and the appeal of the immediate grew at the expense of the future. Activities whose only merit was personal amusement became more popular and acceptable.

In fact, a curious accommodation developed. By the twenties the propriety of certain activities depended on where they occurred. There was a "church morality," which continued to forbid Sunday recreation, card playing, and dancing. Church morality applied when the activity was under the auspices of the church, the school, and organized youth activities. There was also, however, a "community morality," which permitted such activities. The community morality for the most part applied to anything not covered by the former. Local Protestants may have continued to choose not to participate in certain activities on moral grounds, but they were less inclined to take offense when they

HIGH SCHOOL STUDY HALL. The elegance of the filigree work on the desks and the statues were a natural complement to a curriculum which stressed literature, history, and classical languages. *Courtesy of Greene County Historical Society*

SCHOOLTEACHERS IN PHOTO COLLECTION. This collection of Jefferson schoolteachers in the 1890s includes Mrs. E. B. (Minnie) Wilson in the upper righthand corner. Over the next three decades, Mrs. Wilson became a frequent speaker on educational methods, was elected county superintendent of schools, worked in her husband's law firm, and chaired a county committee for local improvements. In *Iowa Illustrated*

CHAUTAUQUA. Chautauqua was a family affair, a week of cultural entertainment, "the most American of institutions," according to President
Theodore Roosevelt. Chautauqua campers made good use of the shade
trees during the hot August afternoons. *Courtesy of Greene County Historical Society*

SODA FOUNTAIN. O. L. Dick's soda fountain was a popular stop for
shoppers at the turn of the century. Already, Coca Cola had found a
following among thirsty local residents. Shortly before WW I, the sale
of ice cream on Sunday became a topic of concern. In *Iowa Illustrated*

UNDERTAKER'S CARRIAGE. Early furniture stores often sold coffins and made funeral arrangements. The Wright Furniture Store offered embalming services and ran a livery stable which had a hearse to rent on occasion. *Courtesy of Greene County Historical Society*

MCCULLY BROS. Grocery staples, like flour, sugar, spices, and canned goods, were available from a wide variety of merchants. The McCully Brothers operated for years on the southeast corner of the square.
OPPENHEIMER'S. Two generations of Oppenheimers operated a respected men's clothing store on the north side of the square. Of German Jewish ancestry, the family was well regarded in the community.

occurred and certainly less inclined to make a public protest. It was not that local residents subscribed to one code or the other, that they were divided into two camps on the issue. Rather, many were comfortable with both sets of rules, even though the two seemed contradictory. "Consistency is the jewel of small minds," Gene Melson chuckled as he recalled the situation.

Did this create a tension in the community? Did residents feel guilty? By and large, they did not. As Melson put it, "My family didn't feel any tension playing cribbage, pitch, and all the rest of it. . . . That's what you did [at the country club]—play cards, dance, and so forth. People were going. There wasn't any feeling of tension. . . . The church didn't take a violent stand about going out there and having fun although the minister, of course, didn't belong and was never taken. . . . He was never invited to go as a guest or anything else. It just wasn't done. It was assumed that he would be offended."[35]

The presence of the minister at a country club event would have violated the terms of the treaty. It was assumed the minister would be offended at the goings-on at the country club, though the members saw nothing really wrong with the activities. What had occurred since the turn of the century was that the affairs of life over which the church had jurisdiction had been restricted. This, of course, had serious implications for the role of the churches in the community and in the lives of their members. It was a serious blow to the authority of the Protestant churches in particular as they had been the foremost exponents of the traditional perspective.

In hindsight, it is easier to identify the postwar decade as an era of rapid and significant changes in community standards than to isolate the causes of the changes. The easy answer is to lay the blame on the wartime experience. Because the Great War immediately preceded the Roaring Twenties, that decade of the raucously new, some have concluded that the war was the cause and the new activity the exaggerated reaction. Returning soldiers brought back with them exposure to less puritanical regions of the nation and Europe. Local citizens supposedly exhausted from the patriotic fervor of the war turned from crusading to the pursuit of personal pleasure.

Frederick Lewis Allen's popular histories of the era are excellent examples of this perspective. He claims that the crusading spirit that sustained the war effort, extended the vote to women, and enacted national Prohibition "was like a bank whose funds were being overdrawn." It held out through January 1920, Allen recounts: "But then, abruptly, the impulse to make over the nation and the world was discovered to have faded away. A people who had had enough of high causes and noble sacrifice to hold them for a long time decided to take things easy, to enjoy themselves; and although there remained many American idealists who would not abandon their quest, they found that they, too, were tired as well as outnumbered. The revolt of the American Conscience was over."[36]

The record in Jefferson, however, is just not that simple. It was not the twenty months of active wartime involvement that produced this reorientation. The war may have hastened its coming, but the buttresses of the old order were showing signs of strain several years before most Jefferson residents even contemplated a serious grievance against the German Empire.[37]

While the war did come at the beginning of the period of the most rapid change, that does not necessarily mean that the war caused what followed. Certainly the war exposed soldiers to new experiences, drew the attention of Jefferson residents to world events, and left the community weary of the demands made on their youth, economic resources, and moral energy. Nevertheless, the nature of the changes in the moral code that were occurring point to the work of more long-term, fundamental influences.

Without question, one such factor was the rapidly changing technology that tremendously increased the contacts of Jefferson residents with the outside world. The virtue of self-denial was under attack from the temptations made possible by automobiles or suggested by the movies and the radio. Images of city life and city definitions of sophistication penetrated into community life on a daily basis. While other factors played a role, the revolution in transportation and communication that brought local residents into contact with the city where traditional Protestant values were less strong was crucial. In their classic study of *Middletown,* Robert and Helen Lynd comment on the broadening effect of technology. "Indeed, at no point is one brought up more sharply against the impossibility of studying Middletown as a self-contained, self-starting community than when one watches these space-binding, leisure-time inventions imported from without—automobile, motion picture, and radio—reshaping the city."[38]

The automobile was one of the most significant factors hastening the change in community values. In 1915 the Presbyterian minister delivered a sermon on the evils of the automobile. The Reverend Caldwell deplored the growing tendency of community residents to seek transient pleasures on wheels at the expense of more lasting spiritual benefits. The sermon was reprinted on the front page of the *Bee* under the headline "Taming the Monster. A Sermon by Rev. Caldwell. Deals with the Automobile and its relationship to Church and Religious Work." The automobile was a monster that was making slaves of local citizens, Caldwell warned.[39]

If it was slavery, it was a servitude that Jefferson took on voluntarily and eagerly. Wilma Downes recalled Sunday night songfests around the pump organ in her family's farm home when boys from around the neighborhood came over. The sessions were gradually discontinued as the boys began to get access to the family car and to drive into town. Nothing prevented the boys from continuing their singing. No one forced them to drive into town. But town was more fun, and the music sessions occurred less and less frequently.[40]

Cars were not only a means of getting somewhere; they were fun in themselves. In the early 1900s the McCullys took a drive nearly every night after supper in their big red Sterling just because it was fun to be going someplace.[41] Forty years later families were still making a tradition of the after-supper drive, now down to the depot to "watch the trains come in." And every generation of small-town teenagers for the last half-century has understood the lure of that simple invitation "to drive around" for awhile. Driving around does not build character. Driving around does nothing to advance one's future interests for time or eternity, but driving around can be fun.

Nor was the contribution of the automobile always good clean fun. Cars liberated townsfolk from the watchful eyes of neighbors or parents. One woman added to an interview (after the tape recorder had been packed up) that her first encounter with alcohol was in an automobile. Her date stopped the car on the way home, reached over to the glove compartment, and pulled out a bootleg flask. What happened then will be lost in history forever because that is where she deliberately ended the narrative. An even more blunt statement came from another Jefferson woman who also went through high school in the mid-1920s. "Young man, we did the same thing in cars then that kids do today."[42]

The influence of the automobile was everywhere. Even at Simpson College in Indianola, a stronghold of the Methodist church that once successfully prohibited trains from running through town on Sunday, officials had to compromise. The college began permitting dances on campus, one Scranton woman remembered, because they felt this was a lesser evil than having their students drive into Des Moines to patronize the big city dance halls.[43]

Grace Wadsworth's insight about rural demands for better schools is relevant here, too. She recalled that farmers realized that the "world was larger" than it had been and that, to deal with it, one needed a better education. The world in which Jefferson existed now increasingly included the cities, either through direct contact or through the images that other new forms of technology were importing to the small towns.

Moving pictures also played a role in changing the moral tone of the community. Movie ads in the *Bee* often stressed the sensational and shocking. During one week in 1925, for example, the Majestic Theater showed three different pictures. On Monday and Tuesday Gloria Swanson starred in "The Wages of Virtue," the ad picturing Swanson in the arms of a handsome sheik. Wednesday and Thursday's attraction was "Gerald Cranston's Lady, the Story of a Purchased Woman." On Friday and Saturday the Majestic showed a special movie, "Broken Laws," which had won the endorsement of the National Women's Christian Temperance Union, the National Federation of Women's Clubs, and "other altruistic organizations." Local ministers, a delegation from the Women's Club, and WCTU members attended a special showing on Friday afternoon. The purpose of the film was to preach "the need for parental discipline and the dangers of the adolescent age." The *Bee* reported: "While the picture showed petting parties and autos parked by the roadside in the early morning hours, the great truths and lessons which it taught counter-balanced any questionable features. . . . Every parent should see the picture, which it is hoped will open their eyes to the danger, and at the same time disgust right thinking young people with many customs now prevalent among those of student age."[44]

The ad promoting "Broken Laws" was eager to inform the public just how awful its characters were.

A pampered son roaring down the Primrose Path! An adoring mother—yielding—catering to his every callow whim! Money—motors—girls—parties doused with gin—irresponsibility—reckless driving—tragedy—arrest—prison—the shadow of the scaffold—and then. . . . Never before have the scarlet curtains that hid the fast life where youthful souls are lost been ripped aside with such terrific force! Never before has jazz-mad/hell-bent civilization seen pictures with such telling vividness![45]

"Broken Laws" was but one example of the films that brought to Jefferson a cinematic presentation of "this jazz-mad, hell-bent civilization" so at odds with the ethic of self-restraint. Using sex to sell a movie was standard practice during the twenties. The movie fare also offered comedies and westerns, and even an occasional biblical or literary presentation, but a surprising number relied on sex as their major attraction. Although censorship sharply curtailed what was actually depicted on the screen, the ad copy was full of descriptions like "lurid," "passionate," or "shocking."

A strong protest from national church organizations led the movie industry to establish an internal code of censorship. The postmaster general, Will H. Hays, headed a review process. It was Hays who piously intoned: "This industry must have toward that sacred thing, the mind of a child, toward that clean virgin thing, that unmarked slate the same responsibility, the same care about the impressions made upon it, that the best clergyman or the most inspired teacher of youth would have."[46] In practice that meant that the moral of the story had to condemn illicit sex and all its practitioners. Seducers and evil women came to unhappy ends and virtue triumphed in the closing reels. Before that, however, audiences ogled at tantalizing flesh, passionate clenches, and steamy kisses.

Movie stars were clearly becoming role models for Jefferson adolescents. One Jefferson woman recalled that local clothing and hairstyles followed Hollywood leads, even to the point where girls yearned for very slinky gowns that hugged the body. She stated: "You didn't wear panties under them because the movie stars didn't wear panties. Didn't wear anything. Everybody was trying to look like Carole Lombard." Regardless of how many followed the lead of Carole Lombard in the underwear division, she was unquestionably a role model for Jefferson youth. It was not simply a case of panties vs. Protestantism, but the movies definitely introduced new standards of behavior that glamorized life-styles based on new foundations (or lack thereof).

The message went deeper than fashion, however. One national study revealed that many young moviegoers were watching the romantic scenes as visual "how-to" instruction. Movies brought a new definition of sophistication. In many cases the message was blatant. Movies glorified the moderns and snickered at those who still clung to Victorian codes. In 1920 Cecil B. DeMille produced "Why Change Your Wife," starring Gloria Swanson as a Victorian wife who temporarily lost her husband to a fashionable flapper. At the beginning of the film Swanson is reading books on "How to Improve Your Mind" and listening to classical music. When her husband is lured away by a short skirt, Swanson decides to devote the rest of her life to charity and good deeds. However, when she overhears a conversation attributing the loss of her husband to her refusal to make herself more attractive, she decides to win her husband back by fighting the other woman on her own turf. She orders a "sleeveless, backless, transparent, indecent" wardrobe and sets about to place herself in the forefront of the fashionable. She succeeds, of course, and she spends her second honeymoon dancing the fox-trot with an adoring spouse. According to historian Mary Ryan, this theme was replayed over and over in the early twenties. Men prefer the modern; Victorian styles are dull and unappealing.[47]

Nor did the plot or characters have to challenge the old code directly to have an impact. In fact, some of the more subtle aspects probably made a more lasting impression. The settings were generally urban locations and presented the cities as exciting, certainly in contrast to the everyday experiences of Jefferson viewers. Little in the movies glamorized church attendance, hard work, thrift, self-restraint, or other hallmarks of the traditional code. It would have been hard to imagine Rudolph Valentino or Theda Bara singing in the choir of a Jefferson church. Both on and off the screen, they represented radically different life-styles, ones the small town found hard to accommodate to the old formula.

Motion pictures also had a hand in bringing about the demise of a hallmark of the old order, that combination of tent meeting, family vacation, and cultural uplift known as chautauqua. In 1874 a huge assembly of Protestant Sunday school teachers met in a campground on the shore of Lake Chautauqua in New York for a week of lectures, sermons, and quality entertainment. So popular was the program that it became an annual event. Soon, traveling chautauqua companies were bringing the show to the small towns, and the Midwest proved most receptive.

The first chautauqua in Jefferson occurred in 1905.[48] Merchants and town professionals pledged up to ten dollars each to cover costs and pay performers if ticket sales did not raise the necessary revenues. A tent went up west of town on Grimmell Road (now across from the hospital) on an acreage owned by the Jefferson Loan Company. Chautauqua week was scheduled in early August when farmers' work loads were somewhat lighter. Families from both town and farm frequently camped on the grounds for the entire week, gathering socially between performances and in the evening. So popular did chautauqua become that the Jefferson Chautauqua Association organized, purchased a permanent grounds, and installed camping facilities that became known as Chautauqua Park.

The programs were deliberately educational and inspirational. In the early years they included sermons, Bible classes, serious lectures on science and child-rearing, and travelogues. String quartets, small orchestras, and vocal soloists brought an artistic dimension to the small town rarely experienced throughout the rest of the year. Political orators toured the chautauqua circuits. Senator Robert LaFollette of Wisconsin and William Jennings Bryan were no strangers to Jefferson stages. Carrie Nation carried her battle against booze to Greene County. State leaders addressed problems of current issues in an age that placed high value on oratorical prowess. Most chautauqua series included a play on one evening, which was often the highlight of the week. As Atherton put it, chautauqua was "festive and folksy and uplifting and cultured."[49] It was, in a word, cultural evangelism, springing from the same source as religious evangelism and manifesting many of the same characteristics.

The shifting climate of the twenties undercut the appeal of the chautauqua. In a survey of annual chautauqua programs, one Jefferson resident documented a marked shift over its twenty-seven-year history from an emphasis on the serious and uplifting to the purely entertaining. Sermons and lectures accounted for about 40 percent to 60 percent of presentations in the early years but fell to from 25 percent to 40 percent toward the end. Morning Bible lectures were discontinued as early as 1912. Entertainment features accounted for an increasing percentage in the final years. In 1908 there was only one humorous performer. By the 1920s entertainments with no serious content accounted for a substantial portion of the program.[50]

Despite the shift toward lighter acts, the chautauqua format could not compete against movie stars and radio entertainers. To hear outstanding speakers and performers had been a once-a-year treat. With the coming of movies and the radio, big-name stars were available on a daily basis. Although the series survived the hard times of the 1920s, the Great Depression proved to be the final blow, and the last chautauqua season was in 1931. As provided in the chautauqua charter in case the programs should discontinue, the campgrounds were donated to the city for a park. About four thousand dollars left in the treasury was transferred to the county for the purchase of Squirrel Hollow Park.

As primary purveyors of traditional morality, the church held sway for many years. But this period of change saw a development in the community that indirectly undercut the churches' preeminence, though that was far from the intention of those who initiated it. As mentioned in earlier chapters, the number of clubs and service organizations grew rapidly through the first third of the century. These clubs organized for purposes unrelated to church activities. Club memberships crossed denominational lines and grouped residents together in new ways.

Prior to 1900 the churches and lodges had had a virtual monopoly on social organization. Kellogg Thomas recalled that his family rarely participated in any organized activities outside those of the Presbyterian church.[51] Other than special holiday occasions, weekly church activities provided the major social functions of the community. Particularly for housewives, whose lives were much more restricted to their duties in the home, church activities were often their only routine contact with persons outside their families. Lacking the daily business associations of the men, they looked forward to Sunday services, circle meetings, and missionary societies to meet their friends.

Beginning shortly before the century mark, however, new groups began to appear, and women's clubs were among the most significant. While these organizations never saw themselves in any way antagonistic to the churches, their presence diluted the role of the churches in community social life. By the 1920s the churches had lost their position as the only organization in which women gathered together outside the home. Church meetings were among many events that might regularly appear on a woman's calendar.

Other elements of the community were also organizing themselves for a variety of purposes unrelated to church activities. One addition to the social scene was the Jefferson Country Club, which formed in 1910, south of town on land donated by banker Henry Haag. The charter members included many prominent citizens. While the charter included as one of the club's goals "to advance the interests of Jefferson," that lofty motive was clearly subordinate to two others, "to promote sociability and encourage athletics and other forms of pleasurable recreation." Paul Stillman, *Bee* editor and charter vice-president of the club, wrote about the formality of the charter: "As a matter of fact, however, the chief avenue of occupation in which the Club will exercise itself will be having a good time and contributing to the joy of life on the part of its members."[52]

The club charter itself is an interesting commentary on social standards of the time. In donating the land Haag required that the charter forbid the use of liquor anywhere on the premises. It also forbade any games or sports on Sunday. The charter specifically spelled out, however, that "dancing, card-playing, tennis, baseball, and other forms of indoor and outdoor amusement shall be permitted, under the direction of the board of Managers, but that no playing of games for money or for prizes having a money value shall be permitted."[53] Members (and the community) knew what was and what was not permitted at the Jefferson club.

Within two decades a second country club was begun to promote a new form of recreation, golf (or "pasture pool" as it was sometimes called by those less than enthusiastic about the sport).[54] While some defended the sport as good exercise, entertainment by 1929 needed to serve no higher purpose, and the game attracted ardent enthusiasts.

The Jefferson Rotary Club was chartered in 1922 as a community service club. According to charter member S. J. Melson, *Bee* editor Paul Stillman called him down to the newspaper one day, gave him a list of prominent Jefferson businessmen, and asked him to sign them up for Rotary. Melson did. A Lions Club came into being the following year.[55] Boy Scouts and Girl Scouts were organized for the youth. The YMCA lasted until 1917 when contributions could no longer sustain the salary of the county director.[56]

In addition to new organizations a new business appeared that offered a service once handled by the churches or neighbors. Traditionally, funeral rites were performed in the home or church. If the deceased had lived in town the body might have been removed to one of the several funeral parlors for embalming, although for farm families, the process often took place in the home. In either case the public service was held in the home or church. By the war churches had begun charging a fee for the use of their sanctuaries in some cases, particularly if they had to fire up their furnaces in midweek for a nonmember's funeral.[57]

When Clyde Slininger opened his funeral home in 1919, there was an initial reluctance to patronize a commercial establishment for a funeral. To help overcome this hesitation Slininger conducted a dedication service for his chapel. Funerals at Slininger's came under the direction of professionals. The minister still conducted the service, but he was no longer responsible for many of the arrangements. Women's organizations from the family's congregation continued to furnish food and assistance during the bereavement, and the pastor offered consolation, but the funeral home handled the details of embalming, the funeral, and interment. Under the new arrangement another important function of the church had been transferred elsewhere. Families came to rely on the services of a commercial establishment for that which had once been supplied by neighbors or their congregation.

The forces of change the churches encountered were not all external. There were debates on religion among theologians themselves. During the summer of 1925, religion was front-page news as a small Tennessee town became the arena of a theological feud that had been simmering for nearly a century. Tennessee had passed a law prohibiting the public schools from teaching evolution or any theory in conflict with the biblical account of creation. With the promise of legal assistance, John Scopes, a young biology teacher in Dayton, deliberately taught a Darwinian theory of evolution in his high school classroom to test the validity of the statute. Clarence Darrow, a brilliant trial lawyer and avowed agnostic, took up Scopes's defense and squared off against the eloquent William Jennings Bryan, champion of biblical fundamentalists.

The sympathies of the *Des Moines Register* were clearly with Darrow and the "modernist" position. As the trial opened, the *Register* ran several stories by noted religious figures arguing that evolution and Christianity are not mutually exclusive. A front-page story by Prof. William H. Norton of Cornell College explained the principles of evolutionist theory and insisted that they do not conflict with Christian belief. Incidentally, he noted, he had been teaching evolution at Cornell for years with no public outcry. Another article reported how Bryan preached a sermon on Sunday to those who believed in the "old-fashioned God" while another report described how a modernist minister was denied the right to address those who had not yet heard "liberal and Progressive" religious concepts. The real question at issue, according to the *Register's* editorial page, was "whether the state should decide by law what part of current scientific thought shall be permitted to reach the minds of the people."[58]

Jefferson newspapers gave the trial minimal coverage, as they did with most national events. The *Herald* published the news of the death of Bryan who collapsed in Dayton from a heart attack shortly after the trial, but the article did not mention Bryan's recent activities on behalf of fundamentalism.[59] Vic Lovejoy, however, wrote an interesting editorial in the *Bee* on the trial, which distinguished between belief in evolution as a natural process and the "monkey origin" theory. Of course he believed in evolution; its evidences were everywhere. Jefferson "evoluted" from a mudhole, farmers have "bred up" their animals into improved breeds, and education and better nutrition have improved the shape and capacity of the human brain. "If that isn't 'evolution', what in thunder is it?" Lovejoy asked, with his usual journalistic reserve. Yet, he immediately added, "to believe (in evolution) is not to concede the 'monkey' theory at all." Having said this, however, he discounted the significance of the Dayton trial and all the discussion. "As a matter of fact, 99 out of 100 people don't 'give a hang' about it at all. God knew what he was doing," Lovejoy declared, "and the process is not for us to quarrel over or quibble about."

His conclusion provides a remarkable insight into some "evolution" of Protestant doctrine itself. Even if the "monkey theory" were clearly proved, Lovejoy asked:

Would science benefit from such a proof, or would man be better off? Certainly not. It would not add a single thing of value to education or human progress, nor would it increase man's respect either for himself or his fellow man. So, what's the use of it all? The only thing which it might accomplish would be to destroy man's belief in the Book of Books. There are those, like Clarence Darrow, who would like to see this happen, but suppose it did? Does any fool think the world would be better off, or humanity happier, if we sweep away entirely man's faith in a hereafter as it has grown up after the centuries of Biblical teaching? As a matter of real fact, opposition to the Bible is from those who want to destroy the Ten Commandments, and with them the great authority for all disciplinary statutes now in use by civilized countries. Any man who seeks to destroy faith in the Bible is either wittingly or unwittingly contributing his efforts to wipe away all law, and leave humanity again in the darkness of remote ages when might was right, and when the only known law was that of brute force.[60]

Reconciling faith with modern science was not a priority of Lovejoy's nor was it with most of the Protestant churches. Faith based on biblical teaching was "useful" to the individual and society, and if science challenged that utility, Christians should ignore it, at least in matters of faith.

During the first decades of the twentieth century, some of America's foremost theologians and Protestant churchmen in urban congregations were preaching what became known as the Social Gospel. They were demanding the active involvement of their churches in programs to establish social justice; the kingdom of God on earth was their goal. In Jefferson with its Protestant faithful divided into four major congregations, however, those who wanted to promote the welfare of the community often found it easier to work through organizations like service clubs and women's clubs rather than the churches. While the individual's motivation to participate may have been rooted firmly in doctrines of Christian responsibility, the avenues through which that service was carried out more and more were organizations other than the churches themselves.

The churches were not becoming irrelevant. They still had a corner on the eternal dimensions of things, and in fact, were becoming increasingly free to devote themselves to otherworldly matters. More of the immediate concerns of Jefferson residents, however, were directed by the other organizations to which they belonged. While no one was openly challenging the traditional moral codes that the churches continued to preach, Jefferson residents were spending more and more of their time in groups and activities not connected with their church.

Moral standards underwent a substantial revision through the early twentieth century. In large part, the historical significance of these changes stems from their relationship to the official stance of the four major churches. What had changed was community behavior, not the Protestant code. Through this period, there seems to be little evidence of any official modification, or even discussion, of the position of the churches on these activities. The changes occurred *in spite of* the official church position. Nor was the condemnation always tacit. According to one of his parishioners, the Reverend Robert Swick, Methodist pastor from 1928 to 1933, rarely delivered a sermon without at least one jab at "bridge-playing ladies," several of whom were loyal members of his congregation.[61]

A similar situation existed in other churches. Conservative Protestants found it more comfortable to ignore changes and to take refuge in familiar formulas than to undertake the painful struggle of reinterpreting the central message of their faith to a rapidly changing world. Modernist Protestants for their part found it easier to pay lip service to the old standards, as long as that was all that was necessary, than to undertake the reformation that would have kept the code a relevant standard for everyday conduct. No one raised the possibility that the traditional norms were peripheral to the essence of the gospel or that the causes that had once given rise to legitimate concerns about activities like dancing or card playing no longer existed in the same form. The Protestant churches continued to preach the same list of "Thou-Shalt-Nots," and the congregation, for the most part, continued to nod its head in assent—at least in church. But the crusading fervor to usher in a reign of righteousness was gone. Service projects continued through outside organizations. The Yankees called a time-out.

CHAPTER 6

World War I
The Noise of War

There is a noise of war in the camp.
— EXODUS 32:17

ON 28 JUNE 1914 A SERBIAN FANATIC ASSASSINATED Archduke Francis Ferdinand, heir to the Austrian throne. Today we look back on that act as the first step in a series of events that put American men into combat against the mighty German army. By no means, however, was United States involvement inevitable when Gavrilo Princip fired those first shots. Had Austria not made impossible demands on Serbia, had Russia not gone to Serbia's support, had Germany not gone to Austria's support, had Britain and France not gone to Russia's support, had the United States not insisted on the commercial rights of nonbelligerents, had Germany not initiated unrestricted submarine warfare — had any of these things not happened, perhaps Floyd Brown of Jefferson might not have been drafted, shipped to France, and killed on the battlefield the day before the armistice was signed.

The chain of events leading to U.S. involvement and the deaths of forty-seven Greene County soldiers forms a logical sequence only in hindsight. That a squabble in the Balkans could draw the United States into a European war seemed a preposterous notion to Greene County residents in 1914. That it could involve even the great powers in Europe in actual fighting strained their credulity. Only two weeks before the start of the war, Vic Lovejoy made a passing reference to the role of war in modern society: "This life is one of progress. We used to enjoy a six-mile-an-hour trotter, but now nobody does who can afford a Ford. We do not hang witches in Salem, and civilized nations go not to war except for righteous cause."[1]

The theme of that week's "Seasonable Sermon" was not the European situation. Lovejoy was merely itemizing the discomforts endured by those foolish enough to think that picnics in the great outdoors were worthwhile recreations. Had he the least inkling of the titanic struggle about to begin in Europe, he probably would have chosen some other comparison for his discussion of the merits of picnics, but in the summer of 1914, Jefferson residents found the prospect of war remote.

When the fighting began in August, the newspapers Jefferson residents were reading expressed little sympathy for either the Allies or the Central Powers. In both the *Bee* and the *Des Moines Register* the kaiser's role was the focal point of the debate – was he or was he not responsible? – but the Allies came in for their share of criticism. Lovejoy observed that Japan's declaration of war on Germany, a pretext to absorb German colonies, was an entirely self-serving action, proving again that "there is blame on both sides."² Greed and jealousy over territorial advantage were the causes of the war, Lovejoy asserted.³ The *Des Moines Capital* expressed a similar sentiment: "Europe has prevented an honest settlement of every war in the Balkans, and Europe is reaping as she has sown."⁴ European alliances, including that between England and France, were formed solely on the basis of self-interest. Lovejoy wrote in late summer of 1914: "The compact entered into last week between England, France, and Russia to the effect that none of them would make terms of peace except with the express agreement of all of them, has the most sinister meaning of any event of the war. It is evidence of the deadly hatred existing between the allies and Germany, and particularly between England and Germany."⁵ Later, Germany, and especially the kaiser, would be assigned the primary responsibility for the onset of the war, but early assessments spread the blame among all the leading powers.

Of course, Jefferson residents who had strong personal ties with a particular European power tended to view the conflict in a more partisan light. The local Catholic priest, Father McAuliffe, was Irish and like many of his fellow countrymen resented the long years of British domination of the island. When he returned to Jefferson from a tour of Ireland in September of 1914, he was upset with the pro-British position that some Irish there were taking and expressed the opinion that other countries had not dealt fairly with Germany. On the other side, Florence Louk gave the *Bee* a letter from her cousin serving in the British army who had written about the Belgians suffering from the German invasion.⁶

The Oppenheimer family is an interesting case. Julius Oppenheimer and his family were Jewish, the only Jewish family in Jefferson, and they had close relatives in Germany. Oppenheimer owned a successful clothing store and was well respected in Jefferson social and business circles. On 5 August, with the outbreak of hostilities among the Great Powers, the *Bee* reported that Oppenheimer had three brothers and two nephews in the German army and a third nephew in Boston who was returning to Germany to enlist. Oppenheimer considered the causes of the war "almost without justice to his former countrymen, who are compelled to take their places in front of foreign guns." Because of his family, the article continued, Oppenheimer "had much to worry him," but a concluding editorial comment noted that "in his troubles, friends sympathize with him in a deep and brotherly way."[7]

Jefferson sympathies also extended to the peoples of Europe who were caught up in the tragedy and suffering of the war, particularly to the people of Belgium. The Belgians were caught between the giants. When Belgium refused to permit the Germans to cross her borders on their way to France, an act that would have compromised her neutrality, Germany attacked, crushed Belgian resistance, and occupied the small nation for the duration of the war. What became known as "the rape of Belgium" did much to generate hostility toward the German army. A Belgian relief fund was collected in Jefferson, with one contributor noting, "Belgium is the only (one) over there for whom I have sympathy."[8]

In discussing the war local editorials consistently differentiated between the people of Europe, who were supposedly powerless to influence public policy and were therefore not responsible for the conflict, and their rulers, hereditary monarchs who pursued their own selfish aims. "The predominating feeling here," stated the *Bee* in August 1914, "is one of sincerest pity for the millions of the rank-and-file in Europe who are thrust without volition and without remedy into a frightful and a useless war." In fact, had there been greater democracy in Europe, the war would likely not have happened. "We have no reason to fear the thrifty, industrious and kindly people of Germany if they are in direct control of their foreign affairs," the paper maintained.

From this perspective the war was a tragic confirmation of the superiority of democracy over autocracy. The war was a natural outcome of political processes that left leaders free to pursue their own aims unchecked by the will of the people. The *Bee* declared: "The quicker Europe is 'shed' of its princes, the better it will be for those who now have no voice in their own personal destiny. . . . Again we say it is only a king's war, a war to perpetuate royalty, a war to acquire territory, a war to grab world wide trade."[9]

This perception strengthened a commitment to U.S. neutrality. America was fundamentally different from European nations. The United States was a democracy whose people would never tolerate participation in a war solely for selfish reasons. For America to have taken sides when neither the Allies nor the Central Powers were fighting for a righteous cause would have been a violation of America's special role in world affairs. On 12 August the *Bee* reprinted an editorial from the *Chicago Herald* that once again drew on the metaphor of America as a "city upon a hill," this time phrasing it as "an image lifted up in a wilderness of war on which the frenzied nations can look and live, if they but follow its example." The *Herald* also applauded President Woodrow Wilson's determination to keep the United States in a position where it can "at the proper moment . . . proffer its good offices to restore peace."[10]

The difficulty the United States faced in the early months of the war was in defining and defending its neutrality. Great Britain controlled the surface of the Atlantic with its powerful navy. In November 1914 Britain declared that the North Sea was a war zone and mined it so extensively with explosives that neutral vessels needed instructions in order to navigate it safely. This, of course, was an open violation of international law, which protected the rights of neutrals.

Germany responded to British naval superiority with the manufacture of "untersee" boats, submarines that could sneak up on larger surface vessels and fire torpedoes at close range. Traditional rules of naval warfare required an attacking vessel to provide safety to the attacked crew and passengers, but this the submarine could not do. The U-boat was a frail craft easily sunk when it surfaced.

On 4 February 1915 the German government announced that the seas around the British Isles were patrolled by U-boats and warned neutrals to cease shipments to the Allies. Germany warned Americans not to sail on Allied vessels. William Jennings Bryan, Wilson's secretary of state, urged the president to forbid such passage to Americans, but the president insisted that American travelers had a right to sail if they wished. Bryan resigned in protest.

As the war dragged into 1915, debate concerned the risks involved in trading with European belligerents. In March the *Register* denounced the British blockade of German ports but urged the United States to remain calm and neutral. The *Bee* argued that the British restrictions represented her fears of the growing commercial might of the United States. "They know that, with a continuation of the war, it will not be long until America outstrips them in commerce. Great Britain will prevent this if possible. . . . It is a matter of life and death to them, and knowing this, can we expect anything but trouble, at some stage of the game?"[11]

On 3 May 1915 a German submarine sank the British liner *Lusita-*

nia, killing 128 American passengers. The *Register* urged the United States to remain calm. Germany had warned Americans of the dangers; the victims knew the risks. Germany was in a deadly struggle for its survival and needed to take desperate action.[12] The *Bee* likewise urged calm and attacked those who thought the *Lusitania* incident justified war against Germany. Nothing would be gained by such action, an editorial maintained. Both papers stressed that *both* Britain and Germany were violating international rules of war. The *Register* even argued that if the United States entered the fight, it must battle both Germany and the Allies because both were violating our rights as a neutral.[13] The *Des Moines Tribune* likewise called for restraint. The honor of the United States, the editorial insisted, had not been attacked "by any agency that a duelist would recognize as composed in mind. To those who cry for war, the country should answer with an unequivocal no. Let those who feel affronted go and enlist in the French army."[14]

When the *Des Moines Capital* argued that the United States needed to preserve humanity's rights, the *Bee* responded hotly that those concerned for such rights should enlist with the warring countries but not to draw the United States into the conflict. Most Americans were not interested in going to war just to protect some theoretical shipping rights. "Rights," the *Bee* declared, was being used as a code word for trade, and trade was not worth the cost of war. The United States should not sacrifice its sons on the altar of greed.[15]

Late in 1915, following several unsuccessful attempts to negotiate a peace settlement and fearing that the United States would inevitably be drawn into the war, President Wilson proposed a policy of "preparedness," enlarging the army, navy, and merchant marine and making plans for industrial mobilization in the event of an American declaration of war. Fearing that preparations would increase the chance of American military involvement, both the *Register* and the *Bee* denounced Wilson's proposals for an increase in military spending. It was unnecessary, they maintained, since the United States was in no danger of being attacked and had no interest in the European conflict that would justify our intervention. Spending for strictly defensive measures had merit in a world at war, the *Bee* admitted, but Wilson's plans were grandiose. The money could be better spent on building roads, a project that was dear to the hearts of many at the time. "Why does he advocate spending $500,000,000 on the navy and $250,000,000 on a 'citizen army'? Why all this chorus, why all this trembling and shaking? We need good roads."[16]

An editorial on 19 April 1916 summarized the *Bee*'s perspective to date:

The Bee is of the opinion that President Wilson is playing a dangerous part in the present German crisis. We hope that we are not lacking in patriotism, but we cannot feel that we have just cause for war with Germany. In looking over the record, it appears that not only the German but all the other powers have done a great many things which have annoyed and embarrassed the United States, but these things have all been done through what they deem the necessities of their life-and-death struggle with one another. We have discovered no instance in which the real motive of any of them was to injure us. When we have gotten hurt, it is because we have been far from home, in the war zone, and have come between the belligerents. It may be that our National honor forces us to stick out for technical observances of the old rules and customs of international usage, to the extent of going to war for them, but we doubt it. When we consider the lives of young Americans which must be sacrificed, and the terrible uncertainties of a struggle which has already well-nigh bankrupted the leading powers of the world, we think America should be very sure she has ample and just cause before becoming embroiled. If any nation with deliberate intent affronts or injures us, we are willing to go to the limit in bringing her to account. But up to this date, no such intentional affront or injustice to the U.S. has been offered by any of the powers.[17]

The nation was far from united, however. In the 1916 election the Republicans nominated the chief justice of the Supreme Court, Charles Evans Hughes, to challenge Wilson. Eastern Republicans like Theodore Roosevelt and Sen. Henry Cabot Lodge of Massachusetts attacked Wilson for cowardice in not declaring war on Germany and demanded substantial increases in military spending. Wilson's supporters campaigned on the slogan, "He Kept Us Out of War," and discovered surprising strengths in midwestern and western states. The *Bee* predictably supported the Republican ticket and forecast a resounding victory for the GOP. However, the *Bee* devoted more column inches to local issues than to either the presidential contest or the European situation. Hughes was praised for his decisiveness and Wilson chided as weak, but the *Bee* denounced those Republicans, particularly Roosevelt, who were urging U.S. entry into the war. More disturbing to Stillman and Lovejoy were the "wet" leanings of Republican gubernatorial candidate William Harding of Sioux City and his refusal to support increased state funding for highways.

As usual, Greene County voted Republican on election day, 2,345 for Hughes to 1,455 for Wilson, but the GOP margin was lower than usual. Dawson and Franklin, with some small German concentrations, supported Wilson for president but returned to the Republican fold for state and local offices. Hughes carried Iowa by a comfortable majority, as Republicans usually did. Nevertheless, the evidence suggests that local sentiment still opposed intervention by the end of 1916.

As 1917 began, prospects for a German victory improved. The Russian army was collapsing in the east, freeing German soldiers for an offensive against the British and French. Allied soldier desertions were rising, and socialist parties in the two nations had begun to call for a truce. The German command calculated that if it could seriously cripple shipping to the Allies, it could mount a successful army offensive to break the stalemate. Even though an unrestricted submarine campaign would almost certainly bring in the United States on the side of the Allies, the German command reasoned that the United States could not mobilize an army in time to counter a massive German offensive. On 31 January 1917 Germany announced that it would henceforth sink all vessels, armed or unarmed, Allied or neutral, in British waters. Unrestricted submarine warfare had begun.

President Wilson immediately broke off diplomatic relations with Germany and urged Congress to authorize him to arm American merchant ships. The *Bee* praised the president for his decisive action. A group of midwestern Republicans, including Senators Robert LaFollette of Wisconsin and Albert Cummins of Iowa, feared that such a measure would almost certainly lead to war and filibustered to prevent Senate action. The *Bee* fumed that if the senators thought they represented Midwest sentiment, they were badly mistaken. It was "standing by the President in a wholehearted way" in the crisis and claimed that the senators in opposition "ought to be kicked out the back door." Permit American vessels to fire on submarines even without a declaration of war, the editors argued. It was one thing for Germany to attack British ships carrying American passengers or goods, but it was quite another to announce that it would sink all American ships in the European war zone.[18]

German-American relations deteriorated rapidly as the submarine took a frightful toll on shipping through February and March. On 4 April the U.S. Senate voted 82–6 for war with Germany. On 6 April the House concurred, 373–50. Republican representative Frank Woods voted against the declaration of war and earned a sharp rebuke from the *Bee*. His vote may have represented the district sentiment in January, but there had been a "radical shift of sentiment here in the Mississippi valley, and a crystallization of the belief that the rights of mankind and the peace and happiness of the world will never be secure until the German military machine has been crushed beyond the possibility of repair."[19] That vote would prove costly to Woods's political future.

Until the early months of 1917, the press had characterized the conflict as a complex, ambiguous, and useless tragedy. While Germany might have played a larger role in bringing on the war, none of the major powers was blameless, none had worthy war aims, and all shared in the dishonor. Wars result when the people are denied a voice in their national affairs, and the United States, the world's leading democracy, must set an example.

When Germany announced plans for unrestricted submarine warfare, the debate in the United States quickly took on a new tone. It is an old saying that truth is the first casualty of any war, and to that, the local experience with World War I sadly bears witness. Several months before any local soldier lost his life in the fighting, community residents began to lose their appreciation for the complexity of the situation. There was a willingness to reduce the affair to an unambiguous struggle between good and evil, in short, to a melodrama. American war aims became the standard by which everything was measured. The original economic, social, and political explanations of the conflict disappeared, replaced as they were by evidences of the fundamental immorality of the enemy. Those trying to defeat the United States lost their human dimensions and became flat personifications of evil. Turning the war into a crusade inspired local residents to sacrifice for the grand cause, but it poorly prepared them to deal with the reality of the postwar world.

What is frightening is how rapidly the reduction occurred. As late as 1916, Stillman and Lovejoy were writing that both the German and Allied restraints on American shipping were occasioned by "their life-and-death struggle with one another" and "in no instance (had) the real motive of any of them been to injure us." With the declaration of war, however, the German military became a monstrous evil, which must be "crushed beyond the possibility of repair." On 4 April 1917, prefacing a reprint of Wilson's address to Congress, the *Bee* insisted that the reason for U.S. entry was not submarine warfare but the German government's "outrages against humanity."[20] The following week, it assured its readers that "future historians will lay the blame of the great war upon the German Imperial Government."[21] The crusade was on.

For men who were concerned about how to demonstrate their masculinity in a socially approved manner, the war offered ample opportunity. Fighting was men's work. Within only a few weeks, a drill corps of Jefferson men organized and reported each Tuesday and Thursday evening at 6:45 at the park. At 7:00 P.M., they began marching drills under the direction of drill veterans. Many of the participants were beyond the age of the draft, but caught up in the initial explosion of patriotism, they paraded around the park and practiced their routines for the coming Memorial Day program. Lovejoy, himself a mem-

ber of the drill corps, let it be known that men in uniform were
engaged in a serious and high-minded work. Young women were especially attracted to soldiers, but "girl life" and "camp life" should be kept
separate. One of his "Seasonable Sermons" intoned: "When a boy joins
the army, it is especially desirable to the service that he cut loose
absolutely from girls, and that girls leave him absolutely alone as long
as he wears the army uniform."[22] Men, and men only, moved into center stage as the primary participants in the glorious cause.

Gone were the ambiguities. By emphasizing the distinction between the German military leadership and the German people, one
could depict the kaiser and his officers as villains without vilifying the
German people, who included many German-Americans. The German
people, the *Bee* declared, were "the most peaceable on earth."[23] There
was no cause for any actions against German-Americans who had left
the fatherland and were now loyal to the United States, a *Council Bluffs
Nonpareil* reprint assured *Bee* readers.[24]

The American public could ascribe to the former all manner of
evils that justified a war. Since 1914, Britain and France had been
manufacturing stories about atrocities committed by the German army,
but Americans had regarded them with a healthy skepticism. The *Register* reminded its readers on several occasions that stories of German
brutalities were coming from Allied sources and warned them of
biased accounts. An American correspondent traveling with the German army reported that there was "no truth" in these stories.[25]
Throughout 1915 and 1916 there was, other than Belgium, only occasional mention of German brutalities.

However, once America entered the war, the stories of German
atrocities multiplied rapidly, and no one challenged their authenticity.
A *Bee* reprint from a London paper reported how the German army
was taking its own dead from the battlefield to render the bodies for
fats and oils and detailed the grisly rendering process.[26] One "Seasonable Sermon" in 1918 was entirely devoted to details of the atrocities
for which Germany "must eventually pay." Lovejoy especially noted
rapes of French and Belgian women and the bayoneting of American
wounded on the battlefields. The Germans had crucified one Canadian
officer on a barn door. "In one butcher shop in Louvain," Lovejoy wrote,
"nine babies were hanged by their little chins upon meat hooks and
allowed to die there. Is that war? Must we allow such crimes to go
unpunished because we have war?"[27]

The kaiser, of course, and the military epitomized German evil
and came in for the most extreme vilification. In a long editorial the
Bee reprinted an interpretation of a sixteenth century prophecy pur-
porting to prove that the kaiser was the long-awaited anti-Christ fore-

told by the Book of Revelation.²⁸ Waxing eloquent in a Fourth of July editorial, the *Bee* reminded its readers that the American colonists had fought for their independence against a German ruler, King George III, whose family had only recently come to England to assume the throne. It was a German King George who was responsible for British acts of cruelty against the colonists. In fact, the editorial stated, England had "a German ruler when America had men like Washington, Jefferson, Franklin, Henry and Hamilton."²⁹ By 1918 Jefferson residents could purchase large books devoted exclusively to pictures and accounts of German atrocities. There was a market among those eager to be horrified.³⁰

To German leaders were ascribed the most hideous traits imaginable, and in the local imagination, that necessarily included unbridled sexuality. An item appeared in the *Bee* reporting how the wife of a famous doctor entered the French city of Noyon shortly after the Germans had abandoned it and found that "every woman between the ages of 14 and 30 had been carried off by the Boches nine days before the retreat began. The young women who were left in Noyon were all about to become mothers by German fathers. . . . Still are there some who wonder why the United States is willing to fight?"³¹ In the summer of 1918 the Jefferson Opera House featured the film, "The Kaiser, the Beast of Berlin." It was advertised as "heretofore unoffered truths of the personal life of the German Demon and the atrocities of his army and navy," which takes the spectator "into the Imperial Palace and the chambers of the Kaiser and unfolds startling, repugnant insights into his private life."³²

While the kaiser and the German officers were the main targets, other German symbols came in for attack. In Franklin Township "Germania" school changed its name to "Liberty," and the *Bee* reported that, as elsewhere in the nation, local residents were calling the German measles the "liberty measles" in keeping with "the ban on all things German."³³

An obvious target of the anti-German campaign was the German language. Coon Rapids, thirty miles southwest of Jefferson, dropped the German language course from its high school in 1917 and substituted a commercial course. The Coon Rapids newspaper called for a ban on all foreign language newspapers because the United States cannot tolerate "hyphenated Americans" during wartime.³⁴ Lovejoy advocated discontinuing the teaching of German in Jefferson schools, and in January the Jefferson School Board voted to discontinue German instruction at the end of the 1918 school year. Lovejoy suggested replacing German with Spanish, which "we need awfully bad to commence the work of Americanizing South America." Or, if there were time for something in addition to Latin, which contains the "essentials of our own language," Lovejoy advocated that the schools ought to emphasize spelling, "in which our students are woefully inadequate."[35]

On 23 May 1918 Gov. William Harding issued an edict prohibiting the use of German in public discourse, including public and private school instruction, public conversation, the telephones, and church services. Those who could not speak English should worship at home, Harding declared. Lovejoy supported the ban on German but objected to its blanket application to all foreign languages. Only German was obnoxious to Americans, Lovejoy argued, but added that Americans did hold a "deep resentment" against Germany at that time.[36]

In some places attacks on German culture carried over to attacks on American citizens of German ancestry. In many areas of the state Germans were victims of patriotic zeal. The *Bee* carried reports of German families from surrounding counties who suffered because of their lack of support for the war effort. Carroll County with its heavy German population reportedly had "problems" with German sympathizers, some of whom were visited by large delegations of patriotic neighbors determined to "give them an opportunity" to buy war bonds or contribute to Red Cross efforts. A Manning resident, John Hell, was arrested and charged with sedition for hosting a party at which Germany was allegedly praised and Wilson and the draft denounced.[37] In Boone, Carl Seiling was "roughed up" for his alleged German sympathies, an incident that drew the following comment from the *Bee*: "Down deep in our heart we have a feeling of sympathy for the former German, who sees his friends and relatives plunged into such a horrible catastrophe, but their condition is a misfortune he cannot help. He certainly cannot be right and have any sympathy for the cause his German friends are fighting for."[38]

Nevertheless, in Greene County, attacks on German-Americans were muted. Unlike surrounding areas, Jefferson had no identifiable German community or German institutions. Greene County Catholics were more likely to be Irish than German, and the small German Lutheran population in the southern part of the county attracted little attention.

Furthermore, the most prominent German family in town had taken timely steps to make its American loyalties well known. As early as 1916, Julius Oppenheimer had displayed an American flag in his clothing store window, the *Bee* reported, "an emblem which Julius says should ornament every business place in the country right at this time." When the United States entered the fighting in 1917, Oppenheimer's store window again displayed the flag, and he ran an ad in the local paper with a tribute to the American flag.[39] During the war, the local food administrator, Charles Cockerill, reportedly asked Oppenheimer why he did not change his name since it was so obviously German. The question drew an angry response from Oppenheimer who retorted that he had no reason to be ashamed of his name. Community sympathies seemed to be with Oppenheimer.[40] German families in Jefferson who were well integrated into the community prior to the hostilities more often received sympathy than censure.

In the Republican primary in the spring of 1918, Congressman Woods was challenged by L. J. Dickinson of Algona for the tenth district nomination to Congress. Dickinson attacked Woods for his votes against an early buildup of the army and navy, an internal espionage act, and, above all, his vote against the war resolution itself. When the ballots were counted, challenger Dickinson had unseated the Republican incumbent by a 12,438–9,958 margin. Greene County gave Dickinson over twice as many votes as Woods, 1,220–561, and was one of the three strongest counties in the Dickinson camp. Dickinson went on to defeat his Democratic opponent soundly in the November election.[41]

The war strengthened Jefferson's sense of community by uniting residents in a common purpose and encouraging sacrifice for the general welfare.[42] The war brought the town together as never before. However, patriotism was not the only force strengthening community ties. The pressure to conform included penalties for those who violated group norms and expectations. "Yellow paint" on doors, barns, or gateposts designated suspected German sympathizers or slackers in the war effort. While the victims of the vigilante brushes suffered no physical harm (and in fact, research can document few actual cases of "yellow painting" at all), the fear of being singled out for the disgrace was enough to motivate residents to support local efforts. Lovejoy condoned the practice when the victims "deserved" it.[43]

A more subtle form of coercion that probably had a greater impact was the practice of publicizing the names of contributors. For example, the *Bee* routinely published the list of those who contributed to the Red Cross *and* how much they gave. In a small town, listing those who contributed also revealed those who did not. By listing how much each donated, the records permitted local residents to evaluate the appropriateness of the contribution. Many local campaigns may have been voluntary, but there were penalties for not participating. The stronger the sense of community grew, the more serious an individual's refusal to support the efforts became.

One of the first demands the war made on Jefferson was for manpower. Because of the intense opposition through 1916 to the "preparedness" campaign, the United States found itself far from ready to enter combat when Congress voted a declaration of war in April 1917. The German military command had estimated that it could mount a successful offensive on the western front before America could mobilize. Considering the time it took the United States to put an army together, one must grant that German estimates were reasonable. The War Department made plans to raise four regular armies of five hundred thousand men each, but it took ten months to get the last local men of the First Army even to basic training camp. Not until the summer of 1918 would these men take their places in the trenches alongside the Allies.

At the beginning of the war there was some minor "action" close to home. On 11 April the *Bee* carried a story of the arrest of a couple in Omaha who had been on a cross-country walk with their baby. They were accused of being German spies when beneath a false bottom in the baby carriage was discovered an elaborate set of drawings of railroad bridges on major lines. A contingent of the state militia was immediately assigned to patrol the railroad bridge over the Raccoon River west of Jefferson to protect it from sabotage by German sympathizers. On 25 April the *Bee* reported that mysterious prowlers and patrol guards had exchanged shots in the night on two occasions. However, in early May the report of the arrest of the couple was announced to have been a false rumor. The couple had not been arrested, and there was no reason to think they were spies. The German high command mounted no subsequent assault on Greene County railroad bridges.

Some were eager to enlist. An officer from Boone appeared at a rally on the courthouse square to sign up recruits for the Boone Military Company. Within two weeks of the declaration of war the *Bee* estimated that fifty men from Jefferson had enlisted in some branch of the service.[44] But volunteer numbers came nowhere near to supplying the total combat forces needed. Within a week after declaring war on Germany Congress passed a law establishing local draft boards and requiring all American men between the ages of twenty-one and thirty-one to register. In Greene County the local draft board was composed of two *ex officio* members, County Auditor B. S. McCully and Sheriff Thomas Caulfield. A third member, Dr. B. C. Hamilton, supervised the physical exams of each registrant. The mechanics of setting up the necessary boards and establishing uniform procedures postponed registration day until 5 June, when 1,546 men in the county registered for the draft. Each man was given a khaki arm band to wear for ten days as "a badge of honor." War fever was running high.[45]

States each accepted a draft quota and divided it among counties proportional to the number of local resident males. Greene County's quota for the First Army was 176 men. To determine the order in which the 1,546 men were called up for service, local draft boards alphabetized their lists by township and then assigned a number to each name on the list. Thus, in Greene County, men in Bristol Township were alphabetized and given numbers from 1 to 73, Cedar Township got numbers 74 through 142, and so on through Willow's 1,477 to 1,546. Meanwhile, the national draft headquarters drew at random 10,000 numbers from a barrel and recorded the order in which they were selected. This list provided the order in which the men were to be called up for classification and the draft. The first number drawn was 258. In Greene County that was Elry Hiram Tam of Franklin Township. The second number was 458, Anton Beschorner of Highland Township. In this manner the entire list of 1,546 names was placed in the order in which they were to be called.[46]

The board received its quota, 176 men. Greene County was given credit for 60 volunteers who had already enlisted, leaving 116 slots to be filled by the draft. To meet that call, the board notified twice that number, the first 232 men on the list, beginning with Elry Tam, to report in late July for examination and classification.

It was also the responsibility of the local board to classify all registrants into one of three groups. Those in good physical condition with no dependents were to be drafted first. For the purposes of classification only those men married before 17 May 1917 could claim their wives as dependents, a policy to discourage hastily arranged weddings for the purpose of remaining civilian. Group two included the physically fit with dependents. The third group was those with physical disabilities.[47] These were the only classifications the local board could make. District boards could grant an occupational deferment, changing a man's status from group one to group two if the man's job were crucial to the war effort.

In Iowa a young man whose labor was necessary for a farm's production might be granted an occupational deferment, but decisions were made case by case. A few men who had been clerking in stores or holding other jobs in town returned to the farms to help out their parents, but their numbers were not great. Some who did found themselves labeled "slackers" or "dodgers." However, the return to the farm was sometimes in response to the very real difficulties of securing hired help, the supply of which had been sharply reduced by the draft. With harvesttime approaching in 1917 the Greene County Farm Improvement Association petitioned Governor Harding to grant farmers

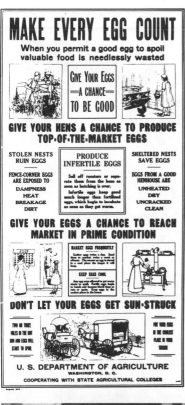

EGG CONSERVATION POSTER. Government posters like this one on egg production probably did not tell Iowa farm families anything they did not already know, but they reinforced farmers' awareness of their critical role in the war effort. *Courtesy of Iowa State Historical Society*

YMCA. The YMCA raised money to provide wholesome entertainment for soldier boys who were far away from home and exposed to temptations of camp life. A song leader at Camp Dodge led some of the troops in an evening session, accompanied by a small brass ensemble. *Courtesy of Greene County Historical Society*

GERMAN WAR CLUB AD. Stories of German barbarism became popular as the war progressed. The government encouraged the belief in ads like this for war bonds. *Jefferson Bee*

THIRD LIBERTY LOAN DRIVE POSTERS. Emotional appeals spurred Liberty Loan sales. *Courtesy of Iowa State Historical Society*

MERLE HAY. Merle Hay, a Glidden youth, was one of the first three Americans killed in World War I. His death brought national attention to his hometown twenty-five miles west of Jefferson, and it also brought the reality of the war home to local residents. *Courtesy of Greene County Historical Society*

DES MOINES SCHOOL/HOSPITAL. During the 1918 flu epidemic, some Greene County mothers traveled to Camp Dodge to care for their sick sons in camp. Des Moines hospitals became so crowded that some Des Moines schools were temporarily converted to care for victims of the killer disease. *Courtesy of Iowa State Historical Society*

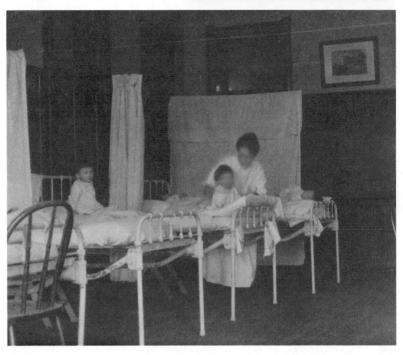

J. K. JOHNSON, OSTEOPATH. According to J. K. Johnson, Jr., who followed his father into a local osteopathy practice, the public had heard about so many bizarre medical practices that a doctor sometimes found it prudent to advertise what he *didn't* do as well as what he did.   JEFFERSON TELEPHONE COMPANY. As early as 1900, Charles G. Cockerill had extended long-distance lines through northwest Iowa as far as Sioux City.

an occupational deferment whenever possible. "We, the Greene County Farm Bureau, earnestly RECOMMEND that the District Exemption Boards especially exempt actual farmers and farm managers whether married or unmarried from military service. We make this request on the broad ground that such men are of more value to the Government in food production in the present war than they could possibly be in the trenches."[48]

Of the first group of 232 called in for classification the board found 122 physically fit with no dependents, giving them the high priority classification. The whole process was public. The *Bee* printed the names of each man examined, his township, and subsequent classification, including the thirty men found to have physical disabilities. Under such public scrutiny and with discretionary judgments severely limited, the local board could hardly have "played favorites" in the selection process even had it wanted to do so.[49]

By modern standards the draft process proceeded at an agonizingly slow pace although contemporary reports praised the careful work of the local board. Not until 21 August, five months after the declaration of war, did the Greene County board certify its first group of registrants eligible for immediate service. Even then, these men had received no orders to report for training. In fact, the construction of the training facilities had not yet begun.[50]

On 5 September the *Bee* reprinted the "Cantonment Notice" from Camp Dodge, the army training facility near Des Moines.

> If you have been called in the first quota of the selective national army and are about ready to depart with the first increment for the camp here, you are probably wondering what to take along.
>
> Don't worry about how you'll get your trunk to the camp. You're not going to be permitted to drag a trunk along. Uncle Sam will have enough material to keep all the idle space in this big cantonment filled. Your trunk will only be in the way, so leave it at home.
>
> A tooth brush, shaving brush, several handkerchiefs, and a change of underwear is about all your Uncle Sam is going to let his thousands of nephews carry to the cantonment sites.
>
> Drafted men will be permitted to take with them only light hand baggage, or better still, bundles containing toilet articles and underclothing. They were cautioned to bring in their orders to report, according to regulations issued today.[51]

The cheerful spirit of the announcement did not seem out of place in central Iowa. Germany and France, by this time, had each lost over one million men in the fighting.

On 12 September the first six draftees of the First Army were ordered to report for induction. These men, representing 5 percent of the county quota, were called up to help build the barracks at Camp Dodge. On 22 September a second call-up sent forty-six men off to Camp Dodge, and several thousand local well-wishers gathered at the Chicago and North Western depot to see them off.[52]

While the draft was in process, the gruesome reality of the war struck home with the news in November that one of the very first American casualties was a soldier from Glidden, twenty-five miles west of Jefferson. Merle Hay, the son of a farm couple, had quit his job as a farm machinery repairman in May to enlist. He was sent first to Ft. Logan, Colorado, and then to Ft. Bliss, Texas, before his company was shipped to France. They were trained through the summer by French veterans and assigned to the line in the fall. The Germans made a surprise attack on 3 November, cutting off Hay's unit and shelling it hard. Five were wounded, twelve reported missing, and three, including Hay, were killed.

His death brought nationwide attention to Glidden. Journalists from all over the nation wanted information on Hay and his family. Since no other American deaths were reported in the next several days, the press had time to concentrate on these first three. The *Glidden Graphic* could not restrain its local pride, even in its expression of sympathy to the family. "It was one chance in a hundred thousand that the first blow of the war should fall upon Glidden. Yet it is a great honor to feel that the first Iowa boy and one of the very first Americans to offer up their lives in France is one of our own. Glidden should take a modest pride in the fact. The bereaved family has a heritage more precious than any that could be bestowed upon them."[53]

Against the somber counterpoint of Hay's death, the draft continued. The Greene County board received word that the final call for the remainder of the quota of the First Army, sixty-four men, was "postponed indefinitely" because the facilities at Camp Dodge were not yet ready. The men selected for the final contin.gent were ordered to be ready within a day's notification, but they spent Christmas and New Year's with their families. On 6 January the waiting men received the news that their call-up could not come before 15 February.

In the meantime, the local board had been continuing to examine and classify the remaining men on the list in the order their numbers had been drawn. By mid-September the board had certified seventy-nine more for service, exempted seventy-nine with dependents, and found sixteen unfit because of physical disabilities. As usual, the name and classification of each man was published in the local paper.[54]

While the last contingent of the First Army was waiting to receive its orders to report for duty, Congress changed the rules. Under new directives, single men with no dependents still remained at the top of the list, but the new orders directed the local board to place all married men, even those who married after 17 May, in a lower-priority classification. Since the new rules went into effect immediately, all husbands awaiting orders to report to Camp Dodge were reclassified. As a result, there had to be a new list. Not until 26 February was that final contingent called, and there was a massive send-off at the C&NW station. War had begun the previous April, but it took ten months to complete the selection and facilities for basic training of the first of four armies the War Department planned.

After a short basic training, the First Army was shipped east, opening Camp Dodge to new recruits. The Second Army assembled much more rapidly, for by then both Camp Dodge and draft procedures were in running order. This time, the county quota demanded 158 men. The first contingent of thirty-four left Jefferson on 30 April, followed by an equal number on 28 May. With these two groups plus ten enlistments at Aero Engineers School in Kansas City, fourteen recruits to Jefferson Barracks in St. Louis, and sixty-six additional enlistments, the county met its Second Army quota.

Through the summer of 1918, the draft continued. On 5 June all new twenty-one-year-olds registered. On 28 June the first twenty-nine men of the Third Army set off for Camp Dodge. In July 119 men headed to Camp Gordon, Georgia, and an additional nineteen for Camp Forest at Lytle, Georgia. Sixteen more reported to Jefferson Barracks in St. Louis. Toward the end of August the board reported that "no more draft calls were in sight," but before the end of the month, the board received new orders for a quota of ninety-six men to leave for Camp Dodge the first week in September.[55]

As the original supply of eligible men evaporated, Congress expanded the draft pool, ordering the registration of all men between the ages of eighteen and forty-six. Local boards were instructed to begin classifying all men between the ages of nineteen and thirty-six. By the end of August the *Bee* reported that 876 men from the county were in uniform, and it ran the entire list.[56]

In the early spring of 1918 Germany launched a strong offensive, its armies bolstered by tough veterans from the eastern front reassigned when the Russian Revolution led to the collapse of the czar's army. By the end of May Germany had pushed within fifty miles of Paris. On 27 May, for the first time, a Greene County family lost a son in actual fighting. Fred Davis, son of the Methodist minister in Churdan, was killed in Picardy. Because Davis had not enlisted from Churdan, his parents having moved there only a few months earlier, he was not officially a county casualty, but the war had struck home. The first

official casualty from Greene County was John McDonald of Jefferson
who died in a hospital at Camp Dodge on 27 October 1917.[57]

The calling up of young men personalized the conflict and stimulated support for the war effort. The United States needed men,
money, and supplies, and Greene County contributed its quotas of all
three. While the draft board continued its work, newspapers reported
a steady chronicle of new taxes, fund drives, and conservation efforts.

Paying for the war was a high-priority concern. In 1913 the Sixteenth Amendment to the Constitution had been ratified, permitting
the federal government to impose a direct tax on individual incomes.
In 1917 Congress authorized a special wartime tax schedule. The rates
grew from 2 percent on incomes over one thousand dollars (two thousand dollars for married couples) to 50 percent on the excess over five
hundred thousand dollars. The following January, an Internal Revenue
Service agent arrived in town to assist any of the five or six hundred
Jefferson residents whom the tax affected. A newspaper article listed
taxable sources of income and eligible deductions and urged those with
questions to see the IRS agent. For the first time local residents encountered the income tax form.[58]

Direct taxes, however, amounted to but a small fraction of the
$33.5 billion the United States spent to pay for its war effort. Over two-
thirds of the cost was paid with borrowed money. Congress authorized
the sale of war bonds and set up national, state, and local committees
to encourage the public to buy them. Five national "liberty loan" drives
took place over a two-year period.

The First Liberty Loan drive began in May 1917. The Greene
County quota was $340,000, based on $20 per person for each of the
17,000 people in the county. County bankers formed a committee to
promote sales of the bonds, even though sales reduced bank deposits
as local residents withdrew savings to buy them. At the time, banks
were paying 4 percent on savings accounts. Local promoters encouraged buyers with the pitch that since the 3.5 percent interest from
the bond was tax deductible, the return on war bonds and on savings
was about the same for those with federally taxable incomes. Patriotism apparently sufficed for those below the tax threshold.[59]

The Second Liberty Loan raised the interest rate to 4 percent.
This time, Greene County's quota was $661,500, calculated on the
basis of $300 per quarter section of land in each school district. Charles
Cockerill chaired the county committee, assisted by S. J. Melson.
Cockerill appointed a local solicitor for each school district to contact

individual homes with pledge cards. The efforts paid off as over half the households in the county purchased bonds in some denomination. Who supported the bond drive (and by inference who had not) became public information as the *Bee* published the list of all Jefferson bond-holders and the amount each had purchased.[60]

The following March, the Third Liberty Loan requested $438,000 from the county. Greene County far exceeded the figure by raising $641,000. These bonds drew 4.25 percent, but the reason for the tremendous success probably lay more with a new twist in the selling. This time the county committee distributed cards to each household that solicited information on the family's financial assets and liabilities. On the basis of this information the family was assessed approximately 2 percent of its net worth. The committee was bound not to make public the information on the cards, and the assessments were only suggestions of what the family's fair share would be. By the end of the campaign, the committee reported, over three-fourths of homes in the county had purchased war bonds, with an average subscription of around $200.[61]

The Fourth Liberty Loan assessed Greene County a staggering $1,187,200, a sum so large that it "took the breath away" from S. J. Melson, the new county bond chairman. The figure represented approximately 2 percent of the county's *total* worth of $60,000,000 listed on the cards from the previous loan drive. Again assigning individual assessments, the committee sold $1,299,300 in bonds, approximately $75 per county resident. Purchase of a bond required a 10 percent payment with the pledge, and the remainder due in installments through 30 January 1919. While the *Bee* no longer printed the names and purchases of bond buyers, the records were no secret in a small town. Lovejoy's "Seasonable Sermons" makes that clear:

The writer has looked over the list of four Liberty Loan issues in the county. The men with the greater values in property are the men who have done the least. This, to us, seems to be a most peculiar thing. . . . As the scale of wealth has increased, the ratio of ownership of bonds has decreased. Men worth from $50,000 on up are the men who have done the "beefing." We do not say that all have, for there are exceptions, as there are to every good rule. But we do say that the chief trouble encountered last Saturday by soliciting boards has been with the men of larger possessions.[62]

A Fifth Liberty Loan drive occurred in the spring of 1919, several months after the armistice. Greene County met its $890,000 quota, but barely, raising $897,900. Most rural districts failed to reach their quotas, but the towns pledged enough to push the county over the top.[63]

In addition to liberty bonds, the federal government borrowed money through the sale of war savings stamps and thrift stamps. In December 1917 the post office offered for sale its first shipment of stamps. A thrift stamp cost $.25 and initially earned 4 percent interest, the going rate at the time for the liberty bonds. With the first purchase of a stamp, the buyer got a thrift card with places for sixteen stamps. When the card had all of its spaces filled, the owner paid an additional $.12, making the completed card worth $4.12, and cashed it in for a $5.00 war savings certificate stamp and a new sheet with places for twenty of these $5.00 stamps. The stamps were in reality small bonds at 4 percent interest, which matured to face value on 1 January 1923. The sheets bearing the $5.00 stamps were registered, could only be cashed by their owner, but could be redeemed at any time with the accrued interest. While liberty bonds came in large denominations, thrift stamps appealed to the small savers.[64] The county was assigned a $326,000 quota of savings stamps, roughly equal to $20 per county resident.

President Wilson declared Sunday, 3 February, as National Thrift Day to promote the sale of stamps. Governor Harding urged Iowans to attend church on that day to provide "spiritual morale" for the drive. The churches willingly participated. The Presbyterian minister preached on the topic "Saving to Serve" while Methodists heard a sermon entitled simply "Thrift."[65] Ladies of the DAR chapter canvassed Jefferson to receive pledges for stamp purchases, and in one week they gathered pledges for $30,000. Schools around the country participated. Jefferson classes alone raised over $1,000, and the *Bee* listed names of student donors.[66]

The interest rate on war savings stamps kept pace with liberty loan bonds. By May new savings stamps were earning 4.25 percent. The Third Liberty Loan campaign based on the family's net worth proved so successful that the concept was applied to savings stamps also. Since May was a busy season for farmers, the county committee mailed out pledge cards and asked residents to commit themselves to purchase war savings stamps equal to 40 percent of their Third Liberty Loan assessment. Again, the commitment was voluntary, but the committee announced that those families who failed to return their pledge cards could expect a call from a committee agent. By June the drive had pledged $225,925. By July the county stood ninth in the state in per capita purchases of stamps.[67]

The total of the five liberty loan assessments and the savings stamps quota came to $3,842,700, or $226 per county resident. War bond and stamp quotas represented 6.4 percent of the county's total worth based on $60 million calculation.

Financial support for the war extended also to semipublic and private charities. The Red Cross held a unique status as the only organization chartered by Congress for military and civilian relief activities. The president of the United States was *ex officio* president of the American Red Cross, and the War Department routinely audited the organization to assure the public of its fiscal integrity. The Red Cross carried on its humanitarian work supported entirely by private contributions, however.

In Greene County Vic Lovejoy chaired the county organization, and the *Bee* spared no effort to make the fund drive a success. A front-page banner headline each week reported how much money had been raised. Red Cross memberships ranged from a one dollar annual membership to patron status for a one hundred dollar contribution. With any membership over two dollars the contributor received a monthly magazine reporting Red Cross activities. Throughout the war the *Bee* ran the names of those who joined or renewed their memberships and the amount of their Red Cross contributions.

The county's first quota was $16,000, but by June, the organization had raised $20,233. Contributions came in part from many small fund-raising events. Jefferson women canvassed the entire town to secure memberships. A Fourth of July picnic that featured games, concessions, and a speech by the head of the Iowa Red Cross, raised $350. A box social in Jackson School District No. 7 added $91.05.[68]

Local Red Cross chapters did more than raise funds, however. The county was asked to make 250 sweaters, mufflers, pairs of wristlets, and pairs of socks for soldiers and needy civilians. Women received yarn and cloth from local Red Cross headquarters and made the articles either there or in their homes. By February the county Red Cross had sent 199 articles.[69] A letter the following summer from an American major in France pleaded for additional assistance to relieve the human suffering caused by the war.

Last winter broke the record for cold, and misery among the people of France was inexpressible. The coming winter is finding us without supplies to meet the situation. . . . [Woolen articles] must come before cold weather and in view of the shortage of fuel and other discomforts they will be of incredible value in both military and civilian work. . . . Get the knitting committees together and have them line up for a rush job.[70]

As a personal touch, many women stuck their names and addresses on a small piece of paper in the toe of a sock or pinned them to a muffler. They sometimes received a thank-you from a soldier who received the item overseas. While the recipients normally expressed gratitude, one strange pair of socks inspired the following from an army buddy of one Jefferson soldier: "The right one's too big/ And the left one don't fit./ Who in hell/ Taught you how to knit?"[71] Most soldiers, however, remembered the Red Cross fondly as the source of tobacco, towels, chocolate, and entertainment as they moved back and forth between the front lines and friendly territory.

In the spring Greene County women supplemented their knitting programs with sewing projects. The local headquarters maintained a bank of sewing machines and kept women busy sewing hospital shirts, pajamas, handkerchiefs, and supplies.[72]

A Junior Red Cross organized in April of 1918 to assist in the effort. School children were taught to knit wash cloths and roll bandages. Local officials praised the program not only for its tangible results but for the opportunity to "teach patriotism" in a practical way.[73]

The humanitarian impulse behind support for the Red Cross was strongly linked to the patriotic fervor generated by the fighting, however, and after the armistice, local officials found it difficult to meet county quotas. The local headquarters closed in December 1918.[74]

Other charities also appealed for funds. The YMCA asked for $8,000 from Greene County toward a $35 million drive "to save the boy who is in the army from the many evils of camp life." Through many private contributions and a fund-raising event at the Methodist Church, the county YMCA raised $14,636. In addition, two Jefferson lawyers, S. J. Sayers and E. B. Wilson, became YMCA volunteers who worked in France for board and lodging only. These "Red Triangle" workers served as counselors to American soldiers overseas. "The work is not exactly religious work," the *Bee* explained, "though only Christian men of high character may go into it." YMCA workers served as surrogate fathers to the soldiers, offering advice, helping to solve problems, and providing wholesome entertainment.[75]

E. B. Wilson wrote from France that his job was to entertain troops in Nice as they awaited shipment back home. In Paris several Jefferson soldiers recalled that the YMCA rented buses for them to tour the city and provided entertainment.[76] Late in 1918 the YMCA joined with Catholic and Jewish charities in a United War Drive campaign to coordinate their activities and raised $61,009 in the county.

In addition to manpower and financial support, Iowans contributed to the war effort by reducing their consumption of resources that the Allies or the army needed, thus permitting more to be shipped overseas. Food was the primary target of conservation efforts. The name of Herbert Hoover, head of the U.S. Food Administration, was converted into a verb as housewives "hooverized" their meals to do with less. A significant factor for his later political career, Hoover established a very positive reputation as an efficient administrator of an essentially voluntary effort rather than as a dictator spying on kitchens or prosecuting housewives. "Hooverizing" was a patriotic gesture, and Hoover emerged from a difficult assignment as a respected national figure.

Four food categories dominated conservation efforts: wheat, meat, sugar, and fats. In August 1917 a committee of Jefferson women canvassed the community with food conservation pledge cards, asking each homemaker to "take the conservation pledge" to cut down on her family's use of these items. Signers promised to serve seven meals a week that used no wheat products at all or fourteen meals with only half a regular portion. By the end of the year stricter guidelines appeared. *All* meals on Tuesday and one meal every day should use no meat, and Saturday was a "porkless" day. There were no legal penalties for violations; the signers were on their honor to meet the guidelines.[77]

Wheat and sugar were the primary concerns of the local food conservation authorities. Charles Cockerill was the county food administrator and relayed messages from Hoover's office to the public. Cockerill appointed a committee of grocers around the county to monitor flour and sugar purchases. While there were no serious shortages locally, Cockerill reported at the beginning of 1918, the committee would try to prevent hoarding and to reduce overall consumption. The rules forbade selling more than one fifty-pound sack of flour and five pounds of sugar to any town customer at one time, unless in exceptional circumstances. Rural customers, who bought less often, could buy twice as much with each purchase. Each grocer made a daily record of flour and sugar sales, which he submitted to Cockerill to spot any buyer trying to circumvent the ruling by making maximum purchases at several stores. "Hoarding" became a federal offense, with a maximum penalty of four years in prison and a fine of ten thousand dollars.[78]

The goal was to reduce per capita flour consumption to six pounds a month and sugar to four ounces a day. At first, the effort was to secure voluntary compliance. Newspapers published recipes for "victory breads" that did not use wheat flour. Royal Baking Powder offered a red-white-and-blue cookbook with war recipes to help the patriotic housewife, and the Jefferson Woman's Club served an "inspirational" lunch at the courthouse, "a practical meal prepared in accordance with U.S. Food Administration ideas." It included "rye bread, corn bread, substitutes for meat, pies unsurpassed, etc." The DAR served hot corn bread, cottage cheese, and coffee as "conservation refreshments" at their meeting in October. A "victory pie" had no upper crust.[79]

As the war progressed, however, stricter measures appeared. In 1918 the government ordered flour mills to include 15 percent bran in their products, stretching a bushel of wheat from forty to forty-five pounds of flour. In February a new rule required a customer to purchase an equivalent weight of a wheat substitute with every purchase of wheat flour. Substitutes included corn flour or meal, barley flour, rolled oats or oatmeal, and buckwheat flour. Four pounds of potatoes and one pound of beans were defined as a flour substitute equivalent to one pound of flour. In March, however, a new regulation removed potatoes from the substitute list. Farmers could bring in their own corn to be ground, but to claim it as a substitute, they had to show a receipt for it to the grocer when they purchased wheat flour.[80]

Sugar conservation followed the same pattern. Grocers reported all purchases of sugar to Cockerill. Town residents were limited to five pounds per purchase and country customers to ten pounds, excepting unusual circumstances when the quotas for both were doubled. Recipes appeared using honey and sorghum as sugar substitutes. There was never a requirement to purchase an equivalent amount of a sugar substitute as there had been with flour, however, since quantities of available substitutes were limited.[81]

To insure that suppliers did not make unreasonable profits on restricted food supplies, the Iowa Food Administration imposed maximum prices on many basic items. County boards made the lists. Profiteering was prohibited on most basic items, including those on the rationing lists.[82]

In the summer of 1918 rumors began to circulate that Cockerill himself was hoarding sugar and flour, storing the excess in his attic for the personal use of his family. On 24 July anonymous "patriots" painted his gateposts yellow during the night. The *Bee,* without identifying Cockerill by name, denounced the action and reported as completely false the rumor that authorities with a search warrant had found fifteen sacks of flour and five hundred pounds of sugar in the attic of "a prominent citizen." There is no record of a search warrant nor any evidence of hoarding, but the tale persisted for years that Charlie Cockerill "got his gateposts painted yellow during the war because he has hoarding flour in his attic." Cockerill was not a popular man with many local residents, and though there was no evidence to support it, it was the kind of rumor that many enjoyed believing.[83]

In addition to conservation, community residents made efforts to grow more of their own food. President Woodrow Wilson urged youth to plant "victory gardens" to demonstrate their support for the soldiers and to increase the food supply on the home front. Arta Brown headed the local War Garden Department and enlisted the aid of several organizations. The Boy Scouts began growing gardens on vacant lots. Many families planted large victory gardens to provide their own vegetables. The *Bee* reported that "one generous citizen locally, who does not wish his name mentioned, has offered to loan any boy the necessary money at six percent to purchase the seed of any of the needed crops."[84]

Conservation and food production were concrete and daily activities through which citizens on the home front could demonstrate their support for the war, and while the efforts substantially relied on voluntary compliance, the record indicates that there was considerable community support.

Patriotism was running high during the summer of 1918. The feature of the chautauqua program was Private Peat, a Canadian soldier who had been injured in front-line action and had been put on the lecture circuit. He described what it was like to be in the trenches. He told of skirmishes in which spunky Canadian troops had routed Germans who outnumbered them 10–1. He told of battles that would have been lost had not God, at the right moment, provided the necessary cloud cover that allowed the Allies to shift around their positions or avoid attack. Private Peat pulled by far the largest audience of the chautauqua week, and receipts from his two performances almost paid for the entire chautauqua expense. Kellogg Thomas, then a high school student, recalled Peat's lectures as his most vivid memory of the entire war experience.[85]

During the fall of 1918 America faced a new enemy, and this time, the battle was fought at home. A vicious epidemic of Spanish influenza spread across the country causing misery and death. In Jefferson so many cases occurred that on 13 October the city council ordered all public assemblies closed, including schools, churches, and movie houses. The council urged parents to keep their children at home to reduce the spread of the disease. Store windows displayed cards instructing customers not to linger after they made their purchases.[86] The measures had little noticeable effect. By November the epidemic was worse. One report estimated the number of cases in the community at four hundred, and flu had caused seven deaths. One of every seven Jefferson residents, according to a newspaper account, had had flu in some form.[87]

On Thanksgiving Day Dr. C. W. Blake was eating dinner with the Winey family on a farm southeast of town. As was his custom, he left word with the local telephone operator where he could be reached. The operator called him in the early evening with a list of fifty-four patients who had come down with the flu that day. Blake asked young Wayne Winey to accompany him on his house calls, and the two spent the entire night visiting the homes of the sick. At one farm north of Jefferson a family of four was too sick even to make themselves the most simple meal. While Blake checked each one, Winey made a soup from ingredients on hand and left it for the family.[88]

There was not much a physician could do except advise patients to stay in bed, keep warm, and wait it out. According to Gladys Finch, Dr. William Young instructed his patients to boil onions and to drink the "tea" as a bacteria killer. She insists that it helped her family ward off the disease.[89] In other homes families kept a solution of water and formaldehyde heating on the stove, the fumes of which permeated the house and supposedly killed flu germs. Sometimes to sanitize a house after flu or some other contagious disease had caused a death, health workers sealed up the doors, windows, and fireplaces and left open all the cupboard and closet doors. They went in and lit formaldehyde candles placed in pails with a little water in the bottom and left the house closed for several days. "It didn't do any good," Winey reflected, "but we didn't know it then."[90]

By December the death toll from the flu had reached thirteen in Jefferson with five additional deaths in the surrounding area. A conservative estimate reported there had been six hundred cases in town. Local officials began placing large warning cards in the homes of the sick but they were not quarantined. Visitors were warned not to enter, but family members were not restricted to the home.

Wilma Winey Slininger was a Jefferson student at Drake University in Des Moines. Classes continued, but students, including soldiers from Camp Dodge, spaced themselves by keeping alternate aisles of desks cleared. The flu was especially vicious in the crowded quarters at Camp Dodge. Slininger recalled seeing long rows of caskets from the camp, four or five deep, lined up at the train depot. Nellie Derry's mother drove to Des Moines to care for her son personally when he came down sick at Camp Dodge.[91]

By New Year's Day the worst had passed. At its first meeting of 1919 the city council lifted the ban on public assemblies. Schools reopened and churches began holding Sunday services again. The Red Cross provided a public nurse at the schools to help identify flu cases. In Scranton a nurse swabbed the throats of teachers as they arrived and gave everyone a daily dose of quinine. Not all country schools had closed because of the flu, but students were not in class during some of the worst of the epidemic because of Christmas vacation. Late in February a new outbreak of the flu occurred in the northern part of the county, but it did not develop into epidemic proportions. By March there were few cases in the area.[92]

The local death toll from the flu far exceeded the number of soldiers killed in combat. While approximately 2,000 Iowans died as war casualties during the entire twenty months of American participation in World War I, state records list 6,543 flu deaths for 1918 alone, and most of these came in the final three months of the year. An additional 1,183 Iowa flu victims died in 1919.[93]

No city council ban on public assemblies, however, could restrict the celebrations that followed the announcement of German surrender. In fact, many Jefferson residents enjoyed the news twice. On Sunday morning, 6 October, a premature report of a surrender brought people into the streets for several hours. The revelries sustained a mortal blow by the news that the peace report was false.[94] On 11 November, however, it was the real thing, and the town has never celebrated anything since with such wild abandon.

The paper reported the exuberant event under the huge headline, "Joy Cometh in the Morning."

The first news of the signing of the armistice arrived at Jefferson by telephone at 3 o'clock Monday morning (November 11). It came from A. D. Howard, who was in Des Moines, who called his brother Ralph Howard, and gave out the good news. However, "hostilities did not commence" in Jefferson until shortly after 5 o'clock, when the big fire whistle cut loose in such glorious notes that everybody knew at once that "it was all over." Crowds commenced to collect upon the public square, other noise making devices joined the glad chorus, and a big bonfire was soon going on the court yard. As the sun arose over this glorious region of America, the demonstration increased, and by nine o'clock, the enthusiasm was at flood tide. The lid was taken off, policemen muzzled and made harmless and there was a hot time in the old town all day. A number of auto trucks were called into use to furnish food for the flames, and when the available supply of kindling and boxes was exhausted, it was no unusual thing to see a truck, piloted by an enthusiastic band of rooters, pulling outdoor toilets, pieces of buildings, and everything inflammable through the streets to the official blaze. A local drayman driving up the street with a load of print paper, had his team unhitched, the horses turned loose, and the paper seized for fuel. However, cooler heads swayed the crowd in time to save the publisher any loss.

Chief among the celebrators were Jefferson's two popular musical organizations, the Jefferson band and the drum corps. The drum corps was on duty all day, dispensing popular airs, its members going home late at night with sore arms and out of breath.

One of the "floats" in the big parade Monday was a rough-box for a casket which was attached to the rear of an automobile and dragged about the streets for several hours during the forenoon. When the demonstration was eased up for dinner, the box, which was labeled Kaiser Bill, was duly dragged to the bonfire and there consigned to the flames. It made a joyous funeral pyre, and its burning was cheered to the echo.

The Kaiser was again the center of attraction in the evening when an improvised gallows was affixed to a light wagon, and his effigy was paraded about the streets for an hour or more. As a climax to this demonstration, the wagon, gallows, Kaiser and all were pulled into the midst of the big bonfire, where the burning was duly and properly performed. The general regret was that the effigy was not the real thing.[95]

Unfortunately, the joyous and enthusiastic celebration did not mean an end to the tragedy. On 4 December Mr. and Mrs. P. O. Brown of Jefferson received a telegram stating that their son Floyd had been killed in a German artillery attack a few hours before the armistice had been signed. A banner headline bordered in black announced the sad news to the community, and the *Bee* printed three letters that the Browns had recently received from their son, the last ending with the cheerful line, "Don't worry about 'Johnny' for he's O.K. and doing nicely." The following week, the paper printed a large picture of Brown in uniform on the front page. On 5 February a letter appeared in the *Bee* that had been written to Brown's parents giving the details of his death. He had been killed instantly by a shell explosion. On 19 February another letter gave the location of his grave twenty miles north of Verdun.[96]

C. Arthur Anderson, a young Paton man, was also killed in the final hours of the war on 10 November. News of his death appeared in the *Bee* on 11 December. On 15 January the deaths of two more soldiers were announced, George Schilling of Franklin Township and Elmer Stockton, a farmhand near Churdan. Both had died of the flu in early October, and for some reason, the telegrams had been delayed for several months. On 30 April 1919 "How James E. Smith Died" told the story of that soldier's death at Chateau-Thierry the previous July. His parents had just received the letter. The 1919 Memorial Day issue listed forty-seven Greene County men who had died in service during the war. Eight had been killed in action, and three had died of wounds received in battle.[97]

Jefferson soldiers did not return home in the same groups in which they had left. They came home a few at a time as they received their discharges. Jake Stevens and his three brothers had enlisted the same day, and their picture had appeared in a Des Moines newspaper. (Stevens recalled, "My brother Fred said that nobody but a bunch of crooks would have their name or picture in the paper.") There was no "welcome committee or anything like that" when they returned, but Jake was not bitter about it. The war was over, and it was time to get things back to normal. Things were a little different than when he left, Stevens recalled. "We went to the Methodist Church, Homer Hensley and I, and nobody knew us. It wasn't too friendly. And it was true that a lot of families that didn't have sons in the war thought we, over in France with the German or French women, were buggers and a lot of them would nearly pull their girls in the house to keep them away from us."[98]

With the armistice came discussion of the peace treaty. When President Wilson proposed a League of Nations to supervise international relations and to prevent future wars, the *Bee* supported him.[99] Some sort of international peacekeeping organization was necessary, and the United States had to continue to be involved in European affairs. Typically, the *Bee* premised its position on moral considerations, arguing that the United States had a responsibility to assume a leading role in world affairs to prevent future carnage.[100] Even when the Senate refused to ratify American entry into the league, the *Bee* continued to urge participation. "The country cannot shake off nor evade the responsibilities we owe to the world's people. We will have it to assume, one way or the other, for the Providence which moves and controls the world will levy upon us our share, the more we kick against doing our part, the greater will be our burden."[101]

By assuming that the spread of American influence brought with it democracy, economic improvement, and moral uplift, Jefferson residents were simply applying to foreign policy the same perspective that guided them in local affairs. The world should be dominated by the enlightened; Christians are responsible for the moral condition of their surroundings. Azor Mills would have been pleased.

During the 1920 presidential campaign, Warren G. Harding issued his call for a return to "normalcy," and Jefferson residents were all for it. And why not? In the world that they knew, it was small towns that had set the norms for the nation. Historian John Garraty interprets the 1920 election as a rejection of Wilson's great causes. "The people, disillusioned by the results of the war, had had their fill of idealism. They wanted, apparently, to end the long period of moral uplift and reform agitation and get back to what Harding called 'normalcy.' "[102]

From another perspective, however, the major battles had been won and it was now time to enjoy the fruits of victory. Germany was defeated, and while there was no permanent peacekeeping force, there was no immediate threat of renewed fighting. At home national Prohibition was finally the law of the land, and American women who now had the ballot were expected to keep it that way. Local residents had enjoyed two decades of rising farm prosperity, substantial technological improvements in transportation, roads, schools, and household comforts. They were not turning their backs on great causes yet to be fought. They had already checked off the major items on their agenda and had not yet drawn up a new list.

Whatever rural Iowa expected normalcy to be, postwar conditions were not what anyone had anticipated. Normalcy was not in the picture. Jake Stevens could not recall much difference in Jefferson between the time he left and when he returned. Things seemed normal. Yes, they had built a new courthouse, and some people now regarded him as a somewhat suspect companion for their daughters, but the town had not changed much from what he could recall.[103]

What had changed, however, was the world in which Jefferson existed. The war had stimulated the growth of new centers of power in American society that did not reflect the small town values of "normal" times. Manufacturing centers in the East and on the West Coast had grown rapidly, attracting European immigrants and rural blacks from the South. Federal regulations had mushroomed, labor unions had grown, the size of business had grown. The entertainment industry had grown. Of more immediate significance, American agriculture had shifted into high gear to provide food and fiber to feed and clothe armies and starving civilian populations. Farmers had invested heavily in more productive machinery, assuming that the prices stimulated by wartime demands would last at least long enough to pay off the debt on the machinery. They were wrong.

CHAPTER 7

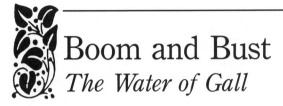

Boom and Bust
The Water of Gall

The Lord our God has put us to silence
and given us water of gall to drink.
— JEREMIAH 8:14

FROM THE TURN OF THE CENTURY through the Great War, Greene County farmers and the small towns dependent on them experienced two decades of economic prosperity that historians now characterize as the "Golden Age of Agriculture."[1] The supply of money was increasing, benefiting farmers by holding down interest rates and making credit easier to obtain. The discovery of gold in Alaska in 1898 put more money in circulation, and the general prosperity of the period reduced the pressures on those like farmers who frequently need credit. The development of an efficient railroad network and the appearance of refrigerated railcars in the latter nineteenth century had opened the East Coast to perishable goods from the Midwest, and the tremendous growth of the eastern cities created a strong domestic demand for farm products.

Furthermore, those city dwellers were turning out manufactured goods in record quantities, which tended to reduce the prices for what the farmers had to buy relative to the prices for which they could sell their products. The value of the ten leading farm crops in the United States rose 72 percent from 1899 to 1919 while a representative list of things farmers had to buy increased only 12 percent.[2] William C. Brown, president of the New York Central Railroad, pointed out in a 1910 speech what these trends meant for the farmer:

I doubt if those who are not like myself, farmers, appreciate just what the past ten years really mean to the farmers of Iowa and the Nation. They are getting sixty-nine per cent more for their wheat, and paying thirty per cent less for binding twine than they did ten years ago.

They are selling their corn for ninety-seven per cent, oats sixty-three per cent and hay for forty per cent more than they received ten years ago, and they

212

are paying twenty-seven and one-half per cent less for barbed wire with which to repair fences and build new.

They are receiving fifty-four and one-half per cent more for butter, milk and cream, and paying forty per cent less for good cream separators than they did ten years ago.

With an average increase of eighty-seven per cent in the price of all kinds of farm produce, they are paying only five per cent more for their binders and mowers, four per cent more for corn binders, three per cent more for hay tedders, and one per cent more for side delivery rakes and loaders.

Sugar costs three per cent and salt four per cent less than it did ten years ago.[3]

As one would expect in such a situation, the value of the fertile farms of central Iowa rose markedly during the period (Fig. 7.1). Trends in Greene County illustrate the pattern. In 1900 the federal census reported the value of farmland in the county at $13,018,450. Ten years later, this figure had climbed 159 percent to $33,634,960. Value for all farm property, including land, buildings, implements, and livestock, rose 130 percent in the same period, from $18,638,884 to $42,782,017. An average acre that sold for $36 in 1900 was worth $94 in 1910.

Across the state, averages reflected the same steady upward

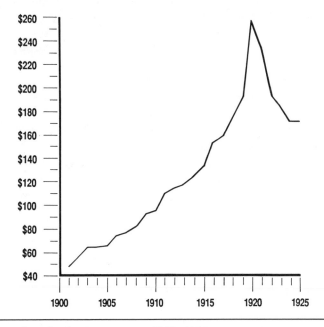

Fig. 7.1. Iowa land prices per acre, 1900–1925

trend. A 160-acre farm purchased for seven thousand dollars in 1900 was worth twenty thousand dollars in 1914. From the turn of the century to the start of European hostilities, the value of an Iowa acre increased an average of almost six dollars every year. Furthermore, farmers were making good money on their crops. A bushel of corn in 1900 brought about thirty cents. In 1914 it was selling for sixty cents.[4]

However, some clouds had begun to appear on the horizon. The technological revolution that had occurred in agriculture had greatly increased the productive capacity of the midwestern farmer, and the economic prosperity of the period put the new inventions within the means of the average farm operation. As a result, the ability to produce food had been increasing at a rate faster than that of the general population growth. Between 1910 and 1914, according to agricultural historians Theodore Saloutos and John D. Hicks, farm prices were leveling off because food production had finally begun to "catch up with the abnormal demands of urbanization." They maintained, therefore, that there "would have been an agricultural recession soon had there been no war."[5]

There was a war, however, and that conflict postponed a decline in farm prices. When the fighting began, the demand for American foodstuffs greatly increased and prices soared. Production in western Europe fell as fields became battlegrounds. Total American exports to Europe rose from $1.5 billion in 1913 to $3.8 billion in 1916, and a large share of the increase represented foodstuffs. American farm income in the same three years rose from $7.8 billion to $9.5 billion.[6] That Iowa farm worth $20,000 in 1914 was selling for $30,000 in the spring of 1919, reflecting an average rise of $12 per acre each year.[7]

When the United States entered the war in 1917, food production became a top priority. In April Gov. William Harding created the Iowa War Emergency Food Committee headed by Raymond Pearson, president of Iowa State College.[8] Under "Iowa's War Plan," the state committee coordinated efforts of farm groups, bankers, local newspapers, service clubs, labor organizations, and merchants to increase resources to agriculture. In August Congress passed the Food Production Act of 1917. It created the U.S. Food Administration, which was headed by Herbert Hoover. The food administration requested a 25 percent increase in Iowa pork production and wheat acreage in the face of a one-third reduction in the farm labor force, which was being diverted into military service.[9]

Greene County farmers responded to the appeal enthusiastically. The "Food Will Win the War" slogan appealed to their patriotism, and guaranteed market prices appealed to their pocketbooks. The food administration was charged with both increasing food production and decreasing domestic consumption. Rationing decreased consumption; price guarantees encouraged production.

One way to boost production was to put more acres under cultivation. Floyd Stevens was a young farmer with a 120-acre farm southwest of Jefferson when the war started. He rented an additional eighty acres and plowed up some of his pasture land to put into corn production. Of his 200 acres he estimated that about half was in crops. With the help of only his brother-in-law, then in his early teens, Stevens worked the additional land in an effort to boost production. It was the farmer's duty in wartime, he recalled. Farmers were told to produce all they could to support the war effort, and Stevens worked hard to do that.[10]

There were other ways to increase acreage. Many fertile acres of Greene County farms were covered with swamps and ponds characteristic of the flat prairies of northern Iowa. Spring rains collected in the ponds, which produced tall, thick grass and several varieties of hearty mosquitoes. A 1908 amendment to the state constitution provided for the creation of drainage districts to facilitate the removal of water to nearby streams and creeks, and with cheap credit and wartime incentives, there were many drainage projects in the county. Crews with special drainage spades dug the lines by hand through the tough sod, carefully maintaining a downward decline toward the outlets. S. J. Melson supervised much of the construction and calculated what share of the cost each of the farms affected should pay. Those fields benefiting most assumed the greatest share of the cost. In many cases farmers were allowed to defer the cost of the installation because of the wartime emergency. According to one account, over half of the state's acres that could have been farmed with adequate drainage were reclaimed and put into cultivation by 1920.[11]

Increasing the available acreage, however, was not the major factor in increasing production, certainly not in Greene County where most of the available acres were already in crops or pasture. Substantial gains had to come from more intensive cultivation of existing fields. Toward this end, the Iowa State Extension Service, the public outreach arm of the land grant college in Ames, played a major role. The extension service greatly expanded its educational efforts to get every possible bushel from Iowa fields. An aggressive campaign to improve seed corn helped boost the 1918 yield for the state by forty-four million bushels above the prewar average, in spite of a hot summer. Agriculture demonstrations spread information about better farming techniques. Extension agents preached more efficient use of corn fodder and encouraged farmers to build silos. Bankers, local merchants, and building suppliers made construction materials available at attractive rates. With the draft shrinking manpower resources, farmers needed an efficient system of securing hired hands. The extension service organized a farm labor bureau in every county to match those wanting work with farmers who needed help.[12]

With labor costly and in short supply midwestern farmers took advantage of high prices to purchase new implements and machinery. Federal census figures report the sharp increase during the first two decades of the century. In 1900 the total of all farm implements and machinery on Greene County farms stood at $584,070. In 1910 it was $1,028,373, but in the next ten years, which included the war, it tripled, climbing to $3,434,629.

Corn yields in 1916 and 1918 were depressed somewhat by dry growing seasons. Nevertheless, with educational assistance, increased technology, and wartime incentives, farmers managed to boost production substantially. An extension department report claimed that Iowa "produced more foodstuffs in 1917 and 1918 than in any other two years previous in her history." Grain production alone, according to extension records, rose 25 percent during the war years.[13]

The intermediate beneficiary of this bounty was the Iowa hog, whose two functions in life—to eat and breed—made for a pleasant though artificially brief existence. During the war years Iowa pork production jumped 25 percent, according to extension figures. Greene County farmers were raising 77,924 hogs in the summer of 1916. In 1919 the number was 83,484. By the summer of 1919 and the peak of market prices, the number of hogs on American farms stood 23 percent above what it had been in 1914.[14]

The real spur to production was, of course, the phenomenal rise in the prices farmers received for each bushel of corn they grew and each hundred pounds of hog they fattened. Greene County pigs may not have appreciated the fact at the time, but the price of meals and snacks was more than twice what it had been in 1914. The food administration never established a guaranteed price for corn, but in November of 1917 it pegged a minimum price for hogs at $15.50 per hundredweight, a figure set to reflect thirteen times the average cost of a bushel of corn.[15] At some midwestern markets hog prices rose to $17.50 in the fall of 1918 and to over $19.00 at their peak the following summer. As the demand for pork increased with the assurance of government price supports, corn and pork prices skyrocketed (Fig. 7.2). For a short period, the price of corn in Greene County hit a record $1.50.[16]

As a result, land prices shot skyward. Beginning in 1919 Greene County, like the rest of Iowa, was swept up in an intense though short-

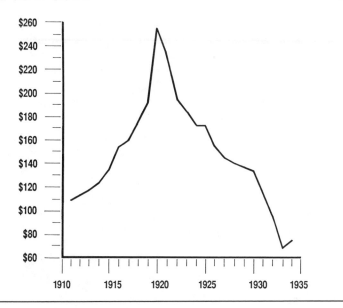

Fig. 7.2.   Iowa land prices per acre, 1910–1935

lived land boom unlike any experienced before or since. While it was triggered by exceptionally high wartime prices, it must be understood in retrospect as a culmination of trends that had been building since 1900. An Iowa State economist, William Murray, claimed that the two decades before the war had "set the stage for this speculative splurge":

Prices of both farm products and of farms had risen so many years without any serious decline that practically everyone believed there was no way for farm values to go but up. And up they went. There was a frenzied effort by farmers, businessmen, doctors, lawyers, bankers, and anyone who could get his hands on enough money to make the down payment on a farm purchase. If you had a farm, you either sold it and bought a larger one, or you mortgaged the farm you had to buy another one. There were some, of course, who did not buy and even some who sold out and bought government bonds but they were few indeed.[17]

Farm economists even figured out a formula that justified the rise in land prices. They identified a relationship between the price of an acre of land and the price of a bushel of corn. In the past land had risen about $2.00 an acre for every cent increase per bushel of corn. In 1890 when corn brought $.20 a bushel, good corn land had sold for $30.00 an acre; in 1912 when corn brought $.55 a bushel, the land that produced it had sold for $100.00 an acre. Therefore, they argued, with corn prices at $1.00 a bushel, the land should bring $190.00 per acre.[18]

Speculators in a land boom anticipate a profit primarily from the resale of the land at higher price, not from the long-term production of the farm. In fact, according to the economist John Kenneth Galbraith, as the land-boom mentality intensifies, "the tendency to look beyond the simple fact of increasing values to the reasons on which it depends greatly diminishes."[19] Such was the case in Greene County. The $94 acre of 1910 became a quaint relic. A study by the Chicago and North Western Railroad based on recorded land sales in Greene County from January 1917 to January 1920 placed the average acre at $194. By 2 May 1920 it had climbed to $233. The federal census conducted in the spring of 1920 reported an acre of Greene County farmland to be worth $271.46. It was hard to pin down the figure precisely because land was changing hands so rapidly. In the first two months of 1919 the county recorder's office received 525 land transactions. In the same period in 1920, at the height of the speculation flurry, the number jumped to 965, an all-time record. This does not mean that 965 different farms changed hands, of course. Sometimes the same farm was bought and resold over and over as speculators capitalized on rising prices to make a quick profit. The *Bee* cautioned its readers not to get caught in any of the phony stock swindles that were making the news. "Loan your surplus money on good first or second mortgages on Greene County land, and you know it is safe."[20]

However, it was not only land and corn prices that had escalated during the war. Prices for nearly everything moved up dramatically. The high cost of living became such a commonplace topic that newspapers abbreviated the subject in headlines, referring simply to the "HCL." Clothing, for example, was especially affected. Some returning soldiers continued to wear their army uniforms, not because they wanted to advertise their military service but because they could not afford to buy replacements. Jake Stevens had mailed his civilian clothes home from Colorado when he was issued his uniform, but the package had been lost in the mail. After the war his uniform was all he had to wear, and clothes were so expensive that he could not afford to buy anything else. During the war he had earned thirty-one dollars a month ("I got thirty-one dollars for being a killer") and upon discharge, a sixty dollar bonus. Jake used his bonus to buy work clothes but needed to get a job to buy "shirts and shoes and stuff so I could go to church." Scranton High School boys banded together to adopt overalls as standard dress because of the high cost of clothing, and the principal gave them his blessing, provided the clothes were neat and clean.[21]

Kellogg Thomas was a victim of the times. When he needed a suit for the junior-senior prom in the spring of 1919, his father told him to go into Oppenheimer's and charge one. He did. After supper, his parents asked him to try it on so they could see how it looked. He recalled: "I tried it on and my father said, 'Well, it looks like a pretty nice suit. How much did it cost?' I said, 'Only ninety dollars.' He said, 'Ninety dollars!!? Well, I'll stop by tomorrow and pay for it, but I think this would be a real good time for you to start buying your own clothes.' " Unfortunately, Kellogg purchased that suit at the peak of the postwar inflation, at a figure much higher than his father was used to spending for a suit of men's clothing.

Everything seemed to cost so much more. Coal prices were high and threatened to go much higher because of striking miners. Salaries for workers were going up, particularly those covered by union contracts. Instead of one dollar a day, section workers on the railroad were reputed to be earning from five to eight dollars a day and wearing silk shirts downtown on Saturday night. Whether or not railroad salaries had increased that much, local residents suspected that they had gone up considerably, and they knew that was in part behind higher ticket prices and freight rates.[22] Teachers demanded more money. The Jefferson school board approved two hikes in teacher salaries to help teachers cope with the "HCL." Rural directors in the summer of 1920 approved a 40 percent pay increase in the paychecks of rural teachers.

Taxes went up right along with everything else, with school taxes leading the way. Pay hikes for teachers were only part of the bill. These were the years of the consolidations of several rural districts to provide high schools. Franklin and Scranton townships each created consolidated districts in 1919, and others followed suit. As predicted, consolidation increased the tax load as districts began work on new buildings. In Franklin, for example, the school tax rate jumped a whopping 364 percent from 1918 to 1920, from 11.18 mills to 51.7 mills for schools alone. In Jefferson, which already had a high school, the levy went up 98 percent. Totals for all school expenditures across the county contrast a 1918 tax bill of $174,878 with a 1920 expenditure of $389,308.

The demand for good roads also resulted in substantial boosts in the annual tax bill while taxes to finance other state and county services also increased. State taxes for Greene County property holders climbed from $59,242 in 1918 to $79,000 in 1920. County taxes jumped from $176,350 to $248,580 in the same period. Various township, city, and town taxes moved from $122,580 to $188,711. These figures, along with the school increases, pushed the total burden of property tax up over 70 percent in only two years, from $532,605 to $905,609. The highest increases came in the rural areas.[23] The state averages for the same period show an only slightly smaller increase. USDA statistics record the average tax on an acre of Iowa farmland in 1919 at $.72 and in 1920 at $1.10, a 53 percent hike.[24]

Furthermore, taxes were but one factor in the farmers' cost of production. Labor, transportation, and machinery also increased. According to a study by *Wallaces' Farmer,* the midwestern farmer invested $19.00 to produce an acre of corn in 1917. In 1918 the cost was $23.00. A progressive farmer might spend as much as $40.00 an acre. The magazine also estimated that a farmer who made a profit of $18.00 per acre on corn in 1917 made no more than $9.00 per acre in 1918 because of rising production costs. The net return per hour of labor in 1917 was $.98 for corn and $1.10 for oats. The next year, comparable figures were $.88 for corn and $.58 for oats.[25] A USDA study later calculated that a farmer's overall production costs doubled during the war.[26]

The phenomenal rise in the prices farmers had been receiving for their crops and livestock since 1914 had been due to the abnormally strong demand for farm products during the war. With the armistice and readjustment, the demand began to return to normal, and farmers were in for a rude surprise. Within two years of the war's ending, midwestern farmers discovered the bitter irony that would dominate the farm scene for several decades: they had become too efficient. Too many farmers farmed too well. They could produce more than the market could absorb at a profitable price to the producer. Even before the war there had been talk of surplus, but in the patriotic fervor and the siren call of $1.50 corn, it had been treason not to bend every effort to seduce just one more bushel from the willing Iowa topsoil.

Like everyone else, farmers rejoiced when the fighting ended, but they did not forget the lessons they had learned from extension demonstrations. Nor did they give up their new, efficient machinery. They did not remove their drainage tile and let the ponds fill up again. Their investments began to pay off in increasing yields, and corn production soared. Greene County farmers harvested a record 43 bushels per acre in 1919 and improved on that in 1920 with 46 bushels. In 1915 county farmers grew 4,500,000 bushels of corn. In 1920 they grew 6,500,000 bushels. What was happening on local farms was occurring all across the state and the Midwest. The supply was rising and the demand falling, producing the inevitable result.

In the spring of 1920 the federal government announced that after 31 May it would no longer support the price of wheat at wartime levels. Other commodity supports followed suit. On 1 July the daily market summary in the *Des Moines Register* listed corn on the Chicago

market at $1.73 a bushel. By 14 July it had fallen to $1.56. The slide
had begun. From then through the rest of the year, it was downhill all
the way in a devastating collapse. On 4 January a bushel of corn sold
for $.69, and it was still going down. For the year 1920, corn averaged
$1.19; in 1921 it fell to $.41 and rose to only $.47 the following year.
For the entire decade of the 1920s, the average was only $.68. Pork
prices followed a similar pattern, and farm income dropped off precipi-
tously (Fig. 7.3).

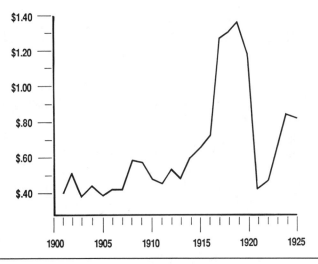

Fig. 7.3.   Iowa corn prices per bushel, 1900–1925

Not all farm products declined at the same rate, but Greene
County farmers were especially hard hit. Dairy farmers witnessed only
a 2 percent dip in the price of butter from 1920 to 1921 while grain
farmers endured a 53 percent decline in income during the same period. Hog farmers' income dipped 39 percent while cattle farmers' returns declined 30 percent. The corn-hog belt of the state, which includes Greene County and north central Iowa, experienced the
sharpest losses.[27]

As crop prices started to slide, runaway land prices came to a
screeching halt. Suddenly, those who had expected to reap a handsome
profit on their land speculations found themselves in real trouble. They
were caught holding title to investments worth much less than the
purchase price, and it was time to pay up. The boom was over; those
still in the game were stuck. In 1915 only 38 percent of Iowa farms

were under a mortgage, but by 1924 over half were under some debt. The debt burden had increased from $54.00 to $100.00 per acre in 1921. At $.41 a bushel, a corn crop could often not even cover the interest on the debt, and farm foreclosures became a sign of the times. One historical analysis illustrates the situation with this example: "Suppose a man had purchased a farm for $20,000 during the last year of the boom, with a mortgage of $10,000 on it. By 1928, his farm would have shrunk in value to about $14,000, while the mortgage would probably have remained the same. Thus the farmer's equity would have declined from $10,000 to $4,000. And how could a $4,000 investment support a $10,000 mortgage?"[28]

Through the remainder of the decade, land prices throughout the state continued to fall as fewer and fewer investors considered land to be a wise choice (Fig. 7.4).

What often happened to those who had spread themselves too thin was that they lost not only their new property but everything else they owned. If the last person to buy a farm could not make the payments, he defaulted, leaving the person from whom he bought it responsible for coming up with his own obligation to his creditors. Furthermore, if a farmer had mortgaged his own farm and then had to sell that to cover his speculations, he put the property on a depressed market and got much less for it.[29]

Fig. 7.4. Iowa corn prices per bushel, 1910–1935

Bankruptcies mushroomed. One Jefferson man had been driving a custom-built car in 1920. Within two years he had scraped enough together to buy a truck to haul coal, and he hauled coal for most of the rest of his life. According to rumor, he had once owned twenty-five farms—at least on paper—but he could neither meet payments nor sell them for enough to pay his creditors. Another man traveled in an expensive Pierce Arrow auto and hired a local pilot to fly him around the country on his many business dealings.[30] By 1922 he had nothing. Paper profits vanished as farm prices plummeted. Throughout the remainder of the decade, prices remained low and failures continued as farm owners found themselves unable to meet interest payments and taxes on their holdings.

In the first wave of the collapse farmers turned to local bankers for credit to tide them over what they hoped was only a temporary slump in prices. In November 1920 a convention of the Iowa Bankers Association and the Iowa Farm Bureau adopted a resolution "that the bankers and farmers in conference assembled pledge to each other their sincere co-operation and help in carrying out their business over this period of ruinously low prices."[31]

Bankers, however, were often in as precarious a financial condition as their customers. Having participated in the boom by loaning money to speculators, local banks watched their assets disappear in the collapse. An epidemic of bank failures swept the state in 1921 and continued through the decade. In 1920 there were suspensions of payment in 167 banks in Iowa. In 1921 the number jumped to 505. It fell to 366 in 1922 but rose and remained over 500 for several years.[32] By mid-decade the state banking convention might have been held in Fort Madison where angry juries had deposited nearly fifty Iowa bankers in the state penitentiary for accepting deposits when they supposedly knew they were insolvent.[33]

Jefferson banks illustrated the state pattern. Every one of the five banks operating in Jefferson in the early 1920s failed, directly or indirectly as a result of wild fluctuations in agricultural markets. Whatever the immediate causes, the underlying difficulty was the same: the collapse of the land boom in the face of a drastic fall in farm prices.

The first to go under was the City Bank on 21 July 1920. It was a private institution, chartered as a bank by neither the state nor federal government. There were no controls on how much it had to retain to cover deposits nor how much it could loan on its capital. Furthermore, in common with most banks of the time, it did not secure financial statements from borrowers. Credit was extended on the basis of reputation, character, and apparent financial security. Because they did not require financial statements, bankers did not know how far some of their customers had spread themselves in the speculation mania.[34] But they soon found out.

A shortage of grain cars in the summer of 1920 made it temporarily difficult for farmers to sell their grain. As a result, many drew on their deposits in local banks to meet their expenses. City Bank was already pressed by the inability of many of its borrowers to make their loan payments, and when the bank tried to borrow money to cover itself, word got out that the bank was in trouble. There was a run as depositors scrambled to retrieve their savings, and the bank had to close. The *Bee* explained the closing this way: "This is the first bank failure in the history of Jefferson, and we think in the history of Greene County. No hint of dishonesty attaches to it. The cause was lack of promptness in making collections, and in letting notes run too long, until in many cases they became worthless, together with doubtful judgment in the extending of credit."[35]

Not everyone in town was as charitable toward bank president M. G. McDuffie, however. Many who lost money were angry, and some wanted blood. Under a state law that prohibits a bank from accepting deposits when it knows itself to be insolvent, McDuffie stood trial the following year. The first vote of the jury was seven to five in McDuffie's favor, but only after five hours of debate did they reach a decision for acquittal. The popular judgment was that McDuffie's fault was lack of judgment rather than criminal intent. When McDuffie was charged with criminal violation, several local lawyers offered their services free for his defense.[36]

McDuffie took a job on a road crew cutting weeds, and he and his wife took in boarders. One resident summarized McDuffie's plight this way: "I think people felt sorry for him because he honest-to-God went broke. And he worked as a common laborer. You admired the guy. He was a proud man, a man of great influence. He took such a financial blow but stayed right in the community, and . . . suffered it out with everybody else."[37] Eventually, City Bank was able to liquidate its assets to repay depositors about seventy-five cents on the dollar, the combined loss standing at approximately $150,000.[38]

The next to go was the Farmers and Merchants Bank. It collapsed on 7 June 1922. Depositors lost about $5,000 when all assets were liquidated and distributed. Although F & M was a national bank regulated by federal banking rules, the underlying causes of its failure were the same as with City Bank: falling crop prices, overdue loans, declining deposits.

The Head family banks, which included both a federal and a state bank, held out until 1925, but on Wednesday morning, 9 December, the First National Bank and its auxiliary savings department closed up and went into receivership. This time there was no run; a few heavy with-drawals on top of a long period of declining assets forced the close. The *Bee* reported that deposits had fallen by $300,000 in the past year, to around $470,000, which was less than half of what they had been in 1918. The *Bee* added: "There are assets of much greater face value, but bank closings give excuse for many not to liquidate their indebtedness, who might otherwise pay a live and working concern."[39] The failure carried down two other banks in the county which the Heads owned, the Farmers and Merchants of Churdan and the Bank of Cooper.

According to the *Bee,* the two brothers running the bank, Mahlon and Roscoe Head, had "striven hard" to sell their land for the past two years, "even below a fair calculation but could not find parties with money to buy land." They tried to salvage some of their holdings by secretly transferring deeds after the failure to another brother, Albert. When this maneuver was uncovered later in the year, it increased the resentment toward the brothers, and the transferred property was ordered to be returned to the receiver.[40]

A particular source of difficulty for the Heads was a $315,000 mortgage on their property held by the Des Moines Savings Bank and Trust Company. Rather than taking out separate mortgages on individual properties, they had lumped their holdings under one blanket mortgage to the Des Moines firm. They could not sell off part to save the remainder, and they could not meet the total obligation. Consequently, they lost everything. In February 1927 the community witnessed a sheriff's sale of the bank fixtures and several personal family items, including the law library of the men's father, Capt. Albert Head. Potential buyers were refused the right to peruse the books prior to the sale on the chance that there might be some money stored in some of the volumes. Also for sale was the family Bible and photograph album, chairs, and railings from the bank. A fifteen hundred dollar burglar alarm system that had never been used sold for eight dollars.[41]

Unlike McDuffie, who stayed in town and worked as a laborer, the Heads moved away shortly after their financial collapse. Many sympathized with McDuffie, but "you didn't feel sorry for the Heads. They brought it on themselves."[42]

The Heads' business failure put a scare into the depositors of the one remaining bank, the Jefferson Savings Bank. From 16 September 1925 to its closing the following January, deposits shrank by more than fifty thousand dollars as skittish depositors pulled out their money. Within a month of the collapse of the First National, with rumors flying about the safety of money in *any* bank, a line started queuing up outside Jefferson Savings as depositors panicked. Ralph Maloney, a young teller just beginning a banking career in Jefferson that would span four decades, had the singularly unpleasant task of facing hostile depositors and counting out a dwindling supply of cash. The bank officers knew what was coming, but there was nothing they could do. Maloney's memory of the event remained vivid:

We ordered $100,000 in cash from some Des Moines bank. We had to put up collateral for it, mortgages and notes, and they shipped up $100,000 and put it in the vault. We hired a couple of guards with shotguns that sat there during the night. Then the next day, it didn't take long to clean that out. I went home that noon. I couldn't eat any dinner. The people were lined up in front wanting their money. And I remember (that) Charlie White went in the bank vault and got little cloth sacks that had gold coins in them. We didn't keep many gold coins around because there weren't too many in circulation but there were probably $200 or $300. I can hear those gold coins when they dumped them on the counter and paid them out to the last depositors. I know the state authorities were there, and they turned the key in the door.

We thought we could make it. If people would have had confidence, which had been badly shaken by the (other closings), our bank could have made it because we paid out 75% under pressure. People got scared. We were a victim of the other banks' closing and all the banks around the county were closing all over, so we couldn't make it.[43]

An interesting footnote is that the bank was not without friends in its hour of need. James Hilton, a future president of Iowa State University, was then serving as extension agent for Greene County. According to his own account, Hilton saw the line stretching down the block and knew what was going on. In his pocket was a small check of Farm Bureau expense money, he recalled, perhaps twenty-five or thirty dollars. "I walked in and here was all this line of people lined up withdrawing their money." Hilton went to the cashier's window and said he wished to make a deposit. "I said it just as loud as I could just so it would have some effect."[44] It did not, and the future president of Iowa State University became the last depositor in the Jefferson Savings Bank.

With the closing of the last bank in the community, Jefferson merchants found themselves hard pressed to pay wholesalers. To keep money in circulation the Milligan grain elevator announced that it would pay cash or acceptable exchange for all corn or other grains delivered to it. Milligan's began to be a clearinghouse for checks while the town was without regular banks.[45] Still, neither merchants nor their customers could get the necessary cash to carry on business as usual. On 28 January, in a united promotion, merchants began a giant sale to attract shoppers who would pay in cash. A special edition of the newspaper, detailing the bank failures and the reasons for the lack of

SILO POSTER. Posters encouraging farmer investment in silos and machinery contributed to the rapid expansion of agricultural production and the resulting postwar surplus. *Courtesy of Iowa State Historical Society*

BANK INTERIOR. The Jefferson Savings Bank was incorporated in 1894 with $25,000 of capital stock issued in shares of $100 each. The cashier's window in this 1896 photo with its fancy but imposing grillwork and marble countertop was typical of the era. In *Iowa Illustrated*

CITY BANK EXTERIOR. The City Bank building with its ornate window treatments and brick was originally constructed with a raised first story. In the late 1920s, the entire building was lowered to ground level. Engineers inserted a system of crossbeams on jacks every two feet. Periodically, each jack was lowered a quarter turn until, a month later, the first floor had descended to sidewalk level. In *Iowa Illustrated*

ROAD GRADER. Keeping country roads passable all year was no small assignment. This road grader, pulled by a steam tractor, tried to fill the worst of the holes and to put a small crown in the center of the road to channel water to the ditch. *Courtesy of Greene County Historical Society*

DANA CHEESE FACTORY DELIVERY CAR. The town of Dana northeast of Jefferson boasted a prosperous cheese factory at the turn of the century. A fire destroyed the building in 1904, but it was back in operation in about six weeks. In 1906, because of some form of "prevailing sickness," the board of health ordered $745 worth of cheese destroyed and closed the factory for six weeks. In 1908, it was reported to have an annual output of over $30,000. Deliveries and milk pickups were made by automobile. *Courtesy of Greene County Historical Society*

THORNTON HARNESS. Fortunately for Thorton, his business was judged by the quality of his harnesses, not the poetry in this 1900 ad. The Spanish American War may have reduced his local competitors for the time being, but within the next two decades, the automobile was going to prove a rival too formidable for most harness and buggy companies.

cash in circulation, was distributed to every household within a thirty-mile radius of the town. Now was not the time to try to hide dirty laundry. Now was the time to encourage shoppers to come to the community that would offer bargains for cash.[46]

The bank closings left a lasting impression on those who saw hard-earned savings vanish. Bess Osgood claimed that she and her husband Paul had the dubious distinction of losing money in every bank that closed in Jefferson. In one instance they barely managed to get their money in before the closing. She recalled: "My step-grandmother had passed away, and she left my brother and me each $500. Paul and I didn't have a car at that time. . . . You could buy a Ford car for $500 or $600. We debated whether to put another $100 with it or put it in the bank. And being thrifty like we were, we decided to put it in the bank. And then the bank went busted and we lost the $500."[47]

Within two months of the collapse of the Jefferson Savings, two new banks opened. The Jefferson State Bank reorganized the assets of the old Jefferson Savings under the direction of the Brenton banks, a prominent financial organization that had originated in Dallas Center. The Iowa State Bank took over the assets of the First National Bank, with Simon Cassady of Des Moines as chairman of the board. The *Bee* waxed eloquent in praise of the new arrangement:

At last, at last! Jefferson is not only to have one bank, but two banks. Jefferson could not ask for any stronger backing for two banks in this city. The financial interests back of these institutions make either one of them much stronger than any bank heretofore in Jefferson. This fact alone should, and will, restore confidence with the people of this locality, who feel that they have had some rough experiences in the past. On the list of owners of both new banks will be found the names of men who are many times millionaires, and well able to give safe and adequate relief to the Greene County financial situation. There is plenty of room in Jefferson for two banks – but two is enough, at least for some years to come.[48]

Gone were the days of securing loans without written financial statements. Tighter controls were placed on the amounts and types of loans that banks could make.

A few weeks after the collapse of the Jefferson Savings, the *Bee* printed a history of banking in the county, with special emphasis on the conditions that led to the recent string of failures. "With lots of money in wartime, we arose to a higher plane, more expensive modes of living, and too exalted ideas in all sorts of valuations," wrote Lovejoy. He refused to single out bankers for "blame" because "if there is sincere heart-searching, there are mighty few who can lay claim to complete exemption from the term. . . . Practically everybody made mistakes of some kind."[49]

Nevertheless, analyzing the reasons for distress did not make it less painful. In 1923 *Jefferson Herald* editors Jon and Ben Frazier claimed that the collapse of the land boom had hurt speculators but not "the farmer who held his land and did the real farming."[50] However, the "real farmers" suffered acutely from the prime factor that brought about the collapse of the land boom—the rapid decline in farm prices. When prices plummeted, farmers found themselves in a squeeze, for while incomes dropped, expenses did not. President Warren Harding's secretary of agriculture, Henry C. Wallace of Iowa, tried unsuccessfully to rally administration support for the farmer by drawing attention to economic realities. Wallace maintained: "In the Corn Belt, the value of an acre of corn in 1921 was 20% under the pre-war value, whereas monthly wages of farm labor were 34% higher, land values 117% higher, implements from 66% to 92% higher, and freight rates about 60% higher."[51] For the most part, the prices farmers had to pay for the goods they bought did not suffer the same rapid deflation.

Furthermore, rural residents could not dismantle their high schools or remove the gravel from their roads and recover the costs of improvements. Nevertheless, it became imperative to cut costs wherever possible, and local taxes were a prime target. Concern for rising tax bills was sufficient to upset two Republicans on the board of supervisors in the 1920 election and to replace them with Democrats promising to keep expenses down.[52] When Democrats won Greene County elections, everyone knew things had reached a crisis.

While salaries in the private sector were rising to try to keep pace with the cost of living, teacher salaries were cut. Twenty-three Jefferson teachers chose to resign their positions at the end of the 1920 school year rather than accept a ten dollar per month cut for 1921. Directors of rural districts lowered minimum rates for beginning teachers from ninety-one dollars a month in 1920 to seventy-eight in 1921. The public demand for an absolutely bare bones budget asserted itself when the supervisors in 1921 voted a pay increase from eighteen hundred to three thousand dollars for the county superintendent of schools. Over one thousand persons signed a petition protesting the increase. The supervisors backed down and returned her salary to eighteen hundred dollars.[53]

Of course, even the most radical cuts in taxes could not have provided all the relief that farmers felt they needed. As prices continued to fall with no promise of improvement, farmers began to look to the federal government for some sort of direct assistance. The system was out of balance. Manufacturing and labor prospered while agriculture suffered. Some called for direct government support of farm prices. Others thought cooperative marketing programs were the best solution while still others trusted the free market system and objected to "socialist" scheming.

In Iowa two major farm organizations, often hostile to each other, dominated the scene in the 1920s. The Farm Bureau and the Farmers Union each had units in Greene County.

The Farm Bureau originated during the war to assist the extension program. The county agent, appointed by Iowa State College, worked with a county committee composed of one director from each township. The bureau helped to disseminate information from the extension program and encouraged local farmers to attend agriculture demonstrations and exhibits. In December 1918 county organizations met in Marshalltown to form the Iowa Farm Bureau, and later the state organization joined in the creation of the American Farm Bureau.

The Farm Bureau essentially took the position that the farmer's best hope for survival was to improve his management. Science and technology had revolutionized factory production, and agriculture needed to adopt the same methods. The Farm Bureau advocated support for agriculture research at land grant schools like Iowa State and dissemination of research findings through county extension agents. Bureau programs emphasized greater production at reduced cost and encouraged members to consider expanding their operations. Inevitably, expansion must mean fewer farms—and fewer farm families—but that was the cost of bringing agriculture into the modern world, according to the Farm Bureau.

Originally, the purpose of the bureau had been educational, but as it grew to represent a sizable proportion of Iowa farmers, it naturally became a mouthpiece for farm interests. As the state and national organizations began to take on more active political roles, the position of the county agent came under increasing scrutiny. Should a government employee be recruiting members into a group actively seeking to influence farm legislation? What was the relationship between the county agent and those farmers who favored solutions different than what the Farm Bureau advocated?

That latter question was frequently raised by the second major farm organization, the Farmers Union. Formed a decade before the war, the Farmers Union attempted to accomplish in agriculture what the trade union movement had done for labor. The Farmers Union wanted all farmers to join together to refuse to sell their product at any price below what would insure them their cost of production and a reasonable profit. Labor unions could strike if their wage demands were not met; a farmers' union could withhold crops from market until its price demands were met. The individual farmer, argued the Farmers Union, was as powerless as the individual worker. Only through collective action could agriculture achieve parity with the concentrated power of business and labor. It was not greater efficiency the farmer needed, especially if that meant squeezing out some farm families who wanted to stay on the farm. The Farmers Union was hostile to the direction of Iowa State research. Teaching the farmer how to produce more during a decade of surplus only aggravated the problem; it made food cheaper for urban residents but did not raise the farmer's income. Any program that did not have as its goal the raising of prices paid to the farmer was viewed suspiciously by Farmers Union advocates.[54]

In an excellent analysis of the farmer's plight Joseph Wall explains how farmers were an awkward combination of both labor and management. On one hand, they were obviously labor. They worked longer hours than factory workers did. But unlike urban workers, farmers could not strike and refuse to produce because they would be striking against themselves since they were, at the same time, management. Many owned their farms or took as their profit a percentage of the harvest of livestock marketed. But unlike the factory owner, farmers could not lay off workers or close down production. They needed to meet mortgage payments and property tax bills. Besides, in a family farm operation, you have to feed your workers regardless. If prices fell production had to increase for the farm just to stay even. Farmers could successfully adopt the tactics of neither urban labor nor management.[55]

James Hilton remembered the Farmers Union as "rabble rousers" and claimed that "the better thinkers, the most successful people" belonged to the Farm Bureau. The Farm Bureau was better organized, with a director in every township, while union membership tended to concentrate in the northern half of the county. The more prosperous farmers tended toward the Farm Bureau rather than the union, which drew heavily from smaller and sometimes marginal operators.[56] Hilton's memory was no doubt colored by the fact that his position as Greene County extension agent was often the focus of Farmers Union attack. The union claimed that the county agent system represented a government subsidy for a rival farm organization and that in promoting more efficient agricultural techniques, the extension service was keeping the farmer in a subservient position.

By the mid-1920s, the formal association of the Farm Bureau and the tax-supported extension service became untenable, and the county agent was restricted to educational activities. In a joint document, *Memorandum of Understanding,* the American Farm Bureau and the Department of Agriculture defined the new relationship.

The county agents will aid the farming people in a broad way with reference to problems of production, marketing, and formation of farm bureaus and other cooperative organization, but will not themselves organize farm bureaus or similar organizations, conduct membership campaigns, solicit memberships, receive dues, handle farm bureau funds, edit and manage the farm bureau publications, manage the business of the farm bureau, engage in commercial activities, or take part in other farm bureau activities which are outside their duties as extension agents.[57]

With conflicting voices speaking for the farmer and with those less directly affected hostile to direct government intervention in the economy, the politics of the 1920s was complex. Though the majority in Greene County was registered Republican, the party spoke with many voices as strong internal divisions arose over the proper role for government. In general, farmers advocated more direct governmental intervention in their behalf and were willing to support candidates who advocated federal action to aid farmers. That included both raising prices and lowering costs by restraining "unfair practices" by railroads, grain buyers, meat packers, and labor unions. On the other hand, merchants and professionals in the small towns were fearful of what they saw as radical schemes that increased regulation and involved government ownership or permanent control of business enterprises.

While small town merchants were also hurt by the farm recessions, they were not hurt as directly as the farmer. To the merchant the situation was not yet so critical that it justified the radical changes that some farm groups advocated. Small town Republicans found themselves torn between their sympathies for the farmer and their traditional fear of government intervention and bureaucracy. That something needed to be done to increase farm income was accepted, but what a government devoted to free enterprise could legitimately undertake was not so clear.

During the war, railroads had been put under strict government control, an action justified as a temporary necessity. After the armistice, debate began on the future of the roads. Some favored outright public ownership while others wanted to continue substantial government regulation. In the postwar reaction against socialism or radicalism, many feared any proposal that smacked of limitations on free enterprise and private ownership. To complicate the picture, the railroads were beginning to feel the competition from automobiles as revenues from passenger service declined. To compensate for lost revenues, the railroads favored increasing freight rates, which had already jumped 50 percent during the war and were slated for another increase in August 1920.[58] Farmers naturally opposed the rate increases and were wary of giving rail management too much of a free hand.

Sen. Albert Cummins of Iowa, who while governor had established a reputation for strong rail regulation, was chairman of the Senate's Interstate Commerce Committee and thus in a powerful position to shape the future of the roads. What emerged from his committee, however, was not a bill that promised much relief from rising freight rates. The Esch-Cummins Act of 1920 returned the roads to private supervision, denied rail workers the right to strike, and provided management with enough discretion in setting rates that higher charges to midwestern farmers were almost certain to occur.[59]

At a state Farm Bureau meeting, a resolution endorsing the Esch-Cummins Act was defeated. Chief spokesman against the measure was a former aide of Cummins, Smith W. Brookhart, who charged that the Iowa senator had betrayed the farmers' interests. So strong was his opposition that he challenged Cummins in the 1920 Republican primary and launched a strange career as the "wild card" of Iowa politics for the decade.

In the primary Brookhart emerged as the champion of the small farmer and the foe of eastern business interests who he claimed were taking unfair advantage of the rest of the country. He picked up the support of labor unions, the *Iowa Homestead* magazine, and several leaders of the farm community. The Farm Bureau did not endorse Brookhart, but it refused to endorse Cummins. Brookhart lost, 115,758 to 96,565, but even so, he commanded surprising strength against an incumbent two-term senator and popular former governor. What must be remembered also is that the primary was in June—a few weeks before the beginning of the plunge in farm prices. These were good times for the farmer, and still Brookhart picked up 45 percent of the vote. Greene County, with almost no labor vote and a strong party tradition, gave Brookhart less support than did any of the neighboring counties, returning a 60 percent majority for Cummins.[60]

During the next two years congressional Republicans began to part company with each other and the White House. Many midwestern Republicans followed the lead of Iowa's junior senator, William Kenyon, in calling for increased federal intervention on behalf of hard-hit farmers. Congress passed the Packers and Stockyards Act governing rates of packing houses and livestock buyers, the Grain Futures Act regulating the grain exchange markets, and the Capper-Volstead Act encouraging farm cooperatives. While none of those addressed the underlying cause of farmers' woes, low prices, they did recognize the imbalance existing between agriculture and other sectors of the economy. Furthermore, they drew the battle lines between the farm bloc and conservative Republicans, including Cummins, who tended to oppose such direct government intervention in the economy.

In 1922 President Harding appointed Senator Kenyon to a position as a federal judge. Iowa voters needed to select a replacement to fill the remaining two years of Kenyon's term, and Brookhart announced his candidacy. So did five other candidates. Brookhart's opponents hoped that no candidate would secure the 35 percent plurality necessary to win the primary so that the nomination would be settled in a state convention where a coalition could defeat the radical spokesman.

Brookhart's campaign focused on two issues, neither popular with conservative Republicans. One called for direct government ownership of railroads, which drew charges that he was a socialist. The second was an extension of the income tax and a shifting of the tax burden toward the wealthy.[61]

Analysis of the voting in the tables that follow reveals the beginning of a split between Greene County Republicans living in town and those on the farm. To clarify the trend the polling places in the county are divided into three groups: (1) Jefferson; (2) the townships containing small towns (Churdan, Scranton, Rippey, Grand Junction, Paton, and Dana) plus surrounding rural areas; and (3) the entirely rural townships. On the basis of this division the sources of Brookhart's strength and weakness become much clearer.

In the 1922 primary Brookhart led the field in Greene County by a narrow margin over his closest primary rival, Clifford Thorne, 1,171 to 1,084. The remaining four candidates together pulled 763 votes. Brookhart's strength lay in the rural townships. There, he won 55 percent of the vote. In Jefferson, the only precincts that contain no farm vote, Brookhart pulled only 22 percent. In the small town townships, those with mixed farm and town voters, Brookhart won 35 percent (Table 7.1).

Once Brookhart won the Republican nomination, party loyalty as-

TABLE 7.1.   Republican primary election, Greene County, 5 June 1922

| | Brookhart | Thorne | Others | Total | %
Brookhart |
|---|---|---|---|---|---|
| Jefferson | 161 | 293 | 270 | 724 | 22 |
| Small town/farm | 442 | 505 | 315 | 1,262 | 35 |
| Rural | 568 | 286 | 178 | 1,032 | 55 |
| Total | 1,171 | 1,084 | 763 | 3,018 | 39 |

Source: *Iowa Official Register, 1923–24,* Des Moines: State of Iowa, 375–76.

serted itself in November. While conservative Republicans in some parts of the state worked against his election, Brookhart swept Greene County with 75 percent of the vote. A spokesman for the embattled farmer with the Republican party endorsement, Brookhart easily carried the state by a 389,751–227,833 margin against Democrat Clyde Herring.

It was customary at the swearing in ceremony of a new senator for the senior senator of the state to escort him down the aisle. Senator Cummins refused to do the honors for his former aide, and "Cotton Ed" Smith of South Carolina, a Democrat but a leader in the farm bloc, performed the honors.[62]

Brookhart was hardly finished being sworn in before he was being sworn at. In the two years remaining of the term, Brookhart managed to establish a name for himself as a champion of radical farm legislation and as a representative "hick." His clothes were sloppy. He postured himself as a man of the people opposed to the plutocracy of special interests. He aligned himself staunchly with the farm bloc and supported direct federal intervention on behalf of the farmers. Perhaps most exasperating for Iowa conservatives, he carefully nurtured his credentials as a Republican even while he drew the wrath of the Republican administration and state party leaders.

Brookhart entered the Republican primary for a full six-year term in 1924, a year that was particularly trying for Midwest Republicans. Wisconsin Sen. Robert LaFollette announced his candidacy for the presidency on a third-party Progressive ticket, which threatened to split the Republican vote. LaFollette and Brookhart had been close allies in the Senate, and it was clear that Brookhart's sympathies were with the Wisconsin senator and not President Calvin Coolidge. Would Brookhart bolt and support LaFollette?

In the primary, conservative Republicans ran Burton Sweet, hoping to unite all anti-Brookhart voters. But the farmers liked Brookhart and recognized him as the best representative of their interests. In Greene County Brookhart carried 56 percent of the vote, predictably much higher on the farm than in town. Jefferson Republicans gave him only 42 percent of their votes, while rural townships supported Brookhart by a whopping 72 percent (Table 7.2).

TABLE 7.2. Republican Senate primary, Greene County, 2 June 1924

	Brookhart	Sweet	Total	% Brookhart
Jefferson	319	440	759	42
Small town/farm	645	563	1,208	53
Rural	636	248	884	72
Total	1,600	1,251	2,851	56

Source: *Iowa Official Register, 1925–26,* Des Moines: State of Iowa, 403.

In the fall election those elements supporting LaFollette and the Progressives endorsed Brookhart—the *Iowa Homestead,* labor unions, and the Farmers Union. Brookhart refused either to remove himself from the Republican party or to endorse LaFollette. On 3 October, however, Brookhart delivered a speech in Emmetsburg in which he openly repudiated Coolidge and the Republican administration—yet still did not endorse LaFollette. Nevertheless, the state Republican Central Committee declared that Brookhart had indeed "bolted" the party and was therefore not entitled to support by the party organization. Many Republican leaders denounced Brookhart and openly endorsed his Democratic opponent, Daniel Steck of Ottumwa. The committee did not officially endorse Steck, just as Brookhart had not endorsed LaFollette.

Many Republican newspapers came out for Steck and published instructions on how to vote for the Democratic candidate and yet support the remainder of the Republican ticket. For example, two weeks before the election, the *Bee* published a sample ballot. Adjacent to the ballot was an article with instructions on how one could mark a Republican ticket and still vote for a Democrat in selected races. For instance, the article hypothesized, suppose one wanted to vote for all Republican candidates except Brookhart. It then gave the way to do just that.[63]

Greene County Republicans were spared none of the political bloodshed. LaFollette failed to capture their imagination, but the farmers did like Brookhart. Nevertheless, crossing party lines was an action not to be taken lightly. Brookhart was the Republican candidate and that carried weight, regardless of what the state central committee might decree. On election day Coolidge walked away with the presidential contest with 67 percent of the vote. LaFollette picked up 1,497 votes, 22 percent, running well ahead of the Democrats' John Davis, who finished a distant third with 790 votes. Even in the rural townships, however, Coolidge beat LaFollette by almost a three to one showing (Table 7.3).

On the same day they voted overwhelmingly for the Republican president, Greene County voters gave Daniel Steck a majority over Brookhart. Steck carried Greene County, 3,534–2,987. Jefferson's third

TABLE 7.3. Presidential returns, Greene County, 1924

	Coolidge (R)	Davis (D)	LaFollette (P)	% Coolidge
Jefferson	1,111	174	290	71
Small town/farm	2,044	311	656	70
Rural	1,444	305	511	64
Total	4,599	760	1,497	67

Source: *Iowa Official Register, 1925–26,* Des Moines: State of Iowa, 515–16.

ward, normally a Republican bastion, gave the Democratic candidate a resounding 409–95 margin! The other two Jefferson wards likewise voted for Steck, bringing Jefferson totals to 930 for the Democrat and 475 for Brookhart. As usual, the farm townships turned in a Brookhart majority, though this time one considerably smaller than in 1922 (Table 7.4).

TABLE 7.4. Senate election, Greene County, 1924

	Brookhart (R)	Steck (D)	% Brookhart
Jefferson	475	930	34
Small town/farm	1,287	1,622	44
Rural	1,225	982	56
Total	2,987	3,534	46

Source: *Iowa Official Register, 1925–26,* Des Moines: State of Iowa, 516.

The vote statewide between Brookhart and Steck was very close, but Brookhart squeaked by in the first tally, 447,594–446,840. Steck demanded a recount, and the issue was taken up by the U.S. Senate when it convened the following spring. To punish Brookhart for his failure to support the Republican ticket, the Senate delayed issuing any decision on the election until April 1926, a year and half after the election. Finally, voting on anything but evidence, the Senate declared Steck the winner and placed him in the seat formerly held by Brookhart.[64]

Brookhart reacted by announcing for the Senate seat held by the aging Senator Cummins who had defeated him in the 1920 primary. This time, however, Brookhart was no political unknown, and Iowa farmers had endured five years of woefully sagging prices. In the June primary Brookhart soundly defeated Cummins, who died a few months later. In Greene County Brookhart received a plurality among Jefferson voters and a majority elsewhere. The three-term Senator Cummins carried only 15 percent of the rural township vote. Howard Clarke, a third candidate hoping to stake out a moderate ground, ran almost as well in the county as Cummins (Table 7.5).

TABLE 7.5. Republican primary election, Greene County, 7 June 1926

	Brookhart	Clarke	Cummins	Total	% Brookhart
Jefferson	352	202	275	829	42
Small town/farm	768	376	391	1,535	50
Rural	711	240	185	1,136	63
Total	1,831	818	851	3,500	52

Source: *Iowa Official Register, 1927–28,* Des Moines: State of Iowa, 331.

So decisive was Brookhart's margin in the state – 208,894 to Cummins's 137,367 and Clarke's 64,392 – that party leaders decided to accept the primary results and to lend their support to Brookhart. In the general election Brookhart easily defeated Democrat Claude Porter, 323,409 to 247,869.

Sentiment for farm relief was growing. By mid-decade the focus of the congressional farm bloc had concentrated on a novel proposal to commit the federal government to a guarantee of high farm prices. The McNary-Haugen bill proposed that the federal government buy at an artificially high price all the grain American farmers could produce. It would sell at that same established price all the grain that the domestic market could use. The remainder, the surplus, would be sold on the foreign market for whatever it would bring. Since the government bought the surplus grain at a high domestic price but sold it at a lower world market price, it needed compensation to prevent the purchases from becoming a drain on the federal treasury. This was supplied through an "equalization fee" charged to farmers on each bushel of grain they sold to the government. According to McNary-Haugen advocates, the farmer would get higher prices and the federal government would come out even, acting only as a buying and selling agent. Consumers would pay higher prices for farm goods, but that was only fair in view of the imbalance between agriculture and the other sectors of the economy.

Critics charged that foreign nations would not sit by passively while the American government dumped its agricultural surplus on the world market. Other nations would erect similar barriers to American products and reduce export markets. Furthermore, opponents pointed out, the plan would encourage farmers to grow more and create even greater surpluses. Soon, if not immediately, the government would have on its hands surplus crops that it could not sell on the world market at any price.

Midwestern congressmen fell into line behind the McNary-Haugen bill. It had the support of the American Farm Bureau, the Farmers Union, a conference of midwestern governors, and numerous farm magazines, including *Iowa Homestead* and the influential *Wallaces' Farmer.* Henry C. Wallace had supported the plan as Harding's secretary of agriculture, and his son Henry A. took up the fight after his father's death in 1924.

In May 1926 the House defeated McNary-Haugen, 212–167, with all of Iowa's delegation voting in support. The Senate voted against it a few weeks later, 45–39. Following the November elections, the Senate again took up the legislation in February and this time passed it by a 47–39 margin. The House also gave its approval, 214–178, and sent it to President Coolidge.

Coolidge was known to oppose the plan, and he vetoed it without hesitation. He attacked it as price fixing, an unlawful tax, and a measure promising a cumbersome government bureaucracy. It was more economic intervention than the federal government should tolerate.[65] On the same day, however, Coolidge signed a bill raising the tariff on pig iron 50 percent, which would, among other things, increase the cost of farm implements and freight rates.

The *Farmers' Union Herald,* no friend of Coolidge even in less stormy times, could hardly find words sufficient to express its indignation. "Ah, the courage of Coolidge is vastly underestimated. He bares his breast to the arrows of outrageous fortune in defense of the steel trust and the banker with an unparalleled calmness and remains— Cool. There is none to make him afraid, for his prayer at eventide runs: 'The Steel Trust giveth and the Steel Trust taketh away; blessed be the name of the Steel Trust.' With such faith, who could know fear?"[66]

Lovejoy's response to the veto in the *Bee* was similar. He wanted revenge. The *Bee* stated:

One of the sure ways of getting "parity" for our western dollar is to assault the tariff, slash duties on articles used by the mid-west, and compel industry to "sell on a world market" as the farmer now has to. This would close numerous factories, throw lots of labor out of employment, but why shouldn't industry and labor get some of the same medicine the midwest has been swallowing the past six years? Never in history has "parity" been obtained by an artificial rise in low-priced articles, but only by lowering the high priced ones. What Iowa needs to do now is to chop the tariff, and chop it deep and hard.[67]

It is impossible to miss in Lovejoy's message his resentment against eastern interests for their treatment of the Midwest. Lovejoy was not at all sure that McNary-Haugen was a sound idea. In fact, he acknowledged that it was "unworkable" but had hoped that Coolidge would sign it anyway for the good psychological effect it would have on farmers. He was angry at Coolidge for the president's consistent rejection of McNary-Haugen without offering any meaningful alternative.

Across the Midwest there was interest in finding a Republican presidential candidate more sympathetic to agriculture than Harding and Coolidge had been. Gov. Frank Lowden of Illinois, a strong supporter of the McNary-Haugen plan, quickly emerged as a favorite, capturing the support of farm leaders and Iowa's congressional delegation. Harvey Ingham, editor of the *Des Moines Register,* championed Lowden. In Greene County, Republicans angry at Coolidge formed a Lowden Club, which drew together members of various factions of the party. Former Jefferson mayor E. R. Wood was elected chairman and county GOP secretary Wayne M. Osborn served as Lowden Club secretary. The group made plans to organize in every township to promote Lowden's candidacy.[68]

Concern for farm relief temporarily peaked in the summer of 1927. By August there was some improvement as the price of corn reached one dollar a bushel. Many farmers were holding out for even higher prices. There was the chance that a killing frost might damage much of the fall harvest, which had been planted late and was in danger of being caught "soft." In November the *Herald* reported that crop prices were good and that local business was improving as the result of a good crop and continuing good prices.[69]

The following May Congress again passed the McNary-Haugen bill, this time with modifications that backers hoped might placate Coolidge's opposition, but to no avail. Coolidge denounced the plan as special-interest legislation. Lovejoy wrote that Congress should have tried something less certain of a presidential veto. Most of the leaders in the fight for McNary-Haugen should have realized that the plan was dead as long as the White House was occupied by someone unwilling to commit the federal government to a positive program on behalf of the farmer.[70]

At the 1928 Republican National Convention in Kansas City, Herbert Hoover easily emerged as the Republican nominee. Lowden had withdrawn before the first ballot, realizing the futility of his case. Nevertheless, twenty-two of the twenty-seven Iowa delegates voted for Lowden against Hoover who, as secretary of commerce, had consistently fought the McNary-Haugen proposal. The Republican platform pledged the creation of a federal farm board to promote better marketing of farm crops, but there was no reference to any type of equalization fee or price guarantee.[71]

The Democrats met a few weeks later in Houston. If their farm plank "did not satisfy the farmer," party leaders proclaimed, then "it is because we do not know how to use the English language."[72] The platform called for a plan like the McNary-Haugen proposal though it did not specifically refer to an "equalization fee."

While the Democrats adopted the plank that midwestern farmers wanted, they nominated a candidate whom many Iowans found impossible to support. Al Smith, governor of New York, was a product of Democratic machine politics in New York City, the son of Irish immigrant parents, a Catholic, and an opponent of Prohibition. Ironically, it was Smith, not the leading opponent of McNary-Haugen within the Coolidge administration, who became the whipping boy of those who feared America was moving too rapidly away from traditional – rural – values.

The Farmers Union column in the *Bee* reported that the Corn Belt

Federation of farm organizations, of which the union was the principal architect, endorsed Smith and warned farmers "to guard themselves against being confused over religion, prohibition or other subjects which might have been brought into the campaign." Farmers, the writer insisted, must "remain aloof from all other questions than the one of equality for agriculture."[73]

The warning was not heeded, however, for too many others had concerns more pressing to them than farm relief. Hoover supported Prohibition; Smith did not. For many that was the deciding issue. Lovejoy claimed that the election "will be fought out on a 'dry' and 'wet' basis and no other." He wrote: "When you inject whiskey into a campaign, all other 'issues' submerge. When the campaign comes on, the democratic politician who tries to talk either 'oil' or tariff will be 'as sounding brass or a tinkling cymbal.' " The *Sioux City Journal* concurred with the *Bee:* "The middle west will not vote for Tammany Hall. It will not vote for liquor. It would much rather vote to sustain the party now in power, and this for the reason that there are worse things than the failure of farm relief legislation."[74]

Midwestern Republicans had not wanted Hoover. They had supported Lowden, sympathetic to the need for more active federal efforts on behalf of farm interests. But when the alternative was Al Smith, it was not a hard choice. Smith unmistakably represented the eastern city, which to midwestern small town and farm residents seemed to pose a threat to cherished values. Columnist Walter Lippmann wrote that opposition to Smith among rural areas "is inspired by the feeling that the clamorous life in the city should not be acknowledged as the American ideal."[75] The *Bee* reprinted an article from *Chicago Tribune* columnist Arthur Sears who stated that the "wet cities are rising to throw off the yoke of the dry rural districts which have ruled the nation for a century and a half."[76]

The way the issues were perceived by local residents is revealing. While it was once common to characterize the 1928 election as an anti-Catholic vote against Smith, such a perspective is far too simple and obscures more fundamental anxieties of Smith's opponents.[77] To many local residents Al Smith represented forces alien to traditional America. No less a figure than Kansas editor William Allen White attacked Smith for his ties to European ethnic groups concentrated in the city: "Smith's leadership comes from the amalgamated Tammanies of our great cities from Boston to San Francisco. This new cult resents the old America. . . . Smith's nomination raises two simple questions: 'Shall Smith Tammanyize America or shall we Americanize Smith's Tammany?' "[78]

Lovejoy picked up on the same theme in early August in an attack on Smith's stand on immigration policy: "It will vastly reduce the immigration from Sweden, Norway, Germany, Britain, Denmark, Holland, and Ireland. It will vastly increase the immigration from Turkey, Bulgaria, Jugo Slavia, Albania, Sicily, Italy, and Spain. Some difference. Since the early days, the northern European has been the builder of America. Now Al wants to change this and flood us with an indigestible gorge of races and people who never had been assimilated by our population."[79] "Balkanizing America" was a phrase that frequently appeared in the local press during the campaign to express the fear of the rise to power of unassimilated ethnic groups.

Rural anxieties expressed themselves on the 1928 ballot in the form of a referendum on an amendment to the Iowa Constitution. The proposed amendment limited representation in the Iowa Senate to no more than one senator per county, regardless of its population. Lovejoy endorsed the proposal, which was "intended to prevent the large cities of Iowa from having too many senators by reason of their preponderant vote." He maintained that "while such a condition would not hurt now, the time is coming when the growth of our cities may make it important."[80] Of course, as an amendment to the state constitution, it applied only to Iowa cities, like Des Moines, Cedar Rapids, Waterloo, and Sioux City. But, to rural residents, these were cities nevertheless. Furthermore, this was a preventative measure to insure that rural forces would always control the legislature, regardless of how large the cities grew.

The amendment carried the state comfortably, with 65 percent of the vote. Greene County voters approved the measure by almost exactly the same ratio, 1,730–920, or 65 percent. The concern was the growing power of the city. It was more than an anti-Catholic vote or an anti-immigrant vote. Heavily Catholic Carroll County gave the measure a 58 percent majority.

In such a political climate Hoover carried the state easily in November, a victory that was part of a national landslide. Hoover won with the biggest vote Iowans had ever given a single candidate, 623,570 votes to 379,311 for Smith. In Greene County the Republican ticket rode to a very comfortable 4,299–2,007 tally. Jefferson and the small towns gave Hoover 71 percent, and even in the rural areas, he carried 63 percent of the vote, regardless of what the Democrats promised for farm relief.

In a larger sense the victory of Herbert Hoover over Al Smith was one of the last triumphs of rural forces over the city. Although defeated, Smith drew urban forces together into a more powerful political force than they had ever been before. As political analyst Samuel Lubell notes, the immigrant vote in the twelve largest American cities prior to 1928 had normally been Republican. In 1920 Harding had a net party plurality of 1,638,000 votes in these dozen cities while Coolidge in 1924 carried them by 1,252,000. In 1928, however, the Democrats nominated someone with whom the urban ethnic could identify. Al Smith was one of theirs. While the rural vote swung to Hoover, Smith carried the cities for the Democrats by 38,000, the beginning of an allegiance with major political significance.[81]

The city was increasingly perceived as a threat not only to the economic well-being of the farm and small town but to the rural view of traditional American values and institutions. Prohibition was the law of the land, but in eastern cities, it was a joke. Chicago was a national disgrace, where booze and lawlessness reigned openly. The inability of the farm bloc to pass relief legislation was frightening for more than its economic consequences. It clearly signaled that the representatives of traditional America were no longer in control of the highest councils of the nation.

What had emerged through the 1920s among the small towns and farms of the Midwest was a sense of injustice, that farmers and the farm community were not being treated fairly. Manufacturing and labor had ganged up on agriculture. Lovejoy wanted to give the East a "taste of its own medicine" for a while. Brookhart's popularity rested in no small part on his capturing the support of those who also resented their "exploitation" by big business, eastern manufacturing tycoons, and labor bosses.

Beneath the struggle for farm relief was a deeper concern, an anxiety that further angered and frightened local residents: the rising power of the eastern city. The fight for farm relief was more than a sectional political struggle. The 1920 census had revealed that farmers, for the first time in the nation's history, had become a minority. As Joseph Wall writes, "Abruptly in 1920, the farmers discovered not only that they were a minority but that they were an oppressed minority."[82] In the following decade the small towns and farmers came to understand more fully what that new status meant.

CHAPTER 8

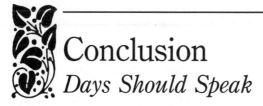

Conclusion
Days Should Speak

Days should speak, and multitude of years should teach wisdom.
—JOB 22:7

IN THE STORY "The Sorcerer's Apprentice," the little apprentice, tired of his daily drudgery, decided to put his scanty knowledge of magic to use. When the sorcerer left the room, he put on his master's cap, said the magic incantations, and ordered a broom to fetch a bucket of water. The broom did, and another and another and another, until the whole room began to flood. The apprentice panicked when he realized that he did not know the command that would stop the process. He chopped the broom into pieces, but each piece grew into a full broom that began carrying buckets. The water rose higher and higher until the apprentice feared he would drown. At the last minute the sorcerer returned, said the magic words, and brought about a "return to normalcy."

Three decades into the twentieth century, many Jefferson residents were eagerly awaiting the return of the sorcerer. The brooms were coming faster and faster. Votes for women had not resulted in the cleansing of the political system and a refinement of civic standards. Instead, many women turned their attention to less lofty pursuits. Some bobbed their hair, shortened their skirts, began smoking, and made it plain that they were as interested in sex as men were. When the *Bee* editor took that little spin around the square in an automobile in 1900, it seemed harmless, but within thirty years, those machines had transformed the landscape, restructured family life, redrawn school districts, and reorganized local government. Prohibition had not ended the evil influence of alcohol. Instead, it had spawned gangsters and crime syndicates who made bootlegging a very profitable enterprise. Why is there never a good sorcerer around when you need one?

247

Agriculture especially suffered from "too much of a good thing." The problem for Iowa farmers was surplus production. The *Bee* addressed the issue directly. Europe could not and would not absorb American grain surplus. Farmers should maintain a production sufficient for the American market only—"and then quit."[1]

Returns from the 1930 census gave telling figures on why the country was swamped with grain. In 1920 Greene county farmers planted 129,233 acres of corn. In 1930 they planted 143,296 acres, an 11 percent increase. However, in 1930 there were 4,000 fewer horses, 8,000 fewer cattle, and 20,000 fewer hogs eating that corn than a decade earlier. The total worth of county farms had fallen from $101,117,093 in the postwar boom to $55,256,345 in 1930, a 45 percent decrease. Tenants were farming a record 58 percent of all Greene County acres. Lovejoy recommended that marginal land in the county be taken out of corn and returned to pasture, but he offered no incentive for the individual owners to do so.[2] No one, it seemed, knew how to stop the brooms.

It took a year for the full impact of the 1929 collapse of Wall Street to reach the rural Midwest, but when it did, a depressed farm economy sank even lower. From $.78 in 1929 the price of a bushel of corn dropped only to $.70 in 1930. In the next two years, however, the bottom fell out, and Iowa farmers faced a truly bleak situation. Not even the collapse in the months after the armistice had been that bad. In 1931 the price averaged $.43 and at some points dipped much lower. Throughout 1932 the statewide average was only $.23.[3] These were the years when some farmers burned corn in their stoves rather than coal because corn was cheaper. Kellogg Thomas recalled that on some winter evenings the countryside smelled like popcorn, a bittersweet commentary on the economy.

The sharp drop in prices brought about another epidemic of rural bank failures in 1931. The Scranton Farmers and Merchants Bank closed in January. A week after the announcement, the *Bee* predicted that depositors would get only 10 percent. Farmers State Bank of Paton folded in March.[4]

In the face of adversity, some clung tenaciously to the old formulas. According to E. A. Milligan, an influential Jefferson grain merchant, the only way to restore long-term economic prosperity was to stick to a free market economy. In the midst of the new round of bank failures Milligan addressed the Jefferson Rotary Club on the farm crisis. He was critical of any plan that would fix prices for farm commodities above what a free market dictated because it would only stimulate greater production. He supported Herbert Hoover's opposition to government guarantees. "Any interference with the free flow of supply and demand is certain to upset the economic structure," he maintained.[5]

Others felt that while the free market might work in the long run, letting the farm economy work itself out of the current mess would be too painful. Instead of guaranteeing farmers a decent price, which would encourage them to produce even more, some argued that it would be cheaper and more effective to pay farmers *not to produce*. The domestic allotment proposal had an interesting "Jefferson connection." The idea originated with W. J. Spillman, an economist in the Department of Agriculture, but the man who worked out the practical details on the proposal was M. L. Wilson of Montana State College. Wilson was a brother of Jefferson lawyer E. B. Wilson. Both had grown up on a farm near Atlantic. Professor Wilson visited his brother in January 1932 on his way to an agriculture conference and dropped in at the *Bee* for an interview. Unlike previous agricultural depressions, Wilson noted, this one was worldwide, a factor that led him to doubt that there could be any improvement in the situation for at least another year. Local residents heard a debate between teams from Kansas State and Iowa State colleges on the domestic allotment proposal. In a poll of the audience a majority opposed the plan but favored some inflation of the currency.[6]

Regardless of what the plan would be, some sort of government action was a necessity. Without some way to get farm prices up and factories running again, the situation appeared hopeless. Midwestern farmers had long been taught that their prosperity depended on a prosperous and fully employed urban labor force. In the fall of 1932, in the darkest months of the depression, Lovejoy wrote, "the thing that the farmer needs worst of all right now is busy industry, busy laboring men, all earning money which they spend for the food and other necessities of life."[7]

But the postwar decade had been a time of unparalleled prosperity for the urban worker, with hard times for the farmer. According to a report by the U.S. Bureau of Labor, farm income in 1933 was less than one-half of the prewar level. The overall cost of living for the average family was equal to what it had been in 1914, but with some important variations among component factors. Food costs were lower, but wages for skilled labor were higher. Hogs in 1914 sold for $7.84; in the beginning of 1933, $2.71. Corn that sold for $.67 in 1914 was on the market for $.20. American farmers who had suffered even when the cities prospered now read reports that one-third of American workers were unemployed. Who would buy farm products?[8]

At both the national and state level there were alarming signs that the political order itself was falling apart. Iowa farmers were showing a measure of their frustration. The state legislature passed a law requiring all cattle to be tested for tuberculosis and those testing positive to be destroyed. In an already strained atmosphere disagreements over the reliability of the test and the amounts awarded for compensation led to confrontations between farmers and the state veterinarians. In the fall of 1931 armed farmers in eastern Iowa drove off vets testing the herds. Governor Dan Turner acted quickly to enforce the law, sending in three regiments of the Iowa National Guard to insure that testing continued. Orville Harris, a Jefferson lawyer, was a captain in one of the regiments and gave a full report in the *Bee* when he returned in September. With the arrival of the troops, he stated, the farmer resistance evaporated. Somewhat sympathetic with the farmers' frustration, Lovejoy nevertheless insisted that the law, whether just or not, must be obeyed.[9]

Confrontations flared elsewhere. In the summer of 1932 twenty thousand angry unemployed veterans marched on Washington demanding increased payments from the federal treasury. President Hoover dispersed the protesters with tear gas and tanks. In Iowa members of the Farmers Holiday Association began sporadic efforts across the state to prevent milk, cream, and livestock from reaching the market. They set up blockades around Sioux City, Council Bluffs, Des Moines, and Cedar Falls and stopped trucks or wagons carrying products into towns. The strike had no long-term effect on farm prices, but it reinforced awareness of farmers' frustration.

As the 1932 election campaigns approached, Republicans knew they were in trouble. Lovejoy denied the assertion that a party in power has the potential to sustain prosperity indefinitely, but he acknowledged that there were many voters who believed it, and that would mean trouble for the GOP. At the national convention party leaders appeared oblivious to how desperate the situation was. The platform committee debated Prohibition. Iowa's governor Turner berated the committee for "twiddling your thumbs and talking about booze . . . with eight or nine million people out of work."[10] But even when Iowa senator Lester Dickinson had the opportunity to address the farm problem as the convention's keynote speaker, he used the occasion to attack the Democrats rather than to make a case for some remedy.

Unfortunately, the Democratic ticket did not excite much hope either. Franklin D. Roosevelt, former governor of New York, did not look like the advance agent of a dramatic change in farm policy, but at least he was not Herbert Hoover. And in the fall of 1932 that was a distinct advantage.

Election night that year came as a nasty shock to Bess Osgood, a Jefferson Republican. Indeed, the experience still rankled half a century later. She recalled:

I used to like to have an Election Day party. We were all Republicans. Well, I had this election party and my uncle from Adel was here. He was a rabid Republican. . . . We had radio and here sat Dr. Franklin and Roy Mayer and Lin Semple and Charlie White and the report came in and their faces started smiling. And my uncle just said, 'Oh, oh boy.' He thought the world was coming to an end. That's when the Democrats came in. I knew there were a lot of New Dealers but I never knew they were these people. . . . There were more New Dealers there than there were old Republicans. And that's the last Election Day party I ever had. . . . I'll never have another one.[11]

And she never did.

Bess Osgood would have taken her chances at any election party that night. Political analysts may argue that Roosevelt did not win the election as much as President Hoover lost it, but in cold vote totals from around the county, the result was the same, 2,747 for the Democrats to 2,360 for the Republicans. Jefferson remained in the Republican column, but the smaller towns and rural townships voted Roosevelt (Table 8.1).

However, after they vented their wrath on Hoover, Greene County voters returned to the Republican fold. In the U.S. Senate race Henry Field carried the county, 2,536–2,235, over the Democrats' Louis Murphy. Smith Brookhart, now running on the Progressive ticket, polled only 172 votes. Gov. Dan Turner was the clear choice over his Democratic challenger Clyde Herring, 2,868–1,948. However, it was a Democratic night in statewide returns, and Murphy and Herring were elected senator and governor respectively.

In the grim four months between Hoover's defeat and Roosevelt's inauguration, there was a growing sense of desperation. Two days

TABLE 8.1. Presidential returns, Greene County, 1932

	Roosevelt (D)	Hoover (R)	Total	% Hoover
Jefferson	609	737	1,346	55
Small town/farm	1,331	1,082	2,413	45
Rural	807	541	1,348	40
Total	2,747	2,360	5,107	46

Source: *Iowa Official Register, 1933–34,* Des Moines: State of Iowa, 229.

G-MEN BY STILL. National prohibition was not nearly as dry as its advocates had hoped, in no small part because of the profits that could come from home distilleries. The enthusiasm of local authorities for raids on local stills varied widely from county to county. *Courtesy of Iowa State Historical Society*

SOUTH SIDE OF JEFFERSON SQUARE, 1900, 1915, 1930. Three shots of the south side of the Jefferson square show the remarkable change that occurred over the first three decades of the twentieth century. What had once served mostly buggies and farm wagons had become a busy transcontinental highway. *Photos for 1900 and 1930 courtesy of Greene County Historical Society, photo for 1915 courtesy of Iowa State Historical Society*

Buy your Dry Goods, Millinery, Cloaks and Furs from Geo. W. Smith, the New Glass Front Store. We are always glad to see you. We always try to please our customers by giving them good goods at moderate prices.

Cor. Main and Cherry Sts. **Jefferson, Iowa.**

SMITH'S DRY GOODS. In 1900, George W. Smith proudly drew attention to his "New Glass Front Store" on the southwest corner of the square. The large picture windows provided more display space and, with the glass door angled across a front corner, greatly improved the natural lighting in the long, narrow store.

after Christmas, Lovejoy wrote: "All in all, this country needs a Mussolini to take action, cram it down our throats and make us like it at the point of a bayonet. Chances are then that he would do us more real good, and real service, than all the whoop-la boys ever presented to us on either a republican or democratic ticket."

He wanted to see a "board of Technocracy" composed of the top economists in the country recommend a plan for recovery. "When they get through," Lovejoy pleaded, "let everybody agree to support their program, for the Lord knows that, whatever it is, it cannot be any worse than we have now."[12]

So desperate did the situation seem to another Jefferson man that he converted a life insurance policy to gold coins, which, with the help of his son who was solemnly sworn to secrecy, he buried in a sack in the basement of their home. He believed that the collapse was imminent.

On 27 April a group of angry, frustrated farmers confronted Judge Charles C. Bradley in his courtroom in LeMars with the demand that he sign no more farm foreclosures. When he refused, they dragged him from the courthouse, took him into the country, and tied a noose around his neck. When cooler heads dissuaded them from proceeding with the hanging, they stripped away his pants and filled them with gravel and poured grease on his head, leaving him dazed along the roadside. By coincidence, on the same day, other members of the Farm Holiday movement broke up a forced farm sale in Denison in spite of resistance of the Crawford County sheriff and fifty deputies. The next day, Governor Herring sent the state militia into both counties to restore order and arrest leaders of the disturbances. Orville Harris again led a militia unit to Denison. Lovejoy called the agitators "thugs and morons" and quoted the former editor of the Storm Lake newspaper who stated: "A country is destroyed by only two things: a lack of regard for authority, and a breaking down of self-reliance."[13] Ominously, both factors were increasing.

While the depression was by far their most immediate and critical problem, underlying anxieties persisted. In particular, rural and small town residents continued their chronic concern with the growing influence of the city. In more and more ways it was obvious that the urban centers, not the farm and small town, were coming to dominate American life. For one thing the cities were simply growing faster. In 1890 approximately one-third of the population lived in cities of over four thousand inhabitants. In 1900 the figure had risen to 40 percent and in 1910 to 46 percent. In 1920 for the first time more Americans lived in cities than in rural areas, and by 1930 57 percent of all Americans were urban.[14]

Late in the 1928 election, Lovejoy spelled out his concerns for the future in a forbidding scenario. Within another twenty years, he predicted, domination of the nation would pass from country to city because of the vast increases in urban population. Immigration barriers would fall as city representatives increased in Congress, and soon the new arrivals would overpower "old America." And the time was coming, whether the "old American stock likes it or not." Urban majorities would abandon high tariffs in favor of cheap food, would vote for liquor, and would support socialism or bolshevism. Democracy ironically would be the demise of democratic institutions.[15]

One of the most distinguishing features of the Yankees of the nineteenth century had been their confidence that theirs was a superior vision and that America's future depended on their ability to impose their order on the life of the nation. Faced with the declining fortunes of New England, they set out to "save America" by converting the West to their standards. To a remarkable degree they succeeded. They established thousands of public schools and private colleges, filled churches and lodge halls with committed believers, and codified their version of morality in the statute books. While there were still the unconverted in their midst, there was no mistaking who was in control.

Twentieth century Yankees faced a similar challenge but in a new arena. Ironically, it was now the eastern city that itself needed conversion. In the decade following World War I, however, it was the cities, not the rural areas, that took the offensive. Urban culture invaded the farms and small towns as technology brought city and country into daily contact. In *Middletown,* Lynd and Lynd emphasized the tremendous impact of "these space-binding, leisure-time inventions imported from without—automobile, motion picture, and radio."[16] "Imported from without" meant, in fact, the eastern city.

Literature took on an antirural tone. In 1915 Edgar Lee Masters's *Spoon River Anthology* briefly resurrected fictional small town residents from their graves in the local cemetery to tell the stories of their warped and stunted lives. Sherwood Anderson's *Winesburg, Ohio* was an only slightly less unflattering account of small town life. H. L. Mencken used the pages of *American Mercury* to keep up a witty diatribe against the American "boobocracy," which included contempt for the farmer and rural life. A good example of Mencken's biting satire is the essay, "The Husbandman," published in 1924. He describes American farmers as "seven million Christian bumpkins." The farmer, according to Mencken, is simply "a tedious fraud and ignoramus, a cheap rogue and hypocrite, the eternal Jack of the human pack. Any city man, not insane, who sheds tears for him is shedding tears of the crocodile."[17]

In 1920 Sinclair Lewis published *Main Street,* a scathing description of the midwestern small town. He wrote: "Not only Gopher Prairie, but ten thousand towns from Albany to San Diego . . . not a dozen buildings which suggested that, in the fifty years of Gopher Prairie's existence, the citizens had realized that it was either desirable or possible to make this, their common home, amusing or attractive." He followed it in 1922 with *Babbitt,* a venomous attack on the dreariness of service clubs, chambers of commerce, and business. In the same acidic vein, *Arrowsmith* and *Elmer Gantry* appeared in mid-decade.

Lovejoy characterized the likes of Masters, Mencken, and Lewis as "scandalmongers" and claimed that "such cheap seekers after notoriety will be dead and forgotten for centuries before the people of the world will cease to sing the praises of men, and the American people, whom they have traduced."[18] Nevertheless, small town residents were aware that their accusers found favor in high places. Lewis accepted the Nobel Prize for Literature in 1930. He had been offered the Pulitzer Prize in 1926 but declined, protesting that there was too much pressure on writers to be "safe, polite, obedient, and sterile."

The assault from the city pressed on other fronts as well. Prohibition, the centerpiece of seven decades of Protestant reform efforts, had become a nightmare. Lovejoy made the comparison between the Civil War South and the city's refusal to enforce Prohibition; both were in direct defiance of federal authority.[19] Repeal of Prohibition was an issue in the 1932 election. Voters knew that the election of the Democrats would boost the chances of wets to end Prohibition, but alcohol was only a sidelight in the referendum on Hoover's economic policies.

When Congress submitted the Twenty-first Amendment to the states for ratification in 1933, Greene County voters remained firm in their support of Prohibition, voting 2,668 against repeal and 1,551 for. The wets carried only Cedar and Willow townships. Protestant Greenbrier voted 95–12 against repeal. But statewide, the amendment carried, 377,275 to 249,943. Sixty counties voted wet while only 39 voted dry, and Iowa became one of the states constituting the necessary majority for ratification. By April the Lincoln Hotel and one Jefferson restaurant had permission to sell 3.2 beer.

Even crime took on an urban flavor. Rural law enforcement officials braced against forays by urban thugs. Where once local officers seemed adequate to handle local crimes, highways and high-powered cars now made it possible for robbers to attack rural targets and within minutes be miles beyond the local jurisdiction. On 23 December 1931 robbers held up a stag party in Perry in the early morning hours with the aid of a machine gun. In 1933 the Greene County Board of Supervisors purchased a Thompson submachine gun for the sheriff "to put a stop to bank robbing, hi-jacking, and other similar operations of organized crime." The report stated that two-thirds of Iowa counties were equipped with the new weapons.[20]

Above all other cities, Chicago became a byword for the criminal element. Lovejoy claimed that murder, robbery, booze, and prostitution were so commonplace in Chicago that the police no longer paid any attention to them. The Sunday lecture at the 1931 chautauqua was "Government by Gangland," a description of conditions in Chicago. Lovejoy even drew Chicago into the Cedar County "Cow War," comparing the occasional lawlessness of frustrated farmers with the routine violence of the city. In the rural perspective, corrupt city officials elected by ignorant blocs of immigrant voters were partners with powerful bootleg syndicates. Tired of trying to reform such a cesspool, Lovejoy urged letting the city "stew in its own juices. It has it coming in seven languages. We see little more hope for Chicago than Abraham saw for Sodom and Gomorrah."[21]

However, rural hostility toward the city was not limited to Chicago and the East. In 1931 the federal government announced that it would build a new veterans' hospital within fifty miles of Ames and urged communities in the area to notify the selection committee of advantages in their town that would be attractive for construction. Boone, Marshalltown, Jefferson, and many other towns soon had visions of building crews and a permanent government work force boosting the local economy. So did Des Moines. When the contract went to Des Moines in September and the rumor circulated that the selection process had been only a ruse, the losers let their antiurban sentiments surface loud and clear. Lovejoy wrote: "Fact is the 'country' need not aspire to such government improvements, for the men who really located the hospital are 'urban minded' and do not consider the country towns like Jefferson as of any use whatever only as loading place for food for 'urban' residents." The following February, Lovejoy devoted one "Seasonable Sermon" to crime in Des Moines.[22]

The future was not promising. As a result of the 1930 census, Iowa lost two representatives in Congress, and state congressional districts were redrawn. A former Jefferson resident living in California urged *Bee* readers not to worry. So many Iowans had moved there that Iowa's interests would be well represented in the California delegation.

With the stock market collapse in 1929, the mood of the nation changed rather abruptly, a transformation that some judged to be a blessing. The past ten years had not been the best of times for the rural Midwest. As the economic condition grew worse, the assault on traditional values and those who held them abated somewhat. After a decade of decline relative to the population, church membership picked up. From 1931 to 1933, according to a *Bee* article quoting the *Christian Herald,* American church rolls increased by a million members, more than four times the growth rate of 1931. Like prodigals returning home, the article maintained, people wanted something to believe in again. "The 1920s are dead. The day of debunking is over."[23]

However, regardless of what people said or believed, American society at the beginning of the 1930s was substantially different from what it had been at the turn of the century. In retrospect, perhaps the most significant change over the entire period was the size of the community of which Jefferson residents were a part. Economically and culturally, the Iowa small towns were becoming integrated into national networks in which the centers of power were far beyond the local city limits. Jefferson merchants worried about chain stores. The radio and daily newspapers made national figures household words. Local athletes played in the shadows of national stars, and the chautauqua stage was no longer competing successfully with the comedians, drama companies, and symphonies of weekly radio shows.

Through all the changes of those decades there were those who never lost faith in the power and responsibility of individuals to influence the world around them. They still felt that life is a struggle; character is the key to success; and the righteous are responsible for the welfare of the community. While economists described current conditions in terms of thousands of failed businesses and millions of unemployed, Vic Lovejoy continued to view the individual as the prevailing force in history. Human selfishness explained the failure of the Federal Reserve Act to end bank failures, the League of Nations to end war, and the Eighteenth Amendment to end booze, wrote Lovejoy in September 1933 (by which time, he was claiming that it also explained the failure of the New Deal to end the depression): "There is no law, no treaty, that selfish human nature will not find a pathway around it. No matter how high and worthy purpose a statute may have, human selfishness has no trouble in largely defeating its objectives if it chooses to do so."[24]

By the same standard, success was the triumph of human character. Life is a struggle, but a noble character can triumph over external adversities. Lovejoy reminded his readers that the means to success lay within reach of each of them. While everyone is occasionally subject to "unseen misfortunes," he wrote in 1932, "the average man has his own 'cure' for financial depression if he but knows it. . . . Many men, by care, good judgment, and business acumen, are unaffected by such conditions because they prepare for them while the preparing is good."[25] His intent may have been to rally hope in the despondent, but his words must also have confirmed to many that their pitifully meager bank accounts were measures of their personal worth. Nevertheless, he returned to the theme frequently. "The menace to government in America today," he later declared, "is instilling into the hearts and minds of everybody that they should expect Uncle Sam to fill their pocketbooks if they haven't brains enough to fill it themselves."[26]

In the Yankee scheme of things, individual success had to be balanced against community welfare, a principle upon which Lovejoy insisted. Personal comfort while others suffered was intolerable. In the spring of 1933 Franklin D. Roosevelt enjoyed such widespread support that even Lovejoy termed the accomplishments of the president's first four weeks "little short of marvelous." In a front-page editorial set in large type, Lovejoy urged his fellow citizens to put the common good above their personal concerns. "President Roosevelt has done wonders to get things started . . . but he cannot do it all." What was needed now, the editorial stated, was for consumers—individual citizens—to start the economy moving again. If you have any money to spend, spend it, Lovejoy pleaded. Buy cars, new clothes, furniture. Help merchants place the orders with wholesalers that will open the factories again. Paint your house or your barn. Put men back to work. Those with the money to do so had a moral obligation to spend it to reinvigorate the economy, Lovejoy wrote. Once again, it was a test between altruism and selfishness, between love and greed. He asked: "Are we going to (spend) or are we going to sit back, pinch our money, refuse to start the wheels of industry, or play the same old hermit game of self-preservation and selfishness? If that is the kind of people we are, we deserve to fail."[27] Azor Mills, a half century earlier, would have applauded the way Lovejoy phrased the issue.

For those who insist that individuals have the ability to direct their own affairs, democracy in modern society has an "irreparable flaw," according to political analyst Robert Dahl.[28] The larger the unit of which one is a part, writes Dahl, the less opportunity most people have to influence it. By 1930 small town residents were, in short, caught in the dilemma of wanting the best of two incompatible worlds. On one hand they wanted what the outside world offered: the factory goods, the services, and the entertainment. On the other hand they did not want to give up the local autonomy of the community in which they had an established identity and opportunity for meaningful participation. But they had to choose and they made their choice, but not without misgivings.

The new order did not totally replace the old. The local community continued to give residents an opportunity to establish an identity and to play out their triumphs and tragedies.[29] For this, though it was no longer as self-contained and self-sustaining as it had once been, the small town commanded a tremendous allegiance from its citizens. That the major transcontinental highway of the world ran quietly through the middle of the town was considered less an honor for Jefferson than a blessing for travelers who might otherwise have missed the opportunity to visit such a splendid community.

For those who defined "normal" as what the world had been at the turn of the century, normalcy by the 1930s was, like the unfortunate Clementine, "lost and gone forever." Some were "dreadful sorry." Others, as always, were oblivious. Still others, especially the young who came of age after the war, were not sorry at all. The new order was exciting, and they were eager to be a part of it. But that, as Kipling says, is another story.

NOTES

All oral histories, except those specifically noted, were conducted in Jefferson during the summer of 1979. The transcripts of many of those will be deposited at the Jefferson Public Library upon publication of the book.

CHAPTER 1.   Introduction: *A Land of Milk and Honey*

1. E. B. Stillman, *Past and Present of Greene County, Iowa* (Chicago: Clarke, 1907), 113.
2. Stillman, *Past and Present,* 67.
3. "1954 Greene County Centennial Edition," *Jefferson Bee,* 26 October 1954.
4. Ibid.
5. Ibid.
6. For a good discussion of the perspectives of Democrats in early Iowa, see David S. Sparks, "The Decline of the Democratic Party in Iowa, 1850-1860," in *Patterns and Perspectives in Iowa History,* ed. Dorothy Schwieder (Ames, Iowa State Univ. Press, 1973) 177-206.
7. Joseph F. Wall, *Iowa: A Bicentennial History* (New York: Norton, 1978), 96.
8. Stillman, *Past and Present,* 66; Leland L. Sage, *A History of Iowa* (Ames, Iowa State Univ. Press, 1974), 128.
9. *Biographical and Historical Record of Greene and Carroll Counties, Iowa* (Chicago: Lewis, 1887), 502. Hereafter cited as *Record.*.
10. *Record,* 467, 503.
11. *Record,* 504; Stillman, *Past and Present,* 38-39, 48.
12. Don Harrison Doyle, in the opening chapter of his *Social Order of a Frontier Community: Jacksonville, Illinois, 1825-1870* (Urbana: Univ. of Illinois Press, 1979), presents an excellent survey of recent historiography on the development of frontier towns. He contrasts historians who stress frontier cooperation in community building as a dominant impulse, like Stanley Elkins and Eric McKitrick, "A Meaning for Turner's Frontier," *Political Science Quarterly* 69 (1954): 321-53, 565-602, and Daniel Boorstin, *The Americans: The National Experience* (New York: Random House, 1965), 113-68, with historians like Allan Bogue, "Social Theory and the Pioneer," *Agricultural History* 34(1960): 221-34 and Robert Dykstra, *The Cattle Towns* (New York: Knopf, 1968) who maintain that towns were more often fashioned by social conflict than by harmonious, uncoerced cooperation.
13. "1954 Centennial Edition.".
14. Sage, *History of Iowa,* 56; Richard L. Power, *Planting Corn Belt Culture: The Impress of the Upland Southerner and Yankee in the Old Northwest* (Indianapolis: Indiana Historical Society, 1953), 10.
15. "1954 Centennial Edition."
16. Stillman, *Past and Present,* 47; Ibid., 60.

17. Ibid., 69.

18. Ibid., 67.

19. For a discussion of Greene County soldiers' participation in the Civil War, see Stillman, *Past and Present,* 78–85.

20. Ibid., 59.

21. Ibid., 68.

22. Vera Mills Haeger in *1954 Centennial Edition;* Stillman, *Past and Present,* 84.

23. George Gallup, letter to author, September 1982.

24. Stillman, *Past and Present,* 137.

25. Ibid., 138. For a discussion of the coordination of curricula among different branches of the Iowa public school system, see Vernon Carstensen, "The University as Head of the Iowa School System," in *Patterns and Perspectives in Iowa History,* 323–58.

26. For a discussion of churches and social order on the Illinois frontier, see Doyle, *Social Order,* 153–67.

27. William G. McLoughlin, "Isaac Backus and the Separation of Church and State in America," *American Historical Review* 73 (June 1968), quoted in Sidney E. Mead, *The Old Religion in the Brave New World* (Berkeley: Univ. of California Press, 1977), 93.

28. Stillman, *Past and Present,* 107–8.

29. Ibid., 440.

30. Lewis Atherton, *Main Street on the Middle Border* (Chicago: Quadrangle Books, 1954), 189.

31. For a discussion of lodges and fraternal orders in Jefferson, see Stillman, *Past and Present,* 140–48.

32. Ibid., 55.

33. Ibid., 88.

34. *Jefferson Era,* 6 April, 1866.

35. Stillman, *Past and Present,* 88; "Jefferson Bee Centennial Edition." 30 December 1966.

36. Stillman, *Past and Present,* 87. Information on the history of the *Herald* was provided by Fred Morain, 19 October 1987.

37. For a table of population figures for all Iowa counties from 1870 to 1970 based on the federal census, see Sage, *History of Iowa,* 311.

38. *Jefferson Era,* quoted in "1966 Centennial Edition.".

39. Stillman, *Past and Present,* 87; *Jefferson Bee,* 6 July 1905.

40. *Record,* 504.

41. Stillman, *Past and Present,* 38–39.

42. *Record,* 506.

43. State of Iowa, *1856 Census..*

44. *Record,* 41. Jefferson was not unique in its diversity of services. It was typical of the frontier small town. The town of Rippey in 1886, for example, with less than a third of the population of Jefferson, boasted two general stores, two groceries, three restaurants, one bakery, one drug store, one hardware store, one harness shop, one hotel, two doctors, one insurance and loan agent, one elevator, three blacksmith shops, three wagon shops, one meat market, one livery stable, one millinery shop, and a coal mine. (*Record,* 521).

45. Atherton, *Main Street,* 232.

46. William G. Murray, "Struggle for Land Ownership", in *Century of Farming in Iowa* (Ames, Iowa State College Press, 1946), 12–13.

47. Earle D. Ross, *Iowa Agriculture: An Historical Survey* (Iowa City: Iowa State Historical Society, 1951), 82, 77.

48. Stillman, *Past and Present,* 69.

49. For a good discussion of prairie farmer politics in the latter nineteenth century, see Allan G. Bogue, *From Prairie to Corn Belt: Farming on the Illinois and Iowa Prairies in the Nineteenth Century* (Chicago: Quadrangle Books, 1963), 280–87.

50. Ross, *Iowa Agriculture,* 115.

51. Ibid., 88.

CHAPTER 2. Social Identity: *To Whom Much Is Given*

1. Joseph F. Wall, *Iowa: A Bicentennial History,* (New York: Norton, 1978), 152.
2. Josiah Strong, *The New Era, or the Coming Kingdom* (New York, 1893), 81, quoted in Robert T. Handy, *A History of the Churches in the United States and Canada* (New York: Oxford Univ. Press, 1976), 280. An excellent treatment of this small town confidence at the turn of the century can be found in Richard Lingeman, *Small Town America: A Narrative History, 1620–Present* (New York: Putnam, 1980), especially Chapter 6, 258–320.
3. Henry A. Wallace, quoted in Don S. Kirschner, *City and Country: Rural Responses to Urbanization in the 1920s* (Westport, Conn.: Greenwood, 1970), 37. Two of the best-known works expressing the Nordic supremacy theme are (Theodore) Lothrop Stoddard, *Rising Tide of Color Against White World-Supremacy* (New York: Scribner's, 1920) and Madison Grant, *The Passing of the Great Race* (New York: Scribner's, 1916). Kenneth Roberts published numerous shorter works on the subject, including "Shutting the Gates," *Saturday Evening Post,* 28 January 1922, and "Worth of Citizenship," *Saturday Evening Post,* 18 February 1922.
4. *Jefferson Bee,* 22 July 1925.
5. Ibid., 8 August 1907.
6. Ibid., 24 November 1904.
7. Frank Stillman, *Jefferson Bee,* 7 July 1904.
8. *Jefferson Bee,* 8 April 1904; 7 February 1912; 24 October 1917.
9. Ibid., 19 November 1916.
10. Ibid., 15 March 1916.
11. *Manchester* (Iowa) *Press,* reprinted in *Jefferson Bee,* 13 January 1915.
12. Charles Beard, *A Basic History of the United States* (New York: New Home Library, 1944), 296.
13. Beard, *Basic History,* 297.
14. Kirschner, *City and Country,* Chapter 2.
15. *Jefferson Bee,* 12 November 1919.
16. *Chicago Tribune,* reprinted in *Jefferson Bee,* 22 October 1919.
17. *New York World,* reprinted in *Jefferson Bee,* 22 October 1919.
18. *Jefferson Bee,* 12 November 1919.
19. Ibid., 19 November 1919.
20. Kirschner, *City and Country,* 48.
21. The Iowa census of 1905 gathered data on the number of members of each denomination, Sunday school attendance, the number of congregations per county, and the value of church buildings.
22. See Richard J. Jensen *The Winning of the Midwest: Social and Political Conflict, 1888–1896* (Chicago: Univ of Chicago Press, 1971).
23. The results of the survey of the religious preference of Jefferson residents were printed in the *Bee,* 13 October 1904.
24. *Jefferson Bee,* 6 October 1915.
25. Interviews with Maxine Trumbo and Gene Melson.
26. Interview with Roy Mosteller.
27. My grandfather, P. O. Morain, told us about the rumors about St. Patrick's Church.
28. *Jefferson Herald,* 20 November 1924.
29. *Jefferson Bee,* 5 December 1915.
30. Interview with Kellogg Thomas.
31. Interviews with Ruth Hensley and Roy Mosteller.
32. Kirschner, *City and Country,* 125–26.
33. Interviews with Wayne Winey and Roy Mosteller.
34. Interview with Pauline Russell. Margaret Cudahy also remembered having been frightened by the Klan as a Catholic girl.
35. My grandfather was the driver in the incident. He told us that a hooded man

looked in his window and said, "Oh, it's you, Perce."; interview with Dr. Dean Thompson.

36. I heard this story from several people. I have used the Brunner family version.

37. Interview with Roy Mosteller.

38. Interview with Wayne Winey.

39. Interview with Charles Hird.

40. Interview with Roy Mosteller.

41. *Jefferson Bee,* 26 February 1908.

42. Interview with Margaret Cudahy.

43. Interview with Kellogg Thomas.

44. Ibid.

45. Interview with Roy Mosteller.

46. Interview with Gene Melson.

47. There are numerous systems to classify occupational categories. Merle Curti's intensive study of a Wisconsin county in the nineteenth century, *The Making of An American Community: A Case Study of a Democracy in a Frontier County* (Stanford: Stanford Univ. Press, 1959) uses a complex system of categories: agriculture, professional, personal service, semiprofessional, business, transportation and communication, labor, and five subcategories of artisan (building trades; metal, wood, leather trades; food processing; clothing; and miscellaneous). Doyle, in *Social Order of a Frontier Community,* collapses Curti's scheme into five. I have divided town jobs into three categories and farming into three. The division was suggested by my father as the major groupings of occupations as they would best be understood by Jefferson residents.

48. *Jefferson Bee,* 6 April 1910.

49. Lewis Atherton, *Main Street on the Middle Border* (Chicago: Quadrangle Books, 1954) 48. A useful model for examining the merchant-professional sector of a midwestern town is provided in Richard Alcorn, "Leadership and Stability in Mid-Nineteenth Century America: A Case Study of an Illinois Town," *Journal of American History* 61 (1974): 685–702. Alcorn compares this group with community norms on several scales, including the length of time they remained in the town.

50. Interview with Berniece Raver.

51. *Jefferson Bee,* 3 July 1918.

52. Joseph F. Wall, "The Iowa Farmer in Crisis, 1920–1936," *Annals of Iowa,* 47 (Fall 1983): 119.

53. Ruth Suckow, *Country People* (New York: Knopf, 1924).

54. Interview with Fred Morain.

55. Carl Hamilton, *In No Time at All* (Ames: Iowa State Univ. Press, 1973), 6.

56. Ibid., 68.

57. *Jefferson Bee,* 23 May 1907.

58. An ad for Mrs. Rydings's cemetery markers appears in the 30 June 1915 *Bee.* An excellent study of female employment is Valerie Oppenheimer, *The Female Force in the United States: Demographic and Economic Factors Governing Its Growth and Changing Composition* (Berkeley: Institute of International Studies, Univ. of California, 1970). See also William Chafe, *The American Woman: Her Changing Social, Economic, and Political Roles, 1920-1970* (New York: Oxford Univ. Press, 1972); Lois W. Banner, *Women in Modern America: A Brief History* (Chicago: Harcourt, Brace, Jovanovich, 1974); and Mirra Komarovsky, *Blue-Collar Marriage* (New York: Random House, 1964). National statistics on percentages of working women often did not include farm women if they worked at home, and as late as the 1910 census, half the American population was still classified as rural. The percentage of rural women in Iowa was, of course, significantly higher. For an early assessment of women's employment in Iowa, see Ruth A. Gallaher, *The Legal and Political Status of Women in Iowa* (Iowa City: State Historical Society of Iowa, 1918).

59. *Iowa Illustrated* (Jefferson Edition) 1, no. 2 (June 1896); *Bee,* 13 July 1905; Gallaher, *Legal and Political Status,* 52. See also Mary Roth Walsh, *"Doctors Wanted: No Women Need Apply": Sexual Barriers in the Medical Profession, 1835-1975* (New Haven: Yale Univ. Press, 1977). Walsh (p. 186) displays a chart listing women physicians as a percentage of the total number of physicians in the nation. A peak came in 1910 with 6

percent, a figure not reattained until 1950. Most female physicians specialized in medicine for women and children.

60. Gallaher, *Legal and Political Status,* 45.

61. Atherton, *Main Street,* 101–2.

62. For more about the feminization of the teaching profession in Iowa, see Thomas J. Morain, "The Departure of Men from the Teaching Profession in Nineteenth Century Iowa," *Civil War History* 26, no. 2 (June 1980): 161–70.

63. *Jefferson Bee,* 12 January 1916.

64. Maxine Morley, letter in *Jefferson Bee,* 20 May 1908.

65. Jensen, *The Winning,* 49.

66. Jensen, *The Winning,* 58–59; *Jefferson Bee,* 20 September 1916.

67. Interview with Lumund Wilcox.

68. The anecdote was related to me by Judge David Harris.

69. Interview with Bess Osgood.

70. Interview with Lumund Wilcox.

71. Interview with Fred Morain.

72. Interview with Fred Morain.

73. The anecdote was related to me by Fred Morain.

74. Sage, *A History of Iowa* (Ames: Iowa State Univ. Press, 1974), 220–21. For short biographies of the Washington delegation from Iowa, Sage is an excellent source.

CHAPTER 3. Gender: *Created He Them*

1. See John S. Haller and Robin M. Haller, *The Physician and Sexuality in Victorian America* (New York: Norton, 1974) especially Chapters 2 and 5. See also Peter Filene, *Him/Her/Self: Sex Roles in Modern America* (New York: Harcourt, Brace, Jovanovich, 1975).

2. *Jefferson Bee,* 25 November 1908.

3. Ibid., 4 March 1908.

4. Ibid., 4 February 1908. My father related that the flowery obituaries were still in vogue when he returned to the Bee in the 1930s after college. It was a difficult tradition to change since no one wanted his or her mother or father to be the first not to be praised, as if omission suggested that the deceased lacked such virtues.

5. Interview with Berniece Raver.

6. Lewis Atherton, *Main Street on the Middle Border,* (Chicago: Quadrangle Books, 1954), 117.

7. *Jefferson Bee,* 22 March 1916; 20 January 1915.

8. This was one of the major indignities of my father's childhood. His reward for practicing and practicing scales and finger exercises was being assigned "The Sweet Violet."

9. *Jefferson Bee,* 7 January 1925.

10. Ibid., 23 November 1905.

11. Ibid., 4 March 1908.

12. Ibid., 25 May 1910.

13. Ibid., 15 December 1915.

14. George Mills, *Rogues and Heroes from Iowa's Amazing Past* (Ames: Iowa State Univ. Press, 1972), 120–23. The story of Sunday's first prayer, delivered silently while he was chasing a fly ball in center field, was printed in the *Bee,* 29 January 1908.

15. *Jefferson Bee,* 5 May 1916.

16. Ibid., 7 January 1904; 14 January 1904. See also 20 January 1915, for the story of one man's conversion by Billy Sunday from a life of booze.

17. Ibid., 10 June 1908.

18. Interview with Floyd Stevens. See also *Jefferson Bee,* 11 November 1908. The YMCA office in Greene County was discontinued in January 1917 for lack of local financial support (*Jefferson Bee,* 10 January 1917).

19. Kathleen Dalton, "Why America Loved Theodore Roosevelt," *The Psychohistory*

Review 8 (Winter 1979): 20. The pioneering work on the relationship between turn-of-the-century reform and status anxieties is Richard Hofstadter's *Age of Reform* (New York: Vintage, 1955). While the conclusion that personal anxieties were the impetus to political reforms has been seriously questioned by later works, the status historians did open a new dimension of inquiry by exploring the insecurities that the new era provoked. See also Glenda Riley and Richard S. Kirkendall, "Henry A. Wallace and the Mystique of the Farm Male, 1921–1933," *Annals of Iowa* 48 (Summer/Fall 1984): 32–55; Howard F. Stein, "Sittin' Tight and Bustin' Loose: Contradiction and Conflict in Mid-western Masculinity and the Psycho-History of America," *Journal of Psychohistory* 11 (Spring 1984): 501–12; and J. L. Dubert, "Progressivism and the Masculinity Crisis," in Elizabeth H. and Joseph H. Pleck, *The American Man* (Englewood Cliffs, N.J.: Prentice Hall, 1980), 305–20.

20. Dalton, "Why America Loved," 21.

21. *Jefferson Bee,* 2 November 1905.

22. Ibid., 7 July 1910.

23. Ibid., 9 September 1904.

24. See Filene, *Him/Her/Self,* 77–104.

25. *Jefferson Bee,* 7 April 1904.

26. *Allison Tribune,* reprinted in *Jefferson Bee,* 5 August 1908.

27. Winifred Van Etten, "Three Worlds," in *Growing Up in Iowa,* ed. Clarence Andrews (Ames: Iowa State Univ. Press, 1978): 147–48.

28. Filene, *Him/Her/Self,* 12.

29. *Jefferson Bee,* 10 May 1888.

30. I have drawn extensively from two histories of Friday Club written and presented to the organization as programs. The first was by Mary Black. The second was by Billie Harding. A copy of each was in the possession of Mrs. Harding at the time of this publication. For a fictional history of a strikingly similar club, see Helen Hooven Santmyer, *And Ladies of the Club* (New York: Putnam's, 1984).

31. According to the Harding history, there was never another prizefight in town after the club's protest.

32. At the time of the 1904 dedication, the *Bee* published a history of the library written by librarian Ida B. Head. Iowa State College president A. B. Storms gave the dedicatory address to an audience of about five hundred, "19/20ths of whom were female," the *Bee* reported. In a review of Storms's address the article stated: "He couples a great, sympathetic voice with a towering mind, while in his manner he is a composite of strength and gentleness. He led his audience along paths of culture and refinement and beside the still waters of genius, and at the close of his remarks, it seemed as if some great and good influence had passed through the place, leaving an aroma of nobility and sweetness behind it" (*Bee,* 21 April 1904).

33. *Jefferson Bee,* 20 July 1910.

34. Interview with Bess Osgood.

35. *Jefferson Bee,* 7 June 1939.

36. *Scranton Journal,* cited in the *Bee,* 2 August 1916.

37. *Jefferson Bee,* 26 July 1916.

38. *New York Times,* reprinted in *Jefferson Bee,* 19 April 1916.

39. The bill was approved on 13 April 1894. Chapter 39, *Laws of the Twenty-Fifth General Assembly of the State of Iowa,* 47. Partial suffrage was possible without a constitutional amendment because of some fine legal distinctions. The constitution defined "electors" as males, and no session of the legislature could alter that definition. Electors voted in "elections," which had been defined by the courts as contests involving candidates for office. Since the constitution spelled out the ground rules only for elections, the laws governing other ballot issues, such as tax levies and bond issues that did not pit candidates against each other, were left under the jurisdiction of the legislature. Suffrage forces seized upon this loophole and successfully lobbied the legislature to grant women the vote in all "non-election" ballot issues, hence the partial suffrage. They made one mistake, however. They forgot to change the wording of the statute that governed the outcome of the balloting. The law stated that for a bond issue to carry, it must be approved by a majority of the *electors* voting on it. In 1918 a supreme court judge ruled

that since electors were defined by the constitution to be males only and since a majority of electors must approve the issue, the law permitted women to express themselves at the polls, but their ballots had no legal standing in determining the outcome. Women could vote, but their votes did not count! By that time, however, women had been voting on local issues for over twenty years, and full suffrage was less than two years away. *Sears v. City of Maquoketa* 166 NW 700, Iowa 1918.

40. *Jefferson Bee,* 31 January 1917; Louise Noun, *Strong-Minded Women: The Emergence of the Women Suffrage Movement in Iowa* (Ames: Iowa State Univ. Press, 1969), 258. *Homestead* editor James M. Pierce was a suffrage advocate, Noun reports, who meekly defended the appearance of the ad in the publication with the statement, "I got $600 for it" (p. 258).

41. *Jefferson Bee,* 6 March 1916; 10 May 1916.

42. Ibid., 9 February 1916.

43. Interview with David Harris.

44. *Jefferson Bee,* 16 January 1918.

45. See Thomas G. Ryan, "Male Opponents and Supporters of Woman Suffrage: Iowa in 1916," *Annals of Iowa,* 45 (Winter 1981): 537–50.

46. *Jefferson Bee,* 7 June 1916.

47. Interview with Kellogg Thomas.

48. Interview with Dorothy Bowley.

49. Interview with Alice Ann Andrew.

50. For a good summary analysis of rural thought of the period, see Dorothy Schwieder, "Rural Iowa in the 1920s: Conflict and Continuity," *Annals of Iowa* 47 (Fall 1983): 104–15.

51. Herbert Quick, "The Women on the Farms," *Good Housekeeping* 17 (October 1913): 427.

52. *Jefferson Bee,* 4 April 1916.

53. Ibid., 31 August 1910.

54. Quick, "The Women," 429.

55. Henry A. Wallace, *Wallaces' Farmer,* 16 December 1927.

56. Interviews with Barbara Hamilton and Francis Cudahy.

57. Interview with Betty Dillavou Durden. I took the liberty with the transcript to edit it into the quoted form. The text is almost entirely a direct quote though the topics have been rearranged for clarity. Ms. Durden reviewed the edited work to insure that the editions did not alter the context in a substantial way. I appreciate her cooperation and thoughtful insights.

58. *Jefferson Bee,* 20 October 1915.

59. Ibid., 19 June 1915.

60. Barbara Hamilton, quoted in Hamilton, *In No Time,* 134.

61. *Jefferson Bee,* 31 May 1916.

62. Interview with Alice Ann Andrew.

63. Interview with James Hilton.

64. Quick, "The Women," 433.

CHAPTER 4. Technology: *Rise Up as Eagles*

1. Interview with Roy Mosteller. Norman T. Moline's study of the impact of automobiles on a small Illinois community, *Mobility and the Small Town, 1900–1930: Transportation Change in Oregon, Illinois,* Research Paper No. 132 (Chicago: Univ. of Chicago Department of Geography, 1971), details turn-of-the-century railroad transportation. He includes a table of travel times from Oregon, Illinois, to other cities. (See pp. 32–34.)

2. Interview with Dr. J. K. Johnson, Jr.

3. Frederick Lewis Allen, *The Big Change* (New York: Bantam Books, 1961), 6.

4. *Jefferson Bee,* 28 September 1905.

5. Allen, *The Big Change,* 6.

6. Cited in Joseph Interrante, "You Can't Go to Town in a Bathtub: Automobile

Movement and the Reorganization of American Space, 1900–1903," *Radical History Review* 21 (Fall 1979): 153.

7. See Michael Berger, *The Devil Wagon in God's Country* (Hamden, Conn.: Archer Books, 1979), 30.

8. Interview with Bess Osgood.

9. *Jefferson Bee,* 8 December 1904; interview with Ken Kinsman. For additional discussion of rural roads, see Dorothy Schwieder, "Rural Iowa in the 1920s: Conflict and Continuity," *Annals of Iowa* 47 (Winter 1984): 109–10.

10. "The Automobiles of 1904," reprinted from *Frank Leslie's Popular Monthly,* January 1904, *Americana Review,* 725 Dongan Avenue, Scotia, New York, 1961.

11. *Jefferson Bee,* 6 July 1905.

12. Interrante, "You Can't Go to Town," 154.

13. Reynold M. Wik, *Henry Ford and Grass Roots America* (Ann Arbor: Univ. of Michigan, 1972), 21.

14. *Jefferson Bee,* 25 August 1904; Berger, *The Devil Wagon,* 25.

15. *Jefferson Bee,* 17 August 1905.

16. Ibid., 12 October 1905.

17. See Interrante, "You Can't Go to Town," 152–53.

18. The article first appeared in the *Bee* in 1906 and was summarized in the 8 August 1917 edition.

19. Interview with Gracelyn Durlam.

20. Edwin P. Chase, "Forty Years of Main Street," *Iowa Journal of History and Politics,* 34 (July 1936): 254.

21. Quoted in Berger, *The Devil Wagon,* 68. Since Wilson was president of Princeton at the time he made the statement, perhaps it is worth pointing out the incorrect grammatical usage. The antecedent of "they" in the second sentence is "automobile", and hence the disagreement between the plural pronoun and its singular antecedent. Such a lapse could be forgiven Wilson the President of the United States but hardly Wilson the president of Princeton University.

22. Daniel J. Boorstin, *The Americans: The Democratic Experience* (New York: Random House, 1973), 548. A 1922 article in *Scribner's* maintained that this rapidly increasing movement among sections of the country was the most wholesome impact of the automobile. See Allen Albert, "Social Influence of the Automobile," *Scribner's* 71, no. 6 (June 1922): 685–88.

23. Allen, *The Big Change,* 100; Berger, *The Devil Wagon,* 44. See also David L. Lewis, *The Public Image of Henry Ford: An American Folk Hero and His Company* (Detroit: Wayne State Univ. Press, 1976), esp. Chapter 3; and Wik, *Henry Ford.*

24. Interview with Roy Mosteller.

25. Lloyd R. Morris, *Not So Long Ago* (New York: Random House, 1949), 296. Model-T jokes were popular. Even Ford officials sometimes encouraged them, believing that the jokes actually promoted sales. (See Lewis, 123–25.)

26. Letter to author, 6 November 1978.

27. *Jefferson Bee,* 14 January 1920.

28. Ibid.

29. *Jefferson Bee,* 18 March 1914. In 1915 the newspaper reported that there were registered 1,519 cars in the county (6 October 1915); by 1920 the ratio had dropped to one car for every five Greene County residents (*Bee,* 14 January 1920).

30. Wik, *Henry Ford,* 21.

31. According to Frederick Lewis Allen, farmers in 1900 who came into a little money were likely to do four things in order: (1) paint the barn, (2) add a porch to the house, (3) buy a piano, (4) send their children to college. By the 1920s, wrote Allen, buying a car came even before painting the barn. One farm woman, asked why she had purchased a car when the family had no bathtub, seemed amazed at the question. "You can't go to town in a bathtub," she replied (see Allen, *The Big Change,* 108; see also Interrante, "You Can't Go to Town").

32. The American Automobile Association, *The Official Automobile Blue Book, 1915: A Touring Hand-Book of the Principal Automobile Routes in the Western States.* Vol.

5, "Mississippi River to Pacific Coast" (Chicago: The Automobile Blue Book Publishing Company, 1915). This copy was in the possession of Billie Harding during the 1979 project.

33. Berger, *The Devil Wagon*, 123.

34. Thomas R. Agg and John P. Brindley, *Highway Administration and Finance* (New York: McGraw Hill, 1927), 32–33.

35. *First Annual Report of the Iowa State Highway Commission* (Des Moines: State of Iowa, 1915), 8.

36. Ibid.

37. Agg and Brindley, *Highway Administration*, 33–34.

38. *Jefferson Bee*, 8 February 1910.

39. Ibid., 8 June 1910.

40. Ibid., 24 August 1910.

41. *Jefferson Bee*, 5 May, 1916; 13 September, 1916; 13 December, 1916. For a discussion of the good roads movement and the election of Harding, see John E. Visser, "William Lloyd Harding and the Republican Party in Iowa, 1916–1920," (Ph.D. diss., Univ. of Iowa, 1957).

42. Peter T. Harstad and Diana J. Fox, "Dusty Doughboys on the Lincoln Highway: The 1919 Army Convoy in Iowa," *Palimpsest* (May/June 1975): 81–82.

43. Ibid., 66.

44. Ibid., 82–83.

45. Ibid., 83–84.

46. Interview with Floyd Stevens.

47. Harstad and Fox, "Dusty Doughboys," 84.

48. Agg and Brindley, *Highway Administration*, 35. See also J. C. Burnham, "Gasoline Tax and the Automobile Revolution," *Mississippi Valley Historical Review* (December 1961): 435–59; Kirschner, *City and Country*, esp. Chapter 5.

49. Interview with Burdette Bowley.

50. Interview with Floyd Stevens.

51. Suckow, *Country People*, quoted in Berger, *The Devil Wagon*, 134.

52. Interview with Dorothy Bowley.

53. Interview with Margery Dillavou; interview with Miriam Clause.

54. Interview with Arvilla Long.

55. Interview with Roy Mosteller. An editorial in the *Bee* discussed the dangers of children driving before they were capable of handling the machines safely (*Jefferson Bee*, 6 September 1916).

56. Interview with Fred Morain; interview with Kellogg Thomas.

57. Interview with Lumund Wilcox.

58. Lewis Atherton claims that the small town shopping area was basically a man's world before the turn of the century, and Hamlin Garland's short story, "A Day's Pleasure," describes the loneliness of a farm wife who had no place to go when she accompanied her husband on a trip to town in midweek.

59. Interview with Walter Stidwell.

60. By the end of the 1920s there were almost always grocery store ads in the *Bee* featuring specials.

61. See Lewis Atherton, *Main Street on the Middle Border* (Chicago: Quadrangle Books, 1954) 237–40. The subject of the small town as a retail center attracted considerable research interest throughout the Midwest. See Neil Salisbury and Gerard Rushton, *Growth and Decline of Iowa Villages: A Pilot Study* (Iowa City: State Univ. of Iowa, Department of Geography, 1963); Carle C. Zimmerman, *Farm Trade Centers in Minnesota, 1905–1929,* Bulletin No. 269 (Minneapolis: Univ. of Minnesota Agricultural Experimental Station, 1939); Paul Landis, *South Dakota Town-Country Relations, 1901–1931,* Bulletin No. 274 (Brookings: South Dakota State College of Agriculture Experimental Station, 1932); Paul D. Converse, *The Automobile and the Village Merchant: The Influence of Automobiles and Paved Roads on the Business of Illinois Village Merchants,* Bulletin No. 19 (Urbana: Univ. of Illinois, College of Commerce and Business Administration, 1928); Vernon B. Morrison, *The Influence of Automobiles and Good Roads on*

Retail Trade Centers, Nebraska Studies in Business No. 18 (Lincoln: Univ. of Nebraska, Committee on Business Research of the College of Business Administration, Extension Division of the Univ. of Nebraska, 1927); John Kolb and R. A. Polson, *Trends in Town and Country Relations,* Bulletin No. 117 (Madison: Univ. of Wisconsin Agricultural Experimental Station, 1933).

62. See Moline, *Mobility and the Small Town,* Chapter 6.

63. Interview with Bess Harding.

64. Interview with Wilma Downes.

65. *Jefferson Bee,* 4 April 1916. The practice of rural students boarding in town continued for some time past the initial introduction of automobiles. In 1917 a short item appeared in the *Bee* stating that Superintendent Smith "wants places for boys and girls who wish to work for their board while attending high school" (*Bee,* 29 August 1917).

66. See the *Jefferson Bee* "1954 Greene County Centennial Edition" for information on various towns and townships.

67. Interview with Ken Kinsman.

68. Interview with Beryl Dillavou.

69. Interview with Grace Wadsworth.

70. Interview with Kellogg Thomas.

71. My mother related that as late as the 1930s, some older students might show up for a course only on Friday afternoons preceding football games to maintain their eligibility.

72. Interview with Kellogg Thomas.

73. See also Moline, *Mobility and the Small Town,* 116–19, who notes similar innovations in his study of Oregon, Illinois, during the same period.

74. Quoted in Berger, *The Devil Wagon,* 132.

75. Interview with Alma Wadsworth.

76. Interview with Gene Melson.

77. Interview with Ross and Gladys Finch. Moline discusses the sponsorship of band concerts by Oregon, Illinois, merchants to attract business (*Mobility and the Small Town,* 111).

78. *52 Years of Progress* (Jefferson: The Jefferson Telephone Company), 8.

79. Ibid., 10.

80. Ibid., 11.

81. Ibid., 37.

82. Ibid., 12.

83. Ibid., 37.

84. *Jefferson Souvenir,* 15 March 1902.

85. Interviews with Barbara Hamilton and Helen Sherwood.

86. *Jefferson Bee,* 8 February 1894.

87. Ibid., 15 February 1894.

88. *Iowa Illustrated* (Jefferson Edition) 1, no. 2 (June 1896).

89. *Jefferson Bee,* 21 November 1907; 27 May 1908.

90. Clayton Brown, *Electricity for Rural America: The Fight of the REA* (Westport, Conn.: Greenwood Press, 1980), xii, xiv.

91. *People—Their Power: The Rural Electric Fact Book,* ed. Erma Angevine (Washington: National Rural Electric Cooperative Association, 1980), 4.

92. Interview with Dorothy Bowley.

93. Brown, *Electricity,* 5, 11.

94. The story of rural electrification is interesting but beyond the time frame of this study. In 1982 I completed a seventy-two-page history commissioned by the Greene County Rural Electric Co-operative entitled *Rural Electrification Comes to West Central Iowa.* It is available at the Greene County REC office.

CHAPTER 5. Morality: *Thine Infinite Iniquities*

1. Sidney Mead, *The Lively Experiment* (New York: Harper and Row, 1963), 136.

2. *Jefferson Bee,* 5 July 1916.

3. Ibid.

4. House File 327, *Iowa Index to House and Senate Bills,* 37th General Assembly, 1917.

5. *Jefferson Bee,* 23 May 1917.

6. Ibid.

7. *Jefferson Bee,* 20 June 1917.

8. Ibid.

9. Senate File 225, *Iowa Index to House and Senate Bills,* 38th General Assembly, 1919.

10. See *Jefferson Bee,* 10 June 1925; 17 June 1925.

11. Ibid., 12 June 1929.

12. House File 446, *Iowa Index to House and Senate Bills,* 45th General Assembly, 1933.

13. Interview with Gene Melson. One of the best interpretations of the motivations of the temperance forces is Norman Clark's *Deliver Us From Evil: An Interpretation of America's Prohibition Movement* (New York: Norton, 1976). Joseph Gusfield, *Symbolic Crusade: Status Politics and the American Temperance Movement* (Urbana, Ill.: Univ. of Illinois Press, 1963) argues that for the temperance elements, Prohibition was important because it symbolized the dominance of the godly.

14. Dan E. Clark, "Recent Liquor Legislation in Iowa," *Iowa Journal of History and Politics* 15 (January 1917): 60–65.

15. *Jefferson Bee,* 12 July 1916. The article was entitled "Booze Scores Again. Leads to Murder in Kendrick."

16. Ibid., 6 December 1915.

17. Ibid., 12 January 1916.

18. Ibid., 10 January 1917.

19. Ibid., 12 January 1916.

20. Lewis Atherton, *Main Street on the Middle Border* (New York: Quadrangle, 1975), 105.

21. See Thomas G. Ryan, "Supporters and Opponents of Prohibition: Iowa in 1917," *Annals of Iowa,* 46 (Winter 1983): 510-522. Ryan identifies three factors that he claims best statistically predict support or opposition to Prohibition: "In the 1917 referendum, three types of counties gave considerably more support to the state prohibition proposal than others. They were Protestant counties, counties in which the largest proportions of men favored women suffrage, and counties with the largest percentage of residents whose families had lived in the United States for at least three generations. Opposition to prohibition was strongest in the most German counties, in the most Catholic counties, and in counties where men demonstrated little support for women suffrage" (pp. 514–15). All three factors predicting support for Prohibition were strong in Greene County.

22. Frederick Lewis Allen, *Only Yesterday* (New York: Bantam Books, 1959), 70.

23. As a child in Jefferson, I had heard the rumors about Templeton's "Chicago Connection." When I was teaching at Iowa State, I supervised an honors student in an oral history project among Templeton residents. Stories of how Templeton Rye reached Chicago speakeasies have deep roots in Templeton folklore.

24. Ryan, "Supporters and Opponents of Prohibition."

25. The election results are taken from the *Jefferson Bee,* 7 June 1916, 17 October 1917, and 23 June 1933.

26. Interview with Blanche Sutton McWilliam.

27. Interview with Gene Melson.

28. Ibid.

29. Interview with Roy Mosteller; interview with Fred Morain.

30. See Carroll L. Engelhardt, "The Common School and the Ideal Citizen," (Ph.D. diss., Univ. of Iowa, 1969).

31. Interview with Alice Ann Andrew.

32. William H. Whyte, *The Organization Man* (New York: Simon and Schuster, 1956), 16. See especially Chapter 3.

33. Reprinted from *Leslie's Magazine* in the *Jefferson Bee,* 16 June 1915.

34. Gusfield, *Symbolic Crusade,* 8.

35. Interview with Gene Melson.

36. Frederick Lewis Allen, *The Big Change* (New York: Bantam Books, 1961), 94.

37. As early as 1959, historian Henry F. May argued that the significant changes in manners and morals preceded the war and were not its result. See May, *The End of American Innocence: A Study of the First Years of Our Own Time, 1912-1917* (New York: Knopf, 1959). A useful review of primary sources supporting May's argument can be found in James R. McGovern, "The American Woman's Pre-World War I Freedom in Manners and Morals," *Journal of American History* 55 (September 1968): 315-33.

38. Robert Lynd and Helen Lynd, *Middletown* (New York: Harcourt, Brace and World, 1924), 271.

39. *Jefferson Bee*, 15 December 1915.

40. Interview with Wilma Downes.

41. Interview with Bess Osgood.

42. Did you really think I was going to tell you who said that?

43. Interview with Helen Sherlock and Odessa Brown.

44. *Jefferson Bee*, 11 March 1925.

45. Ibid.

46. Will Hays, quoted in Allen, *Only Yesterday*, 72.

47. Mary P. Ryan, "The Projection of a New Womanhood: The Movie Moderns in the 1920s," in *Our American Sisters: Women in American Life and Thought*, eds. Jean E. Friedman and William G. Slade (Boston: Allyn and Bacon 1973), 371-72, 373.

48. Information on the history of the Jefferson chautauquas was provided by Gene Melson in a lecture at the "Chautauqua" of the "Autobiography" project, 16 October 1979.

49. Atherton, *Main Street*, 327. See also Melvin Gingerich, "The Washington Chautauqua," *Palimpsest* 26 (December 1945): 370-76; Oney Fred Sweet, "Through Iowa on Chautauqua," *Iowa Journal of History and Politics* 39 (April 1941): 115-47; Harrison John Thornton, "Chautauqua in Iowa," *Iowa Journal of History and Politics* 50 (April 1952): 97-122.

50. Melson lecture.

51. Interview with Kellogg Thomas.

52. *Jefferson Bee*, 6 April 1910.

53. Ibid.

54. In Winifred Van Etten's essay, she puts golf and tennis together as forms of suspect entertainment for small town residents. She writes: "Tennis, like that other foreign game, golf, or pasture pool as we called it, was for effete foreigners like the remittance men. We had the true bumpkin mentality. Whatever was outside our limited experience was bound to be either wicked or ludicrous" ["Three Worlds," in *Growing Up in Iowa*, ed. Clarence Andrews (Ames: Iowa State Univ. Press, 1978), 148].

55. Interview with Fred Morain.

56. *Jefferson Bee*, 10 January 1917.

57. Interview with Wayne Winey.

58. *Des Moines Register*, 14 July 1925.

59. *Jefferson Herald*, 24 July 1925.

60. *Jefferson Bee*, 22 July 1925. On 9 May 1928 the *Bee* ran a long front-page article by "Minister V. W. Gilbert" blasting evolution and Darrow. Gilbert maintained that a belief in the Bible is essential for the moral principles on which civilized society depends.

61. Interview with Gene Melson.

CHAPTER 6. World War I: *The Noise of War*

1. *Jefferson Bee*, 15 July 1914.

2. Ibid., 26 August 1914.

3. Ibid., 29 July 1914.

4. Ibid., 5 August 1914.

5. *Jefferson Bee*, 9 September 1914. This view was shared by numerous other

Iowans. John T. Adams from Dubuque, who ran for Republican national chairman in 1918, sent a letter to the *Dubuque Telegraph Herald* in August 1914 that placed blame for the war on Great Britain's resentment of growing German prosperity. The kaiser and the German people, wrote Adams, were the "most peace-loving people in the world." Germany's only "crime" was her interference with British commerce. The letter returned to haunt Adams four years later in his bid for the GOP chair, but when he wrote it, his views were widely shared. (See *Bee*, 20 February 1918.)

6. *Jefferson Bee*, 16 September 1914; 2 December 1914.

7. Ibid., 5 August 1914.

8. Ibid., 25 November 1914.

9. Ibid., 5 August 1914; 9 September 1914.

10. Ibid., 12 August 1914

11. Ibid., 17 February 1915.

12. *Des Moines Register*, 7 May 1915; 10 May 1915.

13. *Jefferson Bee*, 12 May 1915; *Des Moines Register*, 10 May 1917.

14. Cited in *Jefferson Bee*, 14 July 1915.

15. Ibid., 17 February 1915. See also 21 July 1915.

16. Ibid., 17 May 1916; 13 September 1916; 10 November 1915.

17. Ibid., 19 April 1916.

18. Ibid., 28 February 1917.

19. Ibid., 19 April 1916.

20. Ibid., 4 April 1916.

21. Ibid., 11 April 1917.

22. Ibid., 17 May 1917; see also Filene, *Him/Her/Self*, 105–27.

23. *Jefferson Bee*, 11 April 1917; see also 18 July 1917.

24. Ibid., 11 April 1917.

25. *Des Moines Register*, 7 September 1914. The *Register* had reported on 23 August 1914 that the German government was asking for fairness in the coverage of war events. Editorials on 17 September and 27 September cited news censorship on both sides and advised readers to make no judgment on the validity of atrocity stories coming from official sources of either side.

26. Ibid., 9 May 1917.

27. Ibid., 10 July 1918.

28. Ibid., 23 January 1917.

29. Ibid., 3 July 1918.

30. Interview with Fred Morain.

31. *Jefferson Bee*, 25 April 1917.

32. Ibid., 24 July 1918.

33. Interview with Grace Wadsworth.

34. *Jefferson Bee*, 19 September 1917. A *Bee* editorial on 18 July noted that Newton also banned German and recommended Spanish as a replacement.

35. Ibid., 15 August 1917; see also 16 January 1918.

36. Ibid., 15 June 1918.

37. Ibid., 20 February 1918.

38. Ibid., 28 November 1917.

39. Ibid., 1 March 1916; 11 April 1917.

40. Interview with Loren Durlam.

41. *Jefferson Bee*, 13 February 1918; 4 June 1918.

42. However horrible the carnage or tragic the loss of life that war brings, there is nevertheless an undeniable attraction to the excitement and sense of purpose that it generates. As philosopher Robert Nisbet states, "One of the most impressive aspects of contemporary war is the intoxicating atmosphere of spiritual unity that arises out of the common consciousness of participating in a moral crusade. . . . With the outbreak of war, there is a termination of many of the factionalisms and sectarian animosities which ordinarily reflect the moral perplexities of modern politics. In their place comes what the English philosopher L. P. Jacks has so aptly called the 'spiritual peace that war brings.' To remark cynically that such tranquility is artificial, that it rests upon an unmoral basis,

misses the more important point that tranquility is a foremost goal of modern man and that he is prone to accept it as he finds it. We should be blind if we did not recognize in the war state . . . qualities that stand in the most attractive contrast to the instability and the sense of meaninglessness of modern industrial and political life" (*Quest for Community* [New York: Oxford Univ. Press, 1953], 41).

43. *Jefferson Bee,* 31 July 1918.
44. Ibid., 25 April 1917.
45. Ibid., 6 June 1917.
46. Ibid., 25 July 1917.
47. Ibid., 22 August 1917.
48. Ibid., 15 August 1917.
49. Ibid., 22 August 1917.
50. Ibid., 12 September 1917.
51. Ibid., 5 September 1917.
52. Ibid., 22 September 1917.
53. Joan Muyskens, "Merle Hay and His Town," *Annals of Iowa* 39 (Summer 1967): 31. Hay was buried in Bathelmont, France. In 1921 the body was brought back for burial in Glidden. On a pier in Hoboken, New Jersey, Gen. John J. Pershing placed wreaths on the coffins of Hay and the other two killed in that battle in memorial services for all American soldiers who lost their lives. On 21 July a large crowd assembled for burial services in the Westlawn Cemetery at Glidden. Dr. B. C. Hamilton of Jefferson led a military honor guard, and Ross Finch played "Taps." The state of Iowa erected a large stone memorial to Hay in 1930 (*Annals,* 31).
54. *Jefferson Bee,* 12 September 1917.
55. Ibid., 28 August 1918.
56. Ibid.
57. Ibid., 12 June 1918; 31 October 1917.
58. Ibid., 9 January 1918.
59. Ibid., 30 May 1917.
60. Ibid., 24 October 1917.
61. Ibid., 20 March 1918; 27 March 1918.
62. Ibid., 25 September 1918.
63. Ibid., 21 May 1919.
64. Ibid., 23 January 1918.
65. Ibid., 30 January 1918.
66. Ibid., 6 February 1918.
67. Ibid., 15 May 1918; 10 July 1918.
68. Ibid., 5 June 1918. Jefferson contributions were listed one week and the amounts from each school district around the county were given the following edition.
69. Ibid., 27 February 1918.
70. Ibid., 18 August 1918.
71. Interview with Jake Stevens.
72. *Jefferson Bee,* 10 April 1918.
73. Ibid.
74. Ibid., 25 December 1918.
75. Ibid., 7 August 1918.
76. Interview with Henry Stevens.
77. *Jefferson Bee,* 2 January 1918.
78. Ibid., 9 January 1918.
79. Ibid., 24 October 1917; 31 October 1917. In another project, the local DAR chapter "adopted" Louis Tronchetti, a young Italian immigrant from Jefferson, and sent him presents during his military service since he had no other family in America.
80. Ibid., 6 February 1918; 13 March 1918.
81. Ibid., 2 January 1918.
82. Ibid., 26 June 1918.
83. Ibid., 31 July 1918.
84. Ibid., 13 March 1918; 16 October 1918.

85. Ibid., 6 August 1918.

86. Ibid., 16 October 1918.

87. Ibid., 20 November 1918.

88. Interview with Wayne Winey.

89. Interview with Gladys Finch.

90. Interview with Wayne Winey.

91. Interview with Nellie Derry.

92. *Jefferson Bee*, 8 January 1919; interview with Helen Sherlock and Odessa Brown; *Jefferson Bee*, 26 February 1919.

93. *Report of State Board of Health for the Biennial Period Ending June 30, 1920* (Des Moines: State of Iowa, 1921), 26.

94. *Jefferson Bee*, 9 October 1918.

95. Ibid., 13 November 1918.

96. Ibid., 4 December 1918; 11 December 1918; 5 February 1919; 19 February 1919.

97. Ibid., 11 December 1918; 15 January 1919; 28 May 1919.

98. Interview with Jake Stevens.

99. *Jefferson Bee*, 19 February 1919; 26 February 1919; 7 May 1919.

100. Ibid., 24 March 1920; 20 June 1920.

101. Ibid., 20 June 1920; 11 August 1920.

102. John A. Garraty, *The American Nation* (New York: Harper and Row, 1966), 696.

103. Interview with Jake Stevens.

CHAPTER 7. Boom and Bust: *The Water of Gall*

1. Leland Sage, *A History of Iowa* (Ames: Iowa State Univ. Press, 1974), 249.

2. Gilbert Fite, *American Agriculture and Farm Policy Since 1900,* The American Historical Association (New York: Macmillan 1964), 6.

3. Quoted in Earle D. Ross, *Iowa Agriculture: An Historical Survey* (Iowa City: State Historical Society of Iowa, 1951), 119–20.

4. William G. Murray, "Prosperity and Land Boom," *Palimpsest* 48, no. 10 (October 1967): 461.

5. Theodore Saloutos and John D. Hicks, *Agriculture Discontent in the Middle West* (Madison: Univ. of Wisconsin Press, 1951), 89. Sage makes the same point in his discussion of the subject. (See Sage, *History of Iowa,* 249).

6. Sage, *History of Iowa,* 249.

7. Murray, "Prosperity," 462.

8. In a few weeks Pearson went to Washington, D.C., where he served as an assistant secretary in the Department of Agriculture (Ross, *Iowa Agriculture,* 141).

9. Barton Morgan, *A History of the Extension Service of Iowa State College* (Ames: Collegiate Press, 1934), 54.

10. Interview with Floyd Stevens.

11. Ross, *Iowa Agriculture,* 124. For a history of drainage in Greene County, see the detailed article on the subject by S. J. Melson in the "1954 Greene County Centennial Edition," *Jefferson Bee.*

12. See Morgan, *History,* 54–58.

13. Morgan, *History,* 54.

14. A. B. Gruening, "Agriculture in the World War Period," *Yearbook of Agriculture, 1940,* United States Department of Agriculture (Washington, D.C.: U.S. Government Printing Office, 1940), 277; Morgan, *History,* 54; *Iowa Yearbook of Agriculture, 1916, 1919.*

15. Gruening, "Agriculture," 286.

16. *Jefferson Bee,* 26 January 1921.

17. Murray, "Prosperity," 462.

18. Saloutos and Hicks, *Agriculture Discontent,* 103.

19. John Kenneth Galbraith, "Vision of Boundless Hope and Optimism", in *The 1920s: Problems and Paradoxes,* ed. Milton Plesur (Boston: Allyn and Bacon, 1969), 174.

20. *Jefferson Bee,* 3 March 1920; 4 August 1920.

21. Interview with Jake Stevens; *Jefferson Bee,* 3 March 1920.

22. Interview with Kellogg Thomas.

23. *Greene County Financial Report, 1918, 1920* (Jefferson, Iowa: Greene County).

24. William G. Murray, "Two Depressions," *Palimpsest* 48, no. 10 (October 1967): 473.

25. *Wallaces' Farmer,* 27 December 1918, 1891, quoted in Saloutos and Hicks, 99.

26. Chester C. Davis, "The Development of Agriculture Policy Since the End of the World War," *Yearbook of Agriculture, 1940,* U.S. Department of Agriculture, (Washington, D.C.: U. S. Government Printing Office, 1940), 292.

27. Saloutos and Hicks, *Agriculture Discontent,* 55.

28. Ibid., 194.

29. Interview with Charles Hird. For a detailed statistical study of farm loans in another central Iowa county, see William G. Murray, "An Economic Analysis of Farm Mortgages in Story County, Iowa, 1854–1931," Agricultural Experiment Station Research Bulletin No. 156 (Ames: Iowa State College of Agriculture and Mechanic Arts, January 1933).

30. Interview with Charles Hird.

31. Jerry A. Neprash, *The Brookhart Campaign in Iowa, 1920-1926: A Study in the Motivation of Political Attitudes* (New York: Columbia Univ. Press, 1932), 65.

32. Sage, *History of Iowa,* 254.

33. Interview with Gene Melson.

34. Interview with Ralph Maloney.

35. *Jefferson Bee,* 21 July 1920.

36. Interview with Gene Melson.

37. Interview with Charles Hird.

38. *Jefferson Bee,* 16 December 1925.

39. Ibid., 9 December 1925.

40. Ibid., 24 October 1927.

41. Ibid., 17 February 1927.

42. Interview with Charles Hird.

43. Interview with Ralph Maloney.

44. Interview with James Hilton.

45. Interview with Robert Milligan.

46. *Jefferson Bee,* 28 January 1926.

47. Interview with Bess Osgood.

48. *Jefferson Bee,* 3 March 1926.

49. Ibid., 3 February 1926.

50. Ibid., 25 April 1923.

51. Henry C. Wallace, quoted in Ross, *Iowa Agriculture,* 153.

52. See *Jefferson Bee,* 20 November 1920.

53. Ibid., 20 April 1921. In comparison, the Jefferson chief of police was making $1,200, the street commissioner $1,500, and the county auditor $1,900.

54. I am indebted here to the excellent analysis of the Iowa farm organizations by Joseph F. Wall in "The Iowa Farmer in Crisis, 1920-1936," *Annals of Iowa* (Fall 1983): 120–21.

55. Ibid., 119.

56. Interview with James Hilton. On 30 June 1920 the *Bee* ran a history of the Farm Bureau in Greene County.

57. Morgan, *History,* 66.

58. Sage, *History of Iowa,* 256.

59. Ibid., 254–56.

60. Neprash, *Brookhart Campaign,* 72.

61. Ibid., 51.

62. Sage, *History of Iowa,* 266.

63. *Jefferson Bee*, 22 October 1924.
64. Sage, *History of Iowa*, 266.
65. John D. Hicks, *Republican Ascendancy, 1921–1933* (New York: Harper, 1960), 199.
66. *Farmers' Union Herald*, March 1927, quoted in Saloutos and Hicks, *Agriculture Discontent*, 400.
67. *Jefferson Bee*, 2 March 1927.
68. Ibid., 31 March 1927.
69. Ibid., 17 November 1927.
70. Ibid., 30 May 1928.
71. Sage, *History of Iowa*, 270.
72. Quoted in Hicks, *Republican Ascendancy* 204.
73. *Jefferson Bee*, 24 October 1928.
74. Ibid., 4 April 1928; *Sioux City Journal*, reprinted in *Jefferson Bee*, 4 July 1928. See also *Bee*, 25 July 1928.
75. Walter Lippmann, in Paul A. Carter, "Campaign of 1928 Re-Examined: A Study in Political Folklore," in Plesur, *The 1920s*, 65.
76. *Jefferson Bee*, 1 August 1928.
77. Like Carter's "Campaign of 1928 Re-Examined," another work that challenges the thesis that Smith lost primarily because he was Catholic is Richard Hofstadter, "Could a Protestant Have Beaten Hoover in 1928?," *The Reporter*, 22 (17 March 1960): 31 ff.
78. William Allen White, quoted in *Jefferson Bee*, 25 July 1928.
79. *Jefferson Bee*, 1 August 1928.
80. Ibid., 24 October 1928.
81. Samuel Lubell, *The Future of American Politics* (Garden City, N.Y.: Doubleday 1955), 35–42.
82. Wall, "Iowa Farmer," 118.

CHAPTER 8.   Conclusion: *Days Should Speak*

1. *Jefferson Bee*, 14 January 1931.
2. Ibid., 28 January 1931.
3. Norman V. Strand, "Prices of Farm Products in Iowa, 1851–1940," Research Bulletin 303, Agricultural Experiment Station, Iowa State College, Ames, Iowa, 1942.
4. *Jefferson Bee*, 28 January 1931; 18 March 1931;
5. Ibid., 28 January 1931.
6. Ibid., 7 January 1931; 14 February 1933.
7. Ibid., 27 September 1932.
8. Ibid., 21 February 1933.
9. Ibid., 30 September 1931.
10. Leland Sage, *A History of Iowa*, (Ames: Iowa State Univ. Press, 1974), 280.
11. Interview with Bess Osgood.
12. *Jefferson Bee*, 27 December 1932.
13. C. H. Mitchell, quoted in *Jefferson Bee*, 2 May 1933.
14. William W. Sweet, *The Story of Religion in America* (New York: Harper, 1950), 373.
15. *Jefferson Bee*, 31 October 1928.
16. Robert Lynd and Helen Lynd, *Middletown* (New York: Harcourt, Brace, and World, 1924), 271.
17. The essay is included in Milton Plesur, ed., *The 1920s: Problems and Paradoxes* (Boston: Allyn and Bacon, 1969), 184–93.
18. *Jefferson Bee*, 18 February 1931.
19. Ibid., 29 April 1931.
20. Ibid., 26 September 1933.
21. Ibid., 18 February 1931; 29 April 1931.

22. Ibid., 2 September 1931; 17 February 1932.

23. Ibid., 18 July 1933.

24. Ibid., 5 September 1933.

25. Ibid., 6 January 1932.

26. Ibid., 2 May 1933.

27. Ibid., 28 March 1933.

28. Robert Dahl, *After the Revolution?* (New Haven: Yale Univ. Press, 1970), 142–47.

29. Peter Schrag attributes the "decline of the WASP" in recent American culture to a loss of vitality in the local community, which Anglo-Saxons had traditionally dominated. He writes: "The enervation of WASP culture may derive, more than anything, from a loss of place. The geographic and psychic worlds of the old mainstream become less distinct, but certain special neighborhoods, even if they are a generation away, survive as regions of the mind. The sense of place: Salem and Boston and Concord; Zenith and Winesburg; Yoknapatawpha County. It produced people with accents and fashions and biases – personalities – that they carried around as overtly as parasols and walking sticks. And because they knew who they were, they were quite willing to be eccentric and crazy. . . . But how much of a sense of place can grow in a bedroom suburb? What is the inner sense of Bronxville or Winnetka?" ("The Decline of the WASP," *Harper's Magazine,* April, 1970, 89–90).

INDEX

Adel, Iowa, 5
Agriculture
  butter production, 30
  domestic allotment proposal for, 249
  farm income, 249
  farm size, 59
  "Golden Age," 212
  horse production, 30
  land values, 30, 213–14, 217–18,
    221–22
  mechanization, 30, 216
  politics after WW I, 234–46. *See also*
    McNary-Haugen Bill
  protest movements, nineteenth
    century, 31
  tenancy, 29, 59, 248
  WW I, 214–20
Albert, E. G., 97
Alcohol. *See* Prohibition
Allison, William Boyd, 70
American Automobile Association
    (AAA), road guides, 117–18
American Home Missionary Society, 9
Anderson, Frank, 74
Anderson, Sherwood, 256
Andrew, Alice Ann, 99
Anglo-Saxon tradition, 33, 70–71
Aplington, Iowa, 96
Automobiles
  and community norms, 166
  early models, 110–12. *See also* Model-
    T Ford
  family driving patterns, 125–26
  farmer's response to, 112–14, 116–17
  and farm women, 131
  and high school enrollment, 137
  and local government, 119–21. *See
    also* Road Maintenance; Schools

and long-distance travel, 117–18
  in Midwest, 110, 117
  rentals of, 112
  and retailing and shopping, 132–34
  and rural churches, 138–39
  speed limits of, 112
  and tires, 115–16
  and town women, 126

Bagley, Iowa, 95–96
Baker, Margaret, 44
Bands, 75, 139–40
Banks, 223–32, 248
Baptist Church, 13, 43
Barr, Cleve, 57, 58
Baseball, Sunday games, 148–49
Beecher, Catharine, 9
Berschorner, Anton, 190
"Birth of a Nation," 37
Blacks. *See* Population, Greene County,
    by race; Race
Blake, C. W., 206
Blue Grass Palace (Creston), 32
Blue laws. *See* Sunday observance, laws
    governing
Boone Military Company, 189
Bowley, Dorothy, 145
Boxing prizefights, 81, 91
Boy Scouts, 80, 173, 206
Bradley, Charles C., 255
Bradley, Eva, 63
Brookhart, Smith W., 236–41, 251
Brown, Arta, 206
Brown, Floyd, 177
Brunner, Mike, 48
Bryan, William Jennings, 31, 69, 71,
    173, 180
Buchanan, James, 11

Bus service, 141
Buttrick, Enos, 5–6

Caldwell, C. W., 166
Camp Dodge, 196–97, 207
Camping trips, Raccoon River, 58
Capper-Volstead Act, 236
Card playing, 157–58, 165, 175–76
Carnegie Foundation, 91
Carroll County, Iowa, 6, 68, 155, 158
Carter, E. H., 57
Cassady, Simon, 231
Catholic Church
  county population, 42
  early history of, 22
  Irish membership of, 42
  and relations with Protestants, 43–56
Catt, Carrie Chapman, 96
Caulfield, Thomas, 189
Chautauqua, 36, 170–71
Chicago, 258
Chicago and North Western Railroad,
  25, 26
Christian Church (Disciples), 13
Churches
  membership increase, 259
  and political activity, 67–68
  and rural congregations, 138–39
  and social order, 13, 14
  and state, 14
  and women, 14
Church of Christ, 139
Churdan, Iowa, 25, 26
Civil War, 11–12
Clarke, Howard, 240
Clubs. *See* Service clubs; Women, Club
  movement
Coal Palace (Ottumwa), 32
Coal strike of 1919, 39
Cockerill, Charles, 141–43, 188, 199–
  200, 204, 205
Community clubs, rural, 105
Cook, Mary, 96
Coolidge, Calvin, 238–42
Coon Rapids, Iowa, 186
Cooper, Iowa, 25
Corn Palace (Sioux City), 32
Cottam (black football player), 36
Country Life Commission, 100
County People (Ruth Suckow), 59, 61,
  126
Crime in 1920s, 257

Crooks, V. B., 23
Cudahy, Margaret, 49

Dana, Iowa, 25
Dancing, 158–59, 165, 167. *See also*
  Gobblers' Nob (dance hall); Schools,
  high school prom; Spring Lake
Darrow, Clarence, 173–74
Daughters of American Revolution
  (DAR), 201, 204
Davis, Charles (early settler), 3
Davis, Charles (Extension agent), 105
Davis, Fred, 198
Davis, James, 3
Davis, John, 239
Davis, May, 3, 5
Davis, Truman, 3, 5, 6
Dean, F. M., 141
Delco power systems, 145
Delta Kappa sorority, 92
Democratic Party, 11–12, 68–69, 232
Denison, Iowa, 138, 255
Derry, Fred, 57
Des Moines, Iowa, 258
Dickinson, Lester J., 188, 250
Dillavou, James, 115
Dillavou, Marge, 126
Dillavou, Myrtle, 135
Dolliver, Jonathan, 68, 70
Domestic allotment proposal, 249
Douglas, Stephen, 11
Downes, Wilma, 63
Drainage districts, 215
"Duff Road," 59
Dunning Academy, 13, 85

Eagleson, George, 141
Eastern Star, 22
Edison, Thomas, 143
Elections
  1854, 7
  1856, 11
  1860, 11
  1864, 11
  1876, 31
  1896, 31, 69
  1900, 69
  1904, 69
  1916, 182
  1918, 188
  1920, 232, 236
  1922, 237–38

1924, 239–40
1926, 240–41
1928, 243–45
1932, 250–51
Electricity, 143–46. *See also* Rural Electric Administration
Ethnic groups. *See* Immigration
Extension Service. *See* Iowa State Extension Service

Farlin, Iowa, 25
Farm Bureau, 106, 107, 233, 236, 241
Farmers and Merchants Bank of Churdan, 225
Farmers Holiday Association, 250, 255
Farmers State Bank of Paton, 248
Farmers Union, 233–34, 239, 241
Farm labor. *See* Hired hands
Farm life
  dissatisfied farm women, 99–108
  retirement to, 61
  and social inferiority, 61, 136–37
  superiority of, 99, 101
Field, Henry, 251
Finch, Roy, 58
Finn, A. J., 44, 68
First National Bank, 224–25
Flour milling, 27, 29
Flu epidemic, 206–8
Football, 36. *See also* Schools, extracurricular activities
Foy, E. W., 141
Fraternal organizations, 22–23
Frazier, Ben, 232
Frazier, Jon, 232
Fremont, John C., 11
Friends Church, 139
Funeral homes, 173

Gallup, George, 12, 133
Gallup, Josephus, 12
Gamble, Ed, 107
Gamble, Fred, 107
Gamble, Grace, 126
Garber, Jan, 158
Gender
  and democratic theory, 72
  and traditional roles, 73
Girl Scouts, 173
Gobblers' Nob (dance hall), 131, 158
Good Roads Movement, 122–25. *See also* Road maintenance

Graham, E. G., 150
Grain Futures Act, 236
Grand Junction, Iowa, 25, 110
Greenback Party, 31
Greene County Board of Supervisors, 86, 232, 258
Greene County Farm Improvement Association, 190
Greene County Gazette, 24
Griffith, D. W., 37
Grimmell, Gus, 63

Haag, Henry, 121–22, 154
Hamilton, B. C., 189
Hamilton, Ida, 126
Harding, Bess, 62
Harding, Warren G., 210
Harding, William, 67, 122, 187, 214
Harding, Winifred, 62
Harlan, Iowa, 96
Harris, Orville, 69, 250, 255
Havner, Horace, 149–50
Hay, Merle, 97
Hayes, Rutherford, 31
Head, Albert, 86, 225
Head, Mahlon, 225
Head, Roscoe, 225
Henderson, David B., 70
Herring, Clyde, 238, 255
Hilton, James, 107, 226, 234
Hired hands, 60
Hoboes, 61–62
Holden, J. W., 120
Hoover, Herbert, 203–4, 214, 243–46, 251
Horse and buggy travel, and county lines, 109
Houston, Theo, 92
Howard, A. D., 150–51
Hughes, Charles Evans, 182
Hutchinson, Fred, 58
Hutchinson Bicycle Shop, 58

Immigration, 37–42
  and 1928 election, 245
Income tax, 199
Inflation, post-WW I, 216–19
Ingham, Harvey, 242
Ingleside Club, 92
Iowa Advocate, 24
Iowa Argus, 24
Iowa Homestead, 236, 239

Iowa legislature, urban representation
    restrictions, 245
Iowa State Bank, 231
Iowa State College, 105–6
Iowa State Extension Service, 106–7,
    215
Iowa State Highway Commission, 118,
    120–21, 124, 125
Iowa Transcontinental Road
    Association, 121–22

Jefferson, settlement of, 8, 25–26
Jefferson Bee, 23–24
Jefferson Citizen, 24
Jefferson City Council, 86, 91
Jefferson Country Club, 56–57, 165
Jefferson Culture Club, 86, 92
Jefferson Democrat, 24
Jefferson Era, 23
Jefferson Free Lance, 24
Jefferson Friday Club, 85–92
Jefferson Herald, 24
Jefferson Light, Heat, Power, and
    Water Co., 143
Jefferson Lions Club, 173
Jefferson Record, 23
Jefferson Savings Bank, 225–26
Jefferson Souvenir, 24
Jefferson Standard, 24
Jefferson Star, 23
Jefferson State Bank, 231
Jefferson Woman's Club, 92–93, 96, 204
Johnson, J. K., Sr., 110

Kansas-Nebraska Act, 7
Kenyon, William, 236–37
Kirkpatrick, A. J., 24
Knights Templar, 22
Ku Klux Klan, 47–49

Labor unions, 39, 239
Ladies Reading Circle, 85
Law enforcement, 257–58
League of Nations, 210
LeMars, Iowa, 255
Lewis, Sinclair, 257
Library, Jefferson Public, 86, 91
Library, state traveling, 106
Life insurance, 59
Lincoln, Abraham, 11–12, 125
Lincoln Highway, 113, 123–25
Lincoln Highway Association, 122–25

Lodges, 22–23
Long, Arville, 131
Louk, Frances, 178
Lovejoy, Victor, 24, 25, 69, 70
Lowden, Frank, 242–43
Lowery, Will, 81–82
Lyon, Cap, 57

McCormick, Billy, 68
McCully, B. S., 189
McDuffie, W. G., 154, 224
McKinley, William, 31, 69, 71
McLaughlin, Pete, 58
McNary-Haugen Bill, 241–43
Mail order companies, 28
Mail service, 8
Male role
    and beast image, 75–77
    and character, 74–75
    and music, 75
    and religion, 77–83
    and traditional formulations, 75
Maloney, Ralph, 225–26
Margaret Fuller Club, 92
Martin, Charles, 107
Masons, 22
Masters, Edgar Lee, 256
Melson, Gene, 131
Melson, S. J., 199–200, 215
Menace, The, 46
Mencken, H. L., 256
Meredith, E. T., 122
Methodist Church, 13
    Epworth League, 50
Milligan, E. A., 140, 248
Milligan grain elevator, 226
Mills, Azor, 8–12
Missouri Compromise, 7
Model-T Ford, 58, 114–15, 116
Money, M. H., and M. L., 23
Montgomery Ward and Co., 28
Morain, Fred, 24, 58, 159
Morain, Myrtle, 108
Morain, Perce, 58
Morden, Elizabeth, 63
Morden, Leone, 63
Morden, Roy, 63
Morley, Maxine, 65
Moss, J. E., 125
Mosteller, Roy, 131
Movies
    and community norms, 166–70

and sexual emphases, 168–69
Movie stars, as role models, 169
Movie theaters, and Sunday
performances, 151
Moving day, March 1, 59
Mulct Act, 1893, 154
Murphy, Louis, 251
Murphy, Peter, 50
Myers, Will, 121

Negroes. *See* Population, Greene
County, by race; Race
Nesheim, Victor, 24
"New Jefferson," 8
Newspapers, 23
Nic-O-Let Park, 151
Nineteenth Amendment, 98

Occupation
census data, 1905–1925, 56
clothing industry, 66
domestic service, 64
teaching, 64–65
women, 22
Odd Fellows, 22
Old Settlers Association, 3
Oppenheimer, Chester, 113–24, 159
Oppenheimer, Julius, 178–79, 187
Oppenheimer's Clothing, 60
Osborn, Wayne M., 242
Osgood, Bess, 92, 111, 251

Packers and Stockyards Act, 236
Paton, Iowa, 25–26
Patterson, J. E. (Pat), 68
Pearson, Raymond, 214
Peat, Private, 206
PEO, 92
Phillips, William, 8
Population
Greene County, 7–8, 25
by race, 35
by religion, 42–43
towns, 26
Iowa, 7, 258
rural decline of, 31
urban gains, 255–56
Porter, Claude, 241
Potter, Mary, 83
Presbyterian Church, 13, 43
Primary election, 69
Progressive Party, 238–39

Prohibition, 67, 152–57, 243–44, 250.
See also Churches, political activity;
Women's Suffrage, and prohibition;
and bootlegging, 155–56
and drinkers, concern for, 152
and election of 1916, 152
and European immigrants, 41
and personal morality, 153–54
and referenda, 10, 154–57, 257
and social drinking, 1920s, 155
social ills of, 153–54
Protestant churches, 13, 71. *See also*
Prohibition
and Catholics, 43–56
and community moral norms, 147–48,
160, 165–66, 175–76
and community order, 14
and evolution, 173–75
minister, salaries of, 78
relative strength of, 73
and Social Gospel movement, 175
Public library, 86, 91

Quick, Herbert, 101, 102, 104–8

Raccoon River, 121
Race, 34–42. *See also* Cottam;
Population, Greene County;
Washington, Booker T.
and democratic theory, 36
and foreign policy, 38
Radio, and community norms, 166
Railroads, 7, 27, 235–37
Raver, Berneice, 57
Raver, Earl, 58
Redfield, Iowa, 36
Republican Party, 11–12, 68–70, 235–
45
Retail and professional services, 27
Retirement, farm couples, 61
Rhodes, Charles, 140
Richardson, Guy, 69
Rippey, Robert, 8, 27
Rippey, Iowa, 25–26, 110
Road maintenance, 118–25
expenditures by states, 123
in Greene County, 111, 121
military expenditures for, 8
and 1916 election, 122–23
Robinson, B. F., 8
Roelofsz, H. C., 100, 106
Roosevelt, Franklin D., 250, 260

Roosevelt, Theodore, 69, 81, 100–101
Rotary Club, 172
Royal Arch Masons, 22
Rural anxieties, about city, 39–42, 245–56
Rural Electric Administration, 146
Russell, Mary, 85
Russell, Pauline, 47–48, 50
Rutter, Bertha, 63
Rydings, May, 63

Sabbath observance, laws governing, 148–52
Saturday night, 57
Sayers, Jessie, 126
Sayers, S. J., 203
Schools. *See also* Automobiles, and high school enrollment; Teachers
  bus service for, 131, 136
  consolidation of, 13
  extracurricular activities, 137–38
  high school prom, 158–59
  in Jefferson, 13
Scopes trial, 173
Scranton, Iowa, 25, 26
Scranton Farmers and Merchants Bank, 248
Sears, Roebuck and Co., 28
Separation of church and state, 45–46
Service clubs, 171–73
Sexuality, theory of, 159–60
Shaw, Leslie, 32, 71
Sherman, Hoyt, 8
Simpson College, 167
Sixteenth Amendment, 199
Slavery, 7, 11
Slininger, Clyde, 173
Slininger, Wilma, 207
Slininger Funeral Home, 173
Slothower, A. E., 44
Smith, Al, 243
Smith, "Cotton Ed," 238
Social evolution, theory of, 34
Southern influence, 5–8
  and Civil War, 11
Spillman, W. J., 249
Spring Lake, 121, 158
Stassen, Harold, 4
State Highway Commission. *See* Iowa State Highway Commission
Steck, Daniel, 239–40
Stevens, Floyd, 124, 215

Stevens, Jake, 209–10, 211
Stevenson, John, 69
Stillman, E. B., 13, 24
Stillman, Elizabeth, 85
Stillman, Frank, 24, 36
Stillman, Paul, 24, 25, 69
Storm Lake, Iowa, 76
Strong, Josiah, 33
Suckow, Ruth. See *Country People*
Sunday, Billy, 78–79
Sunday observance, laws governing, 148–52
Sweet, Burton, 238
Swick, Robert, 175–76

Tam, Elry Hiram, 190
Taxes, post-war, 219–20
Teachers. *See also* Schools
  and certification, 64–65
  and males, decline of, 64
  and married women, 65–66
  and moral standards, 65
  and salaries, 65, 232
Telephones, 140–43
Temperance. *See* Prohibition
Templeton, Iowa, 155
"Templeton Rye," 155–56
Thomas, Kellogg, 46, 49–50
Tillman, Ben, 36
Tramps, 61–62
Tronchetti, Louis, 150–51
Tuberculosis testing, 250
Tucker, Bert, 57
Turner, Dan, 250
Twenty-first amendment, 257

Vest, Peter, 74

Wabash, St. Louis, Pacific, 26
Wadsworth, Grace, 63
Wallace, Henry A., 34, 101, 241
Wallace, Henry C., 232, 241
Wallaces' Farmer, 34, 241
Walton, George, 8
Washington, Booker T., 36
Welk, Lawrence, 158
White, Charlie, 226
Wilcox, Lumund, 70, 131
Wilcox, Nancy, 68
Wilson, Charles, 106
Wilson, E. B., 124, 203
Wilson, James ("Tama Jim"), 71

Wilson, M. L., 249
Wilson, Minnie, 63, 96, 106
Wilson, Ned, 58
Wilson, Woodrow, 114, 182, 201
Winey, Wayne, 207
Women. *See also* Automobiles, and
    town women; Farm life, dissatisfied
    farm women
  and careers, factors discouraging, 63
  and churches, significance for, 14
  and club movement, 85–93
  and domestic services, 64
  and occupations, 62–66
  and religion, traditional role in, 77–78
  and separate pay scales, 65
  and taboos, 84–85
  and teaching, 64–65
  and traditional role, 73, 83
Women's suffrage, 93–98
  and Democratic Party, 93
  1916 referendum, 96–97
  opponents, 94, 96, 97
  partial suffrage, 85
  and Prohibition, 97, 157
  qualifications for legislators, 98
  and Republican Party, 93–94
Wood, E. R., 242
Woods, Frank, 183, 188
World War I. *See also* Agriculture, WW
    I; Flu epidemic; Iowa State College;
    Male role; Road maintenance
  anti-German sentiment, 184–88

armistice celebration, 208
Belgium, sympathy for, 179
casualties, 198, 209
declaration of war, 183
and democracy, 179–80
draft, 188–99
farmers, military deferment of, 190
food conservation and rationing, 203–
    5
German atrocity reports, 185
German language, prohibition of, 187
German military, sexual crimes of,
    186
neutralist sentiment, 179–80
Red Cross, 202–3
submarine warfare, 180–81, 183
thrift stamps, 201
Victory gardens, 205–6
"yellow painting," 188

Yankee influence, 8, 256
  and cultural imperialism, 9
  and individual responsibility, 45, 259–
    60
  and League of Nations, 210
  and politics, 11
  and Prohibition, 10
  and reform movements, 45
  and social theory, 22, 79–80, 174
Young, William, 207
Young Men's Christian Association
    (YMCA), 22, 79–80, 173, 203